# 1,000,000 Books

are available to read at

# Forgotten Books

www.ForgottenBooks.com

Read online
Download PDF
Purchase in print

ISBN 978-1-331-20139-7
PIBN 10157646

This book is a reproduction of an important historical work. Forgotten Books uses state-of-the-art technology to digitally reconstruct the work, preserving the original format whilst repairing imperfections present in the aged copy. In rare cases, an imperfection in the original, such as a blemish or missing page, may be replicated in our edition. We do, however, repair the vast majority of imperfections successfully; any imperfections that remain are intentionally left to preserve the state of such historical works.

Forgotten Books is a registered trademark of FB &c Ltd.
Copyright © 2018 FB &c Ltd.
FB &c Ltd, Dalton House, 60 Windsor Avenue, London, SW19 2RR.
Company number 08720141. Registered in England and Wales.

For support please visit www.forgottenbooks.com

# 1 MONTH OF FREE READING

at

www.ForgottenBooks.com

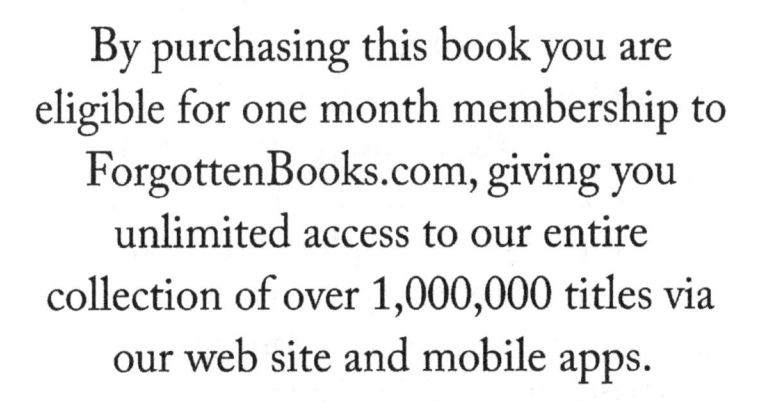

By purchasing this book you are eligible for one month membership to ForgottenBooks.com, giving you unlimited access to our entire collection of over 1,000,000 titles via our web site and mobile apps.

To claim your free month visit:
www.forgottenbooks.com/free157646

\* Offer is valid for 45 days from date of purchase. Terms and conditions apply.

English
Français
Deutsche
Italiano
Español
Português

# www.forgottenbooks.com

**Mythology** Photography **Fiction** Fishing Christianity **Art** Cooking Essays **Buddhism** Freemasonry Medicine **Biology** Music **Ancient Egypt** Evolution Carpentry Physics Dance Geology **Mathematics** Fitness Shakespeare **Folklore** Yoga Marketing **Confidence** Immortality Biographies Poetry **Psychology** Witchcraft Electronics Chemistry History **Law** Accounting **Philosophy** Anthropology Alchemy Drama Quantum Mechanics Atheism Sexual Health **Ancient History** **Entrepreneurship** Languages Sport Paleontology Needlework Islam **Metaphysics** Investment Archaeology Parenting Statistics Criminology **Motivational**

# AN OFFICER

OF

# THE LONG PARLIAMENT

AND

# HIS DESCENDANTS

Oxford
HORACE HART, PRINTER TO THE UNIVERSITY

*AN OFFICER OF THE LONG PARLIAMENT AND HIS DESCENDANTS* Being some Account of the Life & Times of Colonel Richard Townesend of Castletown (Castletownshend) & a Chronicle of his Family   With Illustrations   Edited by Richard & Dorothea Townshend

London   HENRY FROWDE
Oxford University Press Warehouse
Amen Corner, E.C.

MDCCCXCII

# CONTENTS

|  | PAGE |
|---|---|
| INTRODUCTION . . . . . . . . . . | vii |

### CHAPTER I.
THE DEFENCE OF LYME REGIS AND THE SIEGE OF PENDENNIS CASTLE . . . . . . . . 1

### CHAPTER II.
THE IRISH TROUBLES . . . . 33

### CHAPTER III.
THE BATTLE OF KNOCKNONES . . . . . 48

### CHAPTER IV.
PLOT AND COUNTERPLOT AND THE SURRENDER OF CORK . 62

### CHAPTER V.
SETTLING DOWN . . . . . . . 91

### CHAPTER VI.
BRYAN TOWNSHEND, WITH NOTES ON SYNGE . . 143

### CHAPTER VII.
CASTLE TOWNSHEND HOUSE, WITH NOTES ON SOMERVILLE AND TABLES OF THE FIRST HOUSE (I) AND SOMERVILLE (II) . . . . . . . . . . 150

## CONTENTS.

### CHAPTER VIII.

The other Children of Colonel Richard Townesend, viz. John, Francis, Horatio, Philip, Cornelius, Catherine, Dorothea, and Mrs. Owen, with Notes on the Earls of Barrymore and the Copinger and Becher Families. (Tables III–VIII) . . 195

### CHAPTER IX.

Skirtagh House, and Notes on Morris. (Table IX) . 216

### CHAPTER X.

Whitehall House. (Table X) . . . . . 229

### CHAPTER XI.

Derry House, with Notes on Fleming, Corker, and Oliver. (Tables XI, XII) . . . . . . 240

### CHAPTER XII.

Donoughmore House. (Table XIII) . . 267

# INTRODUCTION

'And I but think and speak and do
As my dead fathers move me to.'
R. L. STEVENSON.

THE English Civil War of 1641-49 was essentially a people's war; it was not fought by rival royal houses, nor by rebellious Barons marshalling their feudal retainers. The questions that divided King Charles and his parliament touched the life of every Englishman, and there was hardly an English family that did not take its share in the struggle. The names of the leaders are familiar as household words; but many soldiers now rest forgotten in their 'camps of green' who had their share in winning the freedom that has been handed down to us.

In telling the story of one of these forgotten worthies, it is hardly possible to separate private from public history, however slightly qualified a genealogist may be to make excursions into that dangerously fascinating field. In truth, we know but little of the private life of Colonel Richard Townesend: public records tell of his public services, and we must guess the rest. His descendants, who have left portraits and letters behind them which make us more familiar with their home life, were prominent leaders in the south-west of Munster, a country to which we may apply Professor Freeman's description of South Wales, 'The land was conquered, divided, to a large extent it was settled, but its former inhabitants were neither destroyed, expelled, nor assimilated, . . . genealogy and family history connect themselves more with real history in a district of this sort than elsewhere.'

From time to time different members of the Townshend family in County Cork have begun to draw up some account of their ancestors; but all the memoirs have remained unfinished, and it has fallen to the present editors to try to collect the scattered records and traditions of the line.

It is very difficult to avoid errors when drawing up a sketch of such a scattered family, whose history runs through so many troubled years; but if these fragmentary records induce any other members of the family to correct the mistakes they contain, or to collect new information, the labours of the editors will be amply rewarded.

There is some danger that a family history may resemble a collection of epitaphs; and it may be fairly asked, 'Where are all the bad Townshends?'

To rake up old sins and gibbet the failings of forefathers is not a very grateful or honourable task, and it is even less necessary to do it in Ireland than elsewhere, for facts there speak as plainly as written words.

The Protestant settlers formed a proud and powerful oligarchy, who did very much what seemed right in their own eyes. Those who fell to drinking, gambling, and self-indulgence, very soon died out altogether.

Natural selection had free play, and punished promptly and surely, and only the fit survived.

The fit were not always characters that would precisely suit the nineteenth-century ideals of excellence: undoubtedly they too often shared the faults of their times; but their virtues were their own. It is idle to expect the men of one time or country to match the model of another; but, speaking roughly, the families that have survived the days of rebellion and famine are descended from ancestors who were respectable, honourable, and intelligent gentlemen, who served their generation to the best of their ability.

The unfit dropped out: for example, one family of Elizabethan settlers has left nothing but its name behind it. Its members were once among the principal gentry of the West, yet the story goes, when money was granted by the grand jury to them for improving the highways, they used to lay the coins in rows on the ground, and call on the passers-by to swear that they had seen the money laid out on the road! The last of their name lived in a little cabin by the road side, and when a child from the neighbouring big house peeped in one day, the old lady, for a lady she was in manners and appearance, said, 'Ah, my dear, are you looking for a bit of bread? Not a bit have I in the house.'

But queer stories may be told of most of the old families. It was a jolly, free and easy life, that was led in the last century, and the reckless 'Castle Rackrent' ways brought many a fine property into the Encumbered Estates Court.

One very hospitable Mrs. Townsend loved to keep open house, and when carload after carload of cousins were seen driving up the avenue, an astonished English visitor asked the hostess where she could possibly bestow so many guests. 'Ah!' she answered, 'I needn't trouble at all. I've a very obliging cook and a very accommodating butler, and they'll each take two or three in their beds.'

All were not so hospitable, and the opposite extreme from this good old lady was a Mr. Townsend, who had a fine place, entered by a beautiful avenue of trees. One day a friend met him, and said, 'I was caught in a storm the other day near your house, and I sheltered under that big oak in the avenue.' 'Ah, now, 'tis a pity you stopped there,' exclaimed Mr. Townsend, 'if only you'd gone twenty yards further down the road you'd have found a much thicker tree!'

The younger members of the large families naturally had not much money to spare; one young Townsend, it is said, could get no funds to take him to college, but was so determined to go that he rode all the way up to Dublin, feeding his horse on the grass by the road sides as he went.

In the more remote parts of the country, life was often not merely poor, but rough and squalid. There is a story of a great lady, visiting her rector, a Townsend, and being asked to wait in the parlour, she sat there till her patience was nearly exhausted, when a barefooted girl burst into the room exclaiming, 'Musha, then, did you see the master's razors anywhere?' The great lady thought that it might be some time before

Mr. Townsend's toilet was completed, and said she would call another day.

In a family that numbered several hundred members it could not be hoped that all should succeed in resisting the attractions offered by the wild, jovial life of their less educated neighbours. In parts where there was not much choice of society, the talents and charm which ought to have enabled their possessors to take a high position sometimes proved a curse, and sank them to the level of the peasantry around them.

One young Townsend tried in vain to coax enough of money out of his mother to take to the races, but the old lady was obdurate; at last he seemed to give it up, and changed the subject. 'Mother,' said he, 'did you see the new white cow I've brought back from the fair? she's the greatest cow between this and Cork!' Mrs. Townsend was curious. 'Come along,' said he, and they crossed the farm-yard, and he opened the door of the shed. The old lady went a step inside, when the door banged behind her, and she found that her dutiful son had left her face to face with a great bull. In vain did she rage and entreat; the door was kept fast till she had handed the key of her money-box out through a chink, and then at last she was released.

A wild and lonely life was led by many of the gentry in the isolated country houses on the western sea-coast. Small profits were made by farming, and it seemed as though the English Government levied duties on imports for the special purpose of ruining Irish trade. No wonder that when a French ship was seen weather-bound in the offing, a cow was often hoisted into a boat and rowed out to exchange for a cask of claret, or that the peasants were quick to learn the lesson, and follow the example of their betters.

In Charles Lever's novel, *Sir Jasper Carew*, he mentions a Townshend member of parliament who supported the Irish government in 1782. It would be interesting to know if the name was used by chance, or if the novelist alluded to a real man.

Another Townsend, who has not yet been identified, is described as follows in a 'Letter from the kingdom of Kerry,' 1845[1]:

'Mr. Townsend is one of the water-guard at Sark, and he amuses his leisure hours by diving into the mysteries of natural creation; he is a natural historian of no mean acquirements. The Kerry toads were in his museum placed in the most laughable and extraordinary positions, some as sailors rowing a boat, some as orators, &c. We spent an interesting hour in this simple abode, which is dignified by being the home of an industrious genius and an ardent lover of the works of his Creator.'

Plenty of wild and romantic stories might be collected in the West; but perhaps we have had enough of the sins and follies of the old times, and it is pleasanter to turn to public events and see the share the Townsends took in the progress of their country.

The Editors have to thank many members of the family for their help in preparing this history:—

Mrs. Pierrepont Mundy of Castle-Townshend and Thornbury House, Gloucestershire, for the loan of

[1] *Irish Top. Tracts*, British Museum.

family notes and letters, and of a MS. account of Colonel Richard Townesend and his principal descendants, by the Right Hon. Judge Fitz-Henry Townshend.

Mrs. Edward Townshend of Galway, for valuable information collected by her father, John Sealy Townsend, barrister.

The late Rev. Aubrey Townshend, Vicar of Puxton, for much valuable information, including illuminated pedigree rolls by Major Edward Townshend, and a MS. Life of Colonel Richard Townesend, by John Sealy Townsend.

Mrs. Townsend of Garrycloyne, for the loan of a Memoir of Colonel Townesend's principal descendants, by George Digby Daunt.

The Very Rev. the Dean of Tuam, the Rev. John Hume Townsend, and Mr. Samuel Nugent Townshend, for notes on their branches of the family.

Mrs. Becher of Lough Ine, for the loan of a pedigree; Miss H. Somerville, Miss Reeves, Miss L. Fleming, and the Very Rev. the Dean of Cloyne, for notes and anecdotes.

Mrs. John Townshend, for the loan of letters; Mrs. Pierrepont Mundy, the late Miss Townshend of Whitehall, Mrs. S. Townshend of Harley Street, Mrs. Fleming of New Court, and Colonel Somerville of Drishane, for leave to photograph portraits.

xiv INTRODUCTION.

Among the authorities consulted have been—

CLARENDON. *History of the Rebellion.*
LELAND. *History of Ireland.*
C. G. WALPOLE. *Kingdom of Ireland.*
J. R. GREEN. *Short History of the English People.*
GARDINER. *Puritan Revolution.*
GARDINER. *Great Civil War.*
CROMWELL. *Letters and Speeches,* edited by Carlyle.
D. MURPHY. *Cromwell in Ireland.*
*Lords' Journals.*
*Commons' Journals.*
PRENDERGAST. *Cromwellian Settlement.*
MASSON. *Life of Milton.*
ORRERY. *State Letters.*
BUDGELL. *Memoirs of the Boyle Family.*
LUDLOW. *Memoirs.*
CARTE. *Life of Ormonde.*
*Dictionary of National Biography.*
SIR RICHARD COX. *Hibernia Anglicana.*
EDMUND BORLACE. *History of the Irish Rebellion.*
*Domestic State Papers,* edited by Mrs. Green.
*Carte MSS.,* Bodleian Library.
*Tanner MSS.,* Bodleian Library.
*Extracts from Council Book of Clonakilty.* MSS.
CAULFIELD. *Council Book of Youghal.*
CAULFIELD. *Annals of Kinsale.*
CAULFIELD. *Council Book of Cork.*
REV. W. MAZIERE BRADY, D.D. *Records of Cork, Cloyne, and Ross.*
SMITH. *History of Cork and Kerry.*
TOWNSEND. *Statistical Survey of County Cork.*
BENNETT. *History of Bandon.*

HICKSON. *Old Kerry Records.*

JOHN SEALY TOWNSHEND. *Wills, Custom House and other Dublin MS. Records.*

TUCKEY. *Cork Remembrancer.*

CHARLES HERVEY TOWNSHEND of Newhaven, Conn. *The Townshend Family.*

CARY. *Memorials of the Civil War.*

SPRIGGE. *Anglia Rediviva.*

DONOVAN. *Carbery Sketches.*

Various Pamphlets in the Bodleian Library and in the British Museum, and the Newspapers from 1644 to 1649 in the same Collections.

WHITELOCK. *Memorials.*

GUIZOT. *English Revolution.*

J. T. GILBERT. *Contemporary History of Ireland*, 1641–52.

ROBERTS. *History of Lyme Regis.*

HEPWORTH DIXON. *Life of Blake.*

# LIST OF ILLUSTRATIONS.

PAGE

Facsimile of Lieutenant-Colonel Richard Townesend's Letter to Colonel Ceely .... *Frontispiece*

Fort built at Castletownshend by Colonel Richard Townesend
................................................... *To face page* 91

Castle Townshend . . . . ,, ,, 108
Portrait of Mary, wife of Bryan Townshend . . ,, ,, 143
Portrait of Richard Townshend, of Castletownshend ,, ,, 150
Portrait of Richard Townshend, of Castletownshend, M.P. ,, ,, 153
Portrait of Elizabeth, wife of Richard Townshend ,, ,, 157
Portrait of Samuel Townshend, of Whitehall ,, ,, 229
Portrait of the Rev. Horatio Townshend, of Derry . ,, ,, 258

# GENEALOGICAL TABLES.

I. Richard, Eldest Son of Bryan Townshend . *To face page* 191
II. The Somerville Family . ,, ,, 194
III. Eldest Son of Colonel Townesend . . 196
IV. Third Son of Colonel Townesend . 201
V. Fourth Son of Colonel Townesend . 204
VI. Becher Pedigree, from Judge Fitz-Henry Townshend
................................................. *To face page* 205
VII. Sixth Son of Colonel Townesend . . . 207
VIII. Eighth Son of Colonel Townesend . . . 208
IX. Third Son of Bryan Townshend *To face page* 216
X. Fifth Son of Bryan Townshend . ,, ,, 239
XI. Eighth Son of Bryan and Mary Townshend ,, ,, 240
XII. Youngest Son of Philip Townshend . ,, ,, 265
XIII. Ninth Son of Bryan Townshend . . ,, ,, 271

# CHAPTER I.

## THE DEFENCE OF LYME REGIS AND THE SIEGE OF PENDENNIS CASTLE.

The 27th of July, 1643, was a proud day for the English Cavaliers. Bristol, the great seaport of the West, the second city of the kingdom, had fallen, fallen swiftly and easily, before the assault of Rupert of the Rhine. King Charles should soon have his own again, and round-headed rebels should swing for their treason.

Rupert the headlong believed it with all his heart, and was eager next to dash straight upon London. But Rupert, though now ten years a soldier, was but twenty-four years of age, and Charles with habitual caution said 'no' to the proposals of his ardent nephew. It was decided that Prince Maurice, Rupert's younger brother, should proceed with a part of the army to reduce the West while Charles and Rupert turned north to finish off Gloucester, before finally crushing the rebellion at the centre, Westminster.

Prince Maurice's advance into the West was of the nature of a triumph. Town after town opened its gates to him; nor indeed was it to be wondered at. On Sunday, July 24th, Rupert and Maurice had sat down before the walls of Bristol, and on Tuesday, July 26th, a party of Rupert's horsemen rode over those walls between Brandon Hill and Windmill Fort, and Governor Fiennes hastily surrendered. The very walls of Jericho had held out longer.

Everywhere the news of the Royalist successes was spreading. One Parliamentary army under Waller had just been knocked to pieces at Roundway Down, and another, under the two Fairfaxes, at Atherton Moor. Upon the surrender of Bristol many gentlemen got safe-conducts from the victorious Rupert and returned to their homes. Naturally they exaggerated the courage and fierceness of the Cavaliers who had beaten them.

A wealthy man, Mr. Strode[1], passing through Dorchester, was desired by the magistrates,—anxious enough, poor men, to know what their chances were,— 'to view their works and fortifications and to give his judgment on them.' After he had walked about and looked at them, he said 'that those works might keep out the Cavaliers about half an hour'; and then he told his hearers strange stories of the manner of assaulting Bristol, 'and that the king's soldiers made nothing of running up walls twenty foot high, and that no works could keep them out.'

We can almost hear the superior tone of voice, befitting a man who had just endured the perils of a siege and knew all about it, and see the unhappy faces of the local worthies growing longer and longer. Dorchester surrendered without a blow. Weymouth, Portland, Bideford, Barnstaple, followed its example. Taunton and Bridgewater had done the same thing even earlier.

From Dorchester, Prince Maurice sent a summons, amongst other places, to Lyme Regis, which he deemed an inconsiderable fishing village. It was indeed but a small seaport town, surrounded by hills which completely dominated it, and possessing a little harbour defended by a mole, locally known as The Cobb. It was inhabited however by a daring and

---

[1] Clarendon, iv. 212.

high-spirited race of seafaring folk, proud of their enterprise and their traditions. There must have been many old men still alive in 1643 who could tell of what they had seen in 1588, when the whole bay, as far as eye could see, was covered with ships, and the shores rang with the thunder of the cannon as the great Armada of Spain swept up the Channel and the fleets of England pounded on its rear. Then Lyme had sent out two ships, the 'Jacob' and the 'Revenge,' to help to harry the Spaniard.

Now, when civil war had broken out in England itself, they had chosen their side, and had done their best to fortify their town in the interest of the Parliament, their very women turning out to labour on the works. Colonel Thomas Ceely was appointed to the command, with the title of Governor, and a regiment of ten companies was raised to garrison the place. Whence the officers and men of this regiment came we do not at present know, but the captain of one of those companies was a young man of the name of Townesend [1], who was destined to become in after years the founder of the family of Townsend in County Cork. Of the place of his birth, his parentage, and his previous history, we have no certain knowledge whatever. Castletownsend, which he built, has been destroyed three times, once by siege, once by fire, and once by being 'restored,' and all memorials of his early life appear to have perished utterly. We know from his deposition, made at Cork, February 16, 1654, that he was then thirty-six years old, which would make the year of his birth 1618. He bore the arms of the head of the family in Norfolk, the Presby-

---

[1] So written by himself, though many contemporary records spell the name Townsend.

terian Sir Roger Townshend of Raynham [1], who was brother-in-law to Anne Fairfax, the high-spirited wife of the famous Parliamentary General.

To Prince Maurice's summons Colonel Ceely and his officers returned so peremptory an answer that his Highness resolved not to attack him then, but to leave him alone for the present and pass on to Exeter, which was already hard pressed by Sir John Berkley. There no assault was necessary; Exeter was persuaded to open its gates to the Prince after a fortnight's siege; and the ever-victorious army moved on to Dartmouth. After a month's resistance that town also yielded itself, but by this time autumn was upon them, and wet and exposure had told severely upon the besiegers, who had to camp in the open field. On however went Maurice again from Dartmouth to Plymouth, and here at last his career of conquest was stayed. He beleaguered it all winter long on the landward side, but the Parliament's fleet, under its hard-swearing Lord High Admiral, the Earl of Warwick, kept command of the sea, and the fortress held him at bay.

Meantime the much-alarmed Presbyterians of London and of the two Houses at Westminster had been fitting out new armies to replace those that had been scattered, and had been not only zealously taking the Covenant themselves, but even sending by sea to Scotland to beg their Presbyterian friends across the Border to come quick to their assistance.

Charles, not to be outdone, also looked beyond the

---

[1] Died January 1, 1637. Thomas Townsend of Braconashe, grandson of Sir Roger Townshend of Raynham, married Anne D'Oyley of Shottisham, and Colonel Edward D'Oyley was great-nephew to Dorothy Townsend, Mrs. D'Oyley of Wallingford.' Colonel Edward and Major Charles D'Oyley served with Colonel Richard Townesend in Ireland, and are believed to have been his kinsmen.

boundaries of his English kingdom for aid in his contest with his recalcitrant Parliament. To his wife's own country, France, he looked for some help, but his most cherished hope was that Ireland would swell his forces, and as a matter of fact various Irish regiments for his service were landed in Cheshire, in Wales, and in the West country. Not all of them, by any means, were drawn from the ranks of the Irish loyalists. 'Eight hundred native Irish rebels,' says Whitlock[1], 'landed at Weymouth under the Lord Inchiquin to serve his majesty.'

In the eyes of the King's English subjects this was a grievous wrong on his part. They looked upon the Irish as foreigners, and upon all the Roman Catholic Irish as equally guilty of the fearful massacres of English and Scotch Protestants which had taken place there in 1641 and which were still unavenged. This outrage on the feelings of the Protestants of Great Britain was a blunder which alienated many of his own supporters. The charge of proposing to use an Irish army in England had cost Strafford his head.

The King did not take the warning: on the contrary he endeavoured to carry out the scheme, and he had ultimately to pay the same terrible penalty. But for the present the numbers of his forces were augmented, and it was with considerably increased strength that in January, 1644, Prince Maurice broke up his leaguer before Plymouth and marched back again in the direction of Bristol. His design most probably was to join the King in a combined movement upon London through the southern counties, but he had all spring before him, and that insolent little fisher-village of Lyme, which had defied him in the autumn, lay tempt-

[1] Whitlock, i. 236.

ingly near his path. He would just take it *en route*, and have that triumph at least as a feather in his cap when he rejoined the Court, to wipe out the recollection of Plymouth. He carried with him a powerful siege train, and his united army, of Irish, Cornish, and English, amounted to over 7,000: indeed its numbers are put by some writers as high as 20,000.

Lyme, with its feeble fortifications and its petty garrison, would hardly be likely to detain him more than a single day. But the people of Lyme, in spite of the appalling odds against them, prepared to make him fight for his laurels. Colonel Ceely gathered reinforcements both of men and ammunition when and where he could. On February 21 Colonel Were, who had been sent by Sir William Waller to his assistance, landed at Lyme, and all his forces, together with the garrison of the town, were drawn forth on Lyme Hill. Thence a party under Colonel Peyto was sent to Studcombe House and Axmouth[1] to secure them, and Colonel Were, with his officers and 300 foot, advanced to Studcombe House, intending to fall upon Colyton[2], but by Ceely's orders was held back from so doing. The Royalist commander however, without waiting to be attacked, succeeded in turning the tables on Were, for he captured him and most of his men and took them prisoners to Colyton.

The fugitives who escaped brought the news into Lyme, and Captain Thomas Pine, with a strong party from the garrison, sallied out that same night and reached Colyton. The Royalists were 'in jollity for their success,' and, as the event proved, rather too much so for their own safety, for Pine in his turn surprised them, and took captive the colonel, several

---
[1] Five miles west of Lyme.      [2] Three miles north of Axmouth.

officers, and sixty soldiers, and rescued all the prisoners.

Colonel Ceely's next sally was eastwards, and on March 3, by command of the council of war, Captain Townsend drew out a 'hundred firelocks' and fell upon Bridport[1], where he surprised 150 of the Royalist horse very successfully: this time however Colonel Ceely had no mind to risk a repetition of the Colyton performance, and he and Captain Pine, advancing with horse and foot to Chidwick Hill, secured Townsend's return in safety[2]. But an auxiliary far more important than unlucky Colonel Were reached Lyme Regis before Prince Maurice closed in upon it. When Fiennes surrendered Bristol, after only a few hours' fighting, there was a commander in the strongest of his forts, that on Prior's Hill, who had resisted so stoutly the repeated assaults made on him, and so completely beaten off the Royalist attack on his part of the lines, that he declined to believe the report of the surrender of the town, when it reached his ears. Fiennes in his frantic haste had actually forgotten to apprise him of the treaty, and the brave Captain Blake was within an ace of being hanged by Rupert for what appeared to be a breach of it. He went free however, and in reward for the splendid defence he had made of Prior's Hill he was promoted to be Lieutenant-Colonel and was appointed to Popham's regiment.

When Maurice advanced upon Lyme, and help was wanted, Blake with a handful of his soldiers threw himself into the town and became the heart and soul of its defence. The fortifications of Lyme consisted

---

[1] Ten miles east of Lyme.
[2] Diary of the siege of Lyme appended to a letter from the Earl of Warwick; *King's Pamphlets*, Numero 160, Pamphlet 25, British Museum.

of a dry ditch, a few earthworks hastily thrown up, and three small batteries, named respectively Davies' Fort, Gun Cliff, and the Fort at the Cobb Gate. Two large blocks of buildings, Colway House and Haye Farm, standing on opposite sides of the valley in which Lyme Regis lies, and beyond the line of earthworks which connected the three forts, were occupied as outposts[1].

Prince Maurice, after leaving Tavistock, where he had lingered for a while, moved directly upon Lyme, picking up four of his Irish regiments *en route*. A MS. history of the siege[2] which was discovered in White Lackington House in 1786, says:—

'On the 20th of April the enemy appeared on a certain hill called Uplyme Hill, about two miles distant from Lyme Regis, where the soldiers were mustered, and as it grew near the evening, they drew towards the town about three-quarters of a mile nearer the edge of the hill, and ordered the whole body of horse and foot in view of all the town, as was judged and discovered through the perspective glasses, in abreast three or four troops, in length a mile or thereabouts, to the number of about 4000. In the town were near 500 fighting men, more or less, who were not a jot dismayed at the sight of the enemy, but rather longed to have dealt with them, and so they shouted to the enemy, and the enemy answered them with shouting.'

Haye and Colway House, however, were untenable against such a host, and the outposts had to be withdrawn within the lines.

The Prince now sent a trumpeter to Blake and Ceely with a summons to surrender, but Blake had not come there to yield to a summons, and Colonel Ceely was

[1] Hepworth Dixon's *Life of Blake*, pp. 40, 41.
[2] Quoted by Geo. Roberts in his *History of Lyme*, ed. 1823, pp. 40-64.

a man of a very different quality to Flennes. Their answer was a defiance, to which *Mercurius Aulicus*[1] states they insolently added that they would grant no quarter to any Irish or Cornish.

Such a reply exasperated Prince Maurice to the utmost. He impetuously ordered his trumpeters to sound a general charge. The footmen slung a shower of hand-grenades into the town, and the horse, taking advantage of the confusion caused by their exploding, actually tried to ride over the works and carry the place by a rush. But they were met by volley after volley of musketry from the firelocks, and after a vain effort to face the hail of bullets, they fell back, and drew off out of range. The foot were then formed up in columns and brought up to the attack: again and again they tried to storm, but were met by the same deadly hail, and again and again were driven back with the loss of their best and bravest leaders. Then Maurice himself spurred his horse into their broken ranks, rallied them, and bade them charge once more; but the men were disheartened and would not go on, till in his wrath the Prince formed his cavalry in their rear, and, by pistol shots from behind, drove them forward. But as before, the besieged were ready for them, and meeting their advance with salvoes of musketry and case-shot sent the broken columns reeling back in hopeless disorder. The attempt to take the town by assault had failed.

It was now clear to Prince Maurice that if he was determined to make himself master of this 'little vile fishing town' he must lay regular siege to it. He was loath to postpone his march for the purpose, but dread of the displeasure of Charles, and of the ridicule

[1] A newspaper published at Oxford on the King's side.

which such a failure would draw on him in the censorious circles of the Court, made him even more loath to pass on and leave Lyme untaken. He decided that it must be forced at all hazards; so he made Colway House his headquarters, and threw up batteries for his siege guns on the hills commanding the town. Day after day from these guns he plied the brave defenders with shot, and they on their part by day and night laboured, men and women alike, to build up their ramparts faster than he could beat them down. At times, when there was a lull in the firing, the women even put on red cloaks to make them look like soldiers, and mounted the ramparts, while the outwearied fighting men took their rest.

Time after time Maurice, believing that his cannonade had mastered the fire of the defenders, formed up his columns for new assaults, and sent them desperately on to charge those feeble but firmly held lines, and the best blood in England flowed freely in those fatal trenches. One evening, May 6, under cover of a thick fog, the stormers actually got over the works and into the town, but so steady was the garrison, and so wise were Blake's tactics, that the defenders recovered the lines that had been passed, and cut off the companies which had succeeded in entering the place, so that, taken in front, flank, and rear, they perished almost to a man.

Prince Maurice lost near 500 men that night. Captain Blewitt, one of his best officers, lay dead upon the trench, with two bullets through his body and another in his head. Maurice sent the next day to beg for Blewitt's body, which favour Blake granted on condition that his men were not molested in collecting the arms that lay on the field. Maurice acceded to this, but refused a further request, that he would give up Mr. Harvey, Ceely's brother-in-law, whom he had arrested in the country. Blewitt's corpse, besmeared with blood and dirt, was found and washed and put into a new shroud and coffin; but Maurice declined to give up his prisoner Harvey, saying that they could keep the dead body if they pleased.

Blake was nettled at the insulting message, but he had the coffin taken to the lines opposite Holme Bush, one of Maurice's batteries, and signalled to the heralds to come for it. 'Have you,' said he scornfully, as they approached,—' have you any command to pay for the shroud and coffin?' They answered, 'No.' Curling his whiskers with his fingers, he replied with disdain, 'Nevertheless, take them; we are not so poor but that we can give them to you[1].'

Later in the day there was another parley, and a Royalist general, in an interview with Blake, pointed out to him as an old soldier the weakness of the works, and the certainty that they must soon fall. 'We do not trust in our works,' was Blake's answer; 'and you may tell your Prince, that if he wishes to come into the town with his army to fight we will pull down ten or twelve yards, so that he may come in ten abreast, and we will fight him.'

One can imagine the effect of this spirited reply in kindling the pride of those of Blake's soldiers who heard it, and how the story would fly around from group to group of those who manned the defences.

Provisions and powder now began to run short in Lyme, and by May 23 the garrison were reduced to great straits. But in the nick of time came the stout Earl of Warwick with a little fleet, and brought them

[1] Dixon's *Life of Blake*, p. 47.

enough food and ammunition to enable them to hold out a while longer.

Maurice made a desperate attempt to prevent them from receiving this relief; one of his storming parties actually reached the Cobb, and burned the shallops in the harbour: vainly however, for Warwick and his ships were anchored outside, beyond the range of the batteries; unfortunately, though, the valiant Captain Thomas Pine met his death-wound in repelling them. But by night the supplies were landed, and the besieged took heart again.

On May 27, when Captain Pine was being buried with the honours of a soldier's funeral and volleys were being fired over his grave, the enemy took advantage of it to try once more the 'imminent deadly breach,' only to be hurled back once more with dreadful loss.

The stubborn obstinacy of the defence was at least equalled by the pertinacity of the attack; shame, rage, and the desire to avenge so many brave men's deaths, urged Maurice to a final effort. Three thousand men were chosen from the Cavalier ranks, arranged in three solid columns, and ordered to support one another in the attack. Blake on his side got 300 seamen from the fleet, which brought his forces up to 1200. Maurice began by a heavy cannonade. 'The mariners were at first very fearful and would have withdrawn, but the rest of them (the townsmen) very courageously stood to it, reprehending some of them for their timorousness.' A month's service under Blake had turned the townsmen into seasoned veterans.

Then, when the cannonade was supposed to have done its work, the terrible storming columns came on. There was no flinching this time. It was now or never. But the defenders met them with equal resolution. The women filled the soldiers' bandoliers while they fought. One woman herself fired sixteen musket shots. Men fought hand to hand till the very stream that supplied the town with water ran red with blood. 'The third assault was the most violent, but it was repulsed, and there was a remitting of the former furie, and about 9 an almost general silence.' Maurice's last effort had failed.

Townsend had now become a Major, promoted perhaps on Captain Pine's death, and in the final defeat of the enemy he nearly shared the fate of his late comrade in arms. 'Major Townsend,' says the account of the fighting contained in a letter sent by the Earl of Warwick's secretary to London, 'was shot in the head, but still lives [1].'

Warwick himself, in his own report to the Speaker of the Peers' House, praises the defenders of Lyme in the warmest terms.

'The truth is, next to the protection of Heaven, the courage and honesty of the officers and souldiers were in a manner their sole defence, they being made instrumentall and through God's blessing to the preserving them in safety and cheerefulnesse. When I came amongst the officers I found them all worthy of precious esteem, and modestly submitting to the many inconveniences which a long and hard siege had contracted.'

London was by this time ringing with stories of the valour of the defence, and Essex was specially enjoined by Parliament to move his army to the relief of Lyme. He was slow, but he arrived in Dorset at last; and

---

[1] An exact and true relation in relieving the resolute garrison of Lyme in Dorsetshire, by the Rt. Hon. Earl of Warwicke, Lord High Admiral of England. Besieged by Prince Maurice, the Lord Inchiquin and his Irish rogues, together with the Lord Paulet. *King's Pamphlets*, 160. 23. There are also two copies of this pamphlet in the Bodleian Library.

Maurice, fearing to be taken in the rear, sullenly and reluctantly withdrew his sadly diminished forces. Before dismantling his batteries he fired from them for a whole day red-hot shot into the town, and succeeded in setting several houses in flames, but the fires were put out as fast as they started, and no general conflagration followed.

On June 13 Essex was reported to be at Dorchester, and about two in the morning Maurice drew off his artillery, and his army divided, part to Bristol, and part with himself to Exeter. One story goes that as the last of the great guns was being tugged by the labouring oxen over the brow of the steep hill above Lyme, Blake sent a parting shot after it, which broke up the team, and the gun was in consequence abandoned. *Mercurius Aulicus*, however, will have no such tales.

'And though some false and malicious persons (as there be too many) had caused an unworthy rumour to be raised among us, reporting that the Prince had left four pieces of cannon in the works behind him, yet upon better information it proved nothing, his highness having carefully removed all his carriages before he raised his siege or forsook his trenches.'

At all events the siege was raised, whether Maurice left a gun behind him or no, and Lyme, for the present, was saved. How long it was before Major Townsend recovered from his wound at Lyme we have no means of knowing. The garrison was by no means inactive, though, and began to stir abroad again.

Prince Maurice, on his way to Exeter, had left a strong garrison in Wareham, under Lord Inchiquin's brother, Colonel O'Brien, and Essex on his march west summoned the place on June 21, but being denied, passed it by and went on to Chard.

On August 10, however, the ex-Royalist, Sir Anthony Ashley Cooper, who had lately joined the Parliament, and was now the chief commander of the Dorset forces, drew about 1200 horse and foot out of Lyme, Poole, and Weymouth (which had yielded to Essex), and came before the town and began to storm the outworks. Upon this Colonel O'Brien desired a parley, and presently agreed to surrender the place and return with his men to Ireland.

This very easy victory was an agreeable surprise to the Parliamentary forces; but the reason of it was not hard to explain. Colonel O'Brien was under the influence of his elder brother, and McMurrough O'Brien, Lord Inchiquin, happened just now to be changing sides in the great struggle. His ostensible reason was that he could not endure the cessation or armistice which had been concluded in Ireland between Charles and the rebels who had been guilty of the massacre of 1641. His correspondence with Ormonde, however, in these months of May and June 1644, show that he deeply resented the influence of Lord Muskerry at the Court. 'He has told such a tale of me to his Majesty, as proves exceedingly prejudicial to me, having some shadow of truth in it, and my tale unheard [1],' are his words to Ormonde in a letter in which he says that Muskerry is at Padstow waiting to cross over to Munster by Inchiquin's frigate.

After the death of the late president of Munster, Sir William St. Leger, Inchiquin's father-in-law, Inchiquin himself, who had hitherto fought for the King and had been most energetic in sending over Irish troops to his aid, had expected to receive the vacant appointment, and now Charles had given the place to Muskerry,

[1] Inchiquin to Ormonde, Cork, June 14, 1644; *Carte Papers*.

who was actually the head of the rebels there. The upshot of it all was that on July 17, 1644, Inchiquin formally renounced his service under Charles, and the next day offered his allegiance to the Parliament. It was accepted, and the speedy surrender of Wareham by his brother was but an earnest of what his adhesion might bring. It is believed that the adroit persuasions of Lord Broghill, son of the great Earl of Cork, had no small share in the work of bringing about Lord Inchiquin's defection, which proved a great blow to the royal cause in Munster, of which province the Parliament, after a few months' delay to test the sincerity of their new supporter, appointed him to be President in opposition to Charles's nominee, Lord Muskerry. Inchiquin, as it happened, turned with the tide.

Till this summer of 1644, the course of the war may be said to have been, on the whole, in Charles's favour. But at Marston Moor, in Yorkshire (July 3), Rupert recklessly assailed a superior force of English and Scots (for the Scots had now come), who had the advantage of position as well as of numbers. His army contained the flower of the Cavalier forces and fought most valiantly, but his generalship was at fault: he was utterly beaten and, in a military sense, annihilated.

The loss of a very large number of the King's best officers was irreparable, and the royal cause never recovered from it, although Charles himself marched into the West, and joining the army of Prince Maurice, succeeded in utterly out-manœuvring Essex, whose generalship proved of the feeblest.

The men of Lyme did their best to help poor Essex. Blake, who had thrown himself into Taunton, which he held till the close of the war, with a pertinacity equal to that he had shown at Lyme, harassed Charles's communications as much as he could on the Bristol Channel side, while the Lyme men themselves actually fell upon the rear of the royal army at Chard, and 'there they took eleven brave horses with rich saddles, supposed to be the King's own saddle horses, and divers prisoners[1].' Indeed Clarendon notes that on Charles's return from his successful expedition in the West, one of the things to be provided for before leaving Exeter was to block up the troops of Lyme, 'which were grown more insolent by the success they had had, and made incursions sometimes even to the walls of Exeter'; and some of the Exeter garrison under Sir John Berkley were assigned to this duty[2]. Ceely, however, though Blake had gone to Taunton, showed himself an apt pupil, and when in order to carry out this plan three hundred of the royal forces came to Axminster to fortify it and to straiten Lyme, he fell upon them, and at the second charge routed them, killed Major Walker, two captains, two lieutenants, and several common soldiers, took four pieces of ordnance, many arms and prisoners, and released fifty gentlemen who had been by them taken prisoners from their homes[3].

But no diversion could succeed in helping a helpless general. Essex was driven to surrender his army, he himself making his escape by water to Plymouth. This success of Charles, however, was no real recovery of power for him. In fact, the defeat of Essex was in some sort a gain to the side of the Parliament, for it only led to Essex being himself retired, so that his weakness no longer stood in the way of decisive action. The Self-denying Ordinance was passed, by which

---

[1] Whitlock, 286.  [2] Clarendon, iv. 573, end of Sept. 1644.
[3] Whitlock, 338.

Essex, Manchester, and the rest of the members of either house who held military commands, laid them down, and the New Model Army under Fairfax and Cromwell (who though a member was allowed to keep his military rank) was formed.

In this New Model the hard-fighting Independents had a very much larger share of power than had previously fallen to their lot. Its discipline was strict, and as a military engine it was the most effective organisation that the war had yet produced. The New Model met the army of Charles at Naseby, on June 14, 1645, and after a desperate struggle overthrew it completely. Charles himself showed great personal gallantry, but it was all in vain, and he had to fly the field, a beaten man.

Swiftly and steadily the New Model Army moved across the country, taking town after town, and finally cooped up the scattered remnants of the Royalist armies in the West, driving them back into the counties of Somerset, Dorset, Devon, and Cornwall.

Here, in this district, in this third year of actual warfare, there arose a popular movement which was unlike anything that had yet taken place. For three years the rival armies had marched up and down the country, and the outrages and devastations, the levyings and forced contributions, that the peasantry had endured, now at last caused them to rise up in wrath and cry 'A plague on both your houses. We want peace.' Armed with rustic weapons—they were known as the clubmen—they bade the fighters cease.

It is impossible not to sympathise much with them.

'Delirant reges, plectuntur Achivi.'

King and Parliament might be at loggerheads up in London, but it was hard for John Nokes in a Dorset cottage to see why either of them should seize his stock or waste his fields in order to settle their differences. These West-country peasants had yet to learn that there are no neutrals in a civil war, and that a demand for peace, just when one party has got the other by the throat, is but coming to the rescue of the weaker.

On July 7, 1645, there was a petition read in the House of Peers, from the clubmen, 'that divers garrisons in the County of Dorset and Wilts, might be demolished, or that for such as might be continued they might have liberty to place such persons of their own counties as they should select.'

But now the Parliament was up, and the King was down, and a cessation of arms could only have the effect of giving the King's party time to recover themselves, and preventing the victorious New Model from following up its success at Naseby. The clubmen's proposal stirs the wrath of a good Puritan journalist in the *True Informer*. 'A pretty notion,' he writes, 'and likely to be granted, is it not, think you? The Malignants would be sure to get in those of the Royal parties, and where were then all the Parliament garrisons[1]?'

Precisely: the garrison of Lyme had a very clear idea of where they would be if the clubmen had their way, and they proposed to submit to nothing of the kind. A Parliamentary officer, Colonel Pindar, sent a message to Fairfax, the Lord General, but the clubmen fell upon him, and captured the despatches and stripped him of his horse and arms. Goodall, the messenger, succeeded notwithstanding in making his escape, and on hearing of it, Colonel Ceely with some of his

[1] *King's Pamphlets.*

regiment promptly pursued and overtook them. They proved to be led by an officer of Goring's.

Goring, who was now the King's general in the South-west, a lawless man himself, and a bad disciplinarian, naturally encouraged this irregular popular movement. The triumphant clubmen defied Ceely to fight, but they rued their error. He and his veterans of Lyme fell upon them and routed them, and eighty of the clubmen were killed. Nevertheless they must have made a stout bid for victory, for Ceely himself was wounded, and his Major unhorsed. Doubtless, though his name is not mentioned, it was Major Townesend who accompanied his Colonel on this adventure.

These clubmen, whose numbers rose to as many as ten thousand, were finally dispersed by Cromwell, near Shaftesbury, a month later, but the movement did not entirely die out till Fairfax had driven the King's army of the west to surrender in Cornwall.

The chivalrous Sir Ralph Hopton had, at the eleventh hour, accepted most unwillingly the command of this mutinous and undisciplined army, being urgently pressed to do so by Charles; but the change had come too late; the Royalist cause was now sinking fast, and in March, 1646, he was compelled by his own men to let them give themselves up to Fairfax at Truro.

From this ignominious surrender, however, he excepted the strongly fortified castles of Pendennis and St. Michael's Mount, and even reinforced their garrisons from those among his troops who shared his own determination never to yield to what they deemed the usurping Parliament.

That Parliament had another stroke of luck, for just at this juncture an Irish ship put in at Padstow, on the north coast of Cornwall, and was at once taken possession of by the Parliament men. The master, finding himself in hostile hands, threw overboard a packet of letters, but they were rescued, and proved to contain letters from Lord Glamorgan, who had been sent into Ireland by Charles to get the Irish Catholics to send an army to his aid. Loud were the cries for vengeance all over England when these letters were published.

Ten thousand men had been promised him from Ireland, but before they had time to arrive—if indeed it was ever intended to send them—Charles had no army left for them to join. He had ordered Sir Jacob Astley, who had 3000 men with him at Worcester, to join him at Oxford, where he hoped to assemble a sufficient force to enable him to await the anticipated succours from Ireland. Astley started, but he got no further than Stow-in-the-wold, where he was caught by Brereton and Morgan, 1800 of his troops killed or captured, and the rest dispersed. The old hero was worn out with the fatigues of the conflict, and the Roundhead soldiers brought him a drum to sit upon. 'Now, gentlemen,' said he, as he sat down, to the officers around him, 'you have done all your work and may go to play, unless you prefer to fall out among yourselves.'

Charles had no longer a force in the field, but Oxford and the various castles throughout the country which were held for him, had yet to be reduced by siege.

No sooner had Fairfax received the surrender of Hopton's army at Truro, than he decided to examine the works of Pendennis Castle, with a view to its capture. It stands on a bold promontory 200 feet above the sea, on the western side of the entrance to Falmouth harbour. It was held by Arundel of Trevose, with a strong garrison, and was the most important post to the Royalists in the South-west, both from its impregnable site, and its command of the harbour.

Fairfax sent two regiments, Colonel Ingoldsby's and Colonel Hammond's, to occupy the village of Pennycombequick, and Sir Peter Killigrew's house, Ardwinkle, in order to block up the garrison on the landside. They arrived only just in time to save the house and village from being completely destroyed by Arundel's soldiers; indeed they were too late to prevent most of Ardwinkle being burnt down, as it lay within half musket-shot of the outworks of Pendennis, and it was a matter of great importance to the defence to level it to the ground.

Next day Fairfax himself arrived, and proceeded to view the works; a matter of some risk, for on the north side of the port there lay a king's ship, mounting forty guns. She was stranded, but she could use her teeth for all that, and let fly at the Lord General's party.

'Their shot,' says the narrator of the story, 'by God's mercy did us no harm, though the bullets flew very near us, and one grazed not far from me, which we found, and it was a bullet of some 12lbs. weight. As soon as the General came to Perin,' he continues, 'he caused a summons to be drawn up, and sent it by his drum-major unto the Governor of the castle, requiring him to yield it unto him for the use of the Parliament, using divers reasons to persuade him thereto. But Arundell of Trevesse, who is the governor thereof, gave him a peremptory denial, saying that he was seventy years old and could not have many days to live, and therefore would not in his old years blemish his honour, in surrendering thereof, and would be rather found buried in the ruins thereof than commit so vile a treason (or words to that effect). Questionless the place is very strong, as well by its natural situation (it being almost an island and situated on a rising hill) as by Art and great industry, and it is victualled as they say for nine or ten months, and they have in it about 1000 or 1200 men, all desperate persons and good soldiers; and they have powder and shot great store and at least eighty great guns mounted, besides forty in the ship that lies on the north side the Castle. Therefore the general resolves to block it up by land and sea . . . 2000 foot would keep them in[1].'

Under the superintendence of Colonel Hammond the lines of fortification were drawn across the isthmus, and the garrison was blocked up; but the work was not done without a serious loss, for on March 31 the *Weekly Account* reports that

'This day came the unwelcome news of the death of that religious and truly valiant gentleman Colonel Ingoldsby, who with other commanders going to view Pendennis, received a shot from the enemy who lay in ambush behind a mud wall.'

The wound was mortal, and Ingoldsby died within three hours.

Colonel Hammond having finished the lines and strengthened his forces by the addition of some Cornish troops, left Colonel Richard Fortescue to continue the siege while he proceeded to assail St. Michael's Mount. Admiral Batten blockaded Pendennis by sea, and the place began to be pressed. Stories soon got about as to the behaviour of the garrison.

'As for Pendennis,' says the *Moderate Intelligencer*, 'they are blades of the right sort, and having two hundred tun

---

[1] Truro, March 19, 164$\frac{5}{6}$, T. M. In *Newspapers*, 1646, vol. i, British Museum.

of wine spare not to be daily drunk, and this the governor encourages that their discontents take not overmuch hold on them, which are very great already. They are at sixpence per diem, nor will that hold long.'

They did hold out five long months, nevertheless, after this too triumphant prophecy was in print, but the *Moderate Intelligencer* was no less fallible than our nineteenth-century papers, and the writer may be excused for saying what he thought would please his readers; nor was he the only one just then who did so, for the *Perfect Diurnall* of April 20 reports that—

'A captain in Pendennis came off with eighty men. We understand in Pendennis they have nothing but salt beef tainted, and cannot subsist long. But little bread and their wine almost spent, we hope well of the place.'

Meantime, where was Major Townesend during Fairfax's march into Cornwall? Most probably he was in Dorset with his regiment. Ceely's regiment was not one of those which had been taken to form the New Model Army when the Parliamentary forces were reorganised under Fairfax; neither was it disbanded at that time, like some others, but remained, as it was before, a part of the local forces under the Parliamentary committee for Dorset.

Colonel Ceely himself had been elected to Parliament in 1645 as member for Bridport, in the place of Giles Strangways, who had been disabled for malignancy in 1644. He had gone up to Westminster to sit, but he still retained his colonelcy. The Self-denying Ordinance was really only passed to get rid of Essex and Manchester. It had succeeded in its purpose and now was no longer needed. As soon as the Cavalier forces began to melt away and the Parliament felt its hold on the country strengthened, elections had been held for a number of seats which had been vacated like Bridport.

The Ordinance did not apply to the members chosen at these elections, and among the 'Recruiters,' as these new members were called, were many officers of the army, not a few of them Independents.

Colonel Ceely being occupied with his Parliamentary duties, the rank of Lieutenant-Colonel was conferred upon Major Townesend, and he was placed in command of the regiment; and now, when Pendennis held out contrary to the hopes of the besiegers, he was summoned with his regiment to take a part in the blockade. This proved to be a matter of some time. Various efforts were made by the King's partisans in France to throw supplies into Pendennis, but the vigilance of Batten defeated them all. Hope of succour by land there could be none, for Charles had no longer an army. In fact Charles himself had become a prisoner, for at the end of April he fled from Oxford to escape the advance of Fairfax upon that city, and threw himself into the hands of the army of the Scots at Newark.

But, succour or no succour, old Arundel of Trevose, 'game to the toes,' as the rhyming phrase went, was fixed in his determination to hold out to the bitter end. In July his condition was almost desperate. Some ships from St. Malo were sent to relieve him if possible, but contrary winds drove them back to Morlaix. Perhaps had they reached the English shore they might have found the task beyond their powers, for Admiral Batten kept a most vigilant guard. Every night he sent ten large boats and barges well manned to patrol the harbour entrance within range of the castle, drawing them off at daybreak.

'One morning,' says Sprigge, 'when he was newly drawn off, a shallop got in by stealth, which caused great triumph in the castle: but 'twas conceived (and Colonel Fortescue was so informed by good hands) that little relief was in it, save a hogshead or two of wine.'

Summoned once more to surrender by Colonel Fortescue, Arundel refused without a special warrant from the King, asking his besieger to let him send to the King for it, 'as but a common courtesie.' Fortescue did not understand it so, and declined to allow any communication. Arundel repeated his request, naming this time Prince Charles (afterwards Charles II, now with the queen in France), as one whose warrant he would obey. Fortescue was equally obdurate. Arundel had killed all his horses for food and made a sally in boats to try to bring in relief. He was beaten back with loss. An agent from the King of Spain came and proposed, Colonel Fortescue allowing him to enter for the purpose, that the Roman Catholics of the garrison should take service in Flanders under the King of Spain. They thanked Fortescue for his courtesy, and replied to the agent, 'that at present they were engaged, but should they be once free, next to their present master they would serve his Majesty of Spain.'

In the intervals of treating, hostilities were carried on with vigour, and though short of food the besieged had plenty of powder to expend, 'making 200 great shot in the space of three days at our men,' says Sprigge, 'but without any great execution, only three of our men being slain thereby.'

On July 26 a shallop from the castle eluded Batten's vigilance and escaped to bear to the Prince the news of their hopeless condition. Fires were kept at night on the ramparts to guide their deliverers if ever they should come, but there were none to deliver them.

The game was up. Arundel sent a letter to Colonel Fortescue to ask whether he had power to treat with him, and if that were so whether he could make good the conditions he might grant. Fortescue answered that he had power to treat and to make good the agreement. Arundel paused once more, but the sight of his half-starved soldiers decided him to accept a treaty. To persevere longer would only be to sacrifice the lives of so many faithful and brave men in vain. He submitted to the inevitable, and appointed commissioners to treat on his behalf,—Sir A. Shipman, Lieut.-Col. R. Arundel, Col. Wm. Slaughter, Col. Charles Jennings, Col. Lewis Tremain, Nevill Bligh, Joseph Jeune, and Lieut.-Col. Brocker.

To meet them the Col. R. Fortescue[1] sent Col. John St. Aubyn, the High Sheriff, Sir John Ayscue, Kt., Col. Robert Bennet, Lieut.-Col. Edward Herle, Lieut.-Col. Thomas Fitch, Lieut.-Col. Richard Townesend, Major T. Jennings and Capt. W. Maynard.

[1] Richard Fortescue is frequently mentioned during the Civil Wars as a Parliamentary officer of distinction, but no clue has been found to his place in the Fortescue family. As his landed estates were in Berkshire he may have belonged to the Salden House, who were connected with that county. The *Thurloe State Papers*, Whitlock's *Memoirs* and the Rawlinson MS. in the Bodleian are the chief sources of information concerning him. He was a Colonel in 1644 (*Thurloe S. P.* III, pt. 4, p. 649).

In August 1646 he took Pendennis Castle, and was made Governor, and his name occurs in various expeditions and services until December 1654, when he is first mentioned in Thurloe. He was Commander-in-Chief in Jamaica, June 24, 1655, and Major-General. He was appointed to succeed General Venables as Governor in the event of the death of the latter officer, which took place soon after the arrival of Fortescue in the Island. There are several letters extant that passed between Cromwell and Fortescue. Fortescue's will was signed July 25, 1648; he died November 1655, and his will was proved by Mary his wife July 29, 1657. See Rawlinson MS. in the Bodleian, printed 27. 647.

*History of the Family of Fortescue*, by Thomas Fortescue, Lord Clermont.

They met on Monday, August 10, and parleyed, the Royalists making demands, the Roundheads offering propositions in vain, till Wednesday noon, and then, says the *Moderate Intelligencer*,

'Their commissioners brake off in great discontent, and away. We might then give you the demands of each, but it will be superfluous. Colonel Fortescue finding this unexpected rupture, contrived a way to bring on the treaty again, which took. Then upon this they began again Friday 14th, and agreed all by the 15th towards night save the time of surrender. The 16th they agreed on articles and signed them.'

Lieutenant-Colonel Townesend hastened to apprise his Colonel of the fact in a letter which has happily been preserved among the Tanner MS.[1] in the Bodleian :—

'*Colonel Richard Townesend to Colonel Thomas Ceely.*

'Sir,

'I am just now going to meet the commissioners appointed to treat about the surrender of Pendennis: the articles are agreed upon by both parties and to be signed this morning, they are to march out to-morrow or Tuesday at furthest; the soldier hath very honourable conditions—colours flying, trumpets sounding, drums beating, bag and baggage: and at the rendezvous which is within two miles to lay down their arms, their goods to be viewed ; and if any man of the country can upon good proof make any of those goods appear to be his, then and there to receive it, and the soldier in whose custody it is found shall lose all that he hath. The sum of the rest is according to the account I gave you the last week.

'Sir, you have always expressed a great deal of care and love towards your regiment; now it hath pleased God to finish the western work, and to bring it into a condition, no

[1] Vol. lix. fol. 481.

soldier in the kingdom in the like. I have often writ you that the most part have not wherewith to cover their nakedness, yet never received from you the least engagement to supply us, to incite those to it that shoule relieve us. I need not urge our service nor the faithfulness of it, well known to the most part, though not well considered by any.

'I desire to receive directions how to dispose of the regiment, and positively what employment and future maintenance we may expect: the committee of this county hath expressed a great respect towards us, and some of them desire to continue us here till the great affairs of the kingdom are better settled. Be pleased to afford a line or two concerning the Irish proceedings.

I remain, Sir,<br>Your faithful servant,<br>RICH. TOWNESEND.

August 16,
at Truro, 6 in the morning.'

The letter is addressed on the back,

'These for Colonell Thomas Ceely, a member of the House. Haste, post haste, for the especial service of the Kingdom.'

The terms were liberal, and so was the treatment of the defeated party; possibly too much so, for we read that

'The hunger-starved soldiers of Pendennis who came out thence, regaling too freely on victuals and drink, brought themselves into incurable diseases whereof many died, so that more men and women died by too often putting their hands to their mouths than by clapping their hands to their swords [1].'

Pendennis surrendered on August 16. On the following day Raglan submitted to Fairfax in person [2],

---

[1] Hall's *Parochial History of Cornwall*, quoted by Capt. S. P. Oliver.
[2] Sprigge, *Ang. Rediv.* pp. 302-334; Rushworth, *Hist. Collections*, pt. iv. vol. i. 295.

and all England acknowledged the authority of the Parliament. We need not wonder at Colonel Townesend's desire to be informed by the member for Bridport as to the Irish proceedings. The war was over in England, but in Ireland, on the part of the Parliament, it can hardly have been said to have begun as yet in earnest. They did not however lose time about it.

The *Perfect Diurnall* for August 24, says:—

'A thanksgiving was ordered for the surrender of Ragland and Pendennis: the three regiments at the taking of Ragland to be sent to Munster and shipped from Pendennis.'

It goes on to say:—

'£500 given by Fortescue at Pendennis to the adverse party to be repaid to him, as also £500 advanced by Batten for the same purpose.'

The sagacious Roundhead commanders had built a golden bridge for their enemy's retreat.

The Raglan regiments were sent to Munster, but those employed at Pendennis were not destined for that service as yet. Fortescue's regiment rejoined the main body of the New Model Army of which it was a part, and Colonel Townesend's, instead of remaining in Cornwall under the committee there who wished to keep them, was marched back into Dorset.

It was not however stationed permanently at Lyme, the garrison of which was now disbanded, the war being over, like so many others all over England. It was probably used in different parts of the county to support the authority of the Dorset committee. The only actual information about it however for the remainder of this year that we possess relates not to any services it may have performed in enforcing sequestrations or suppressing clubmen, but to the fact that the worthy committee were careful to provide their soldiers with spiritual refreshment, for in their minute-book, which is fortunately still preserved in Dorset, we may read in the crabbed handwriting of the time :—

'John Tucker has the public faith for one hundred twenty one pounds and two shillings due unto him as chaplain unto Colonell Towensend's (sic) regiment by order of the Lord Ffairfax his commission unto him directed for that place wherein he did officiate from the 20th day of April, 1646, unto the 15th day of April, 1647, at the rate of 8*d*. per diem. (dated) Jan. 29, 1649 (i.e. 1650).'

Eightpence a day seems cheap for a minister, and would come to but £12 for the 360 days mentioned, instead of £121. But if the rate should be read as eight shillings a day, the total comes out rather too much, as that would amount to £144 for the same period. However that may be, the entry at least establishes the fact that the regiment was kept at the charges of the Dorset committee for the year subsequent to the surrender of Pendennis.

That year was one which proved to be fraught with a struggle within the walls of Parliament hardly less important than the one which had just been decided in the field.

'You may go play now, gentlemen,' said Astley, unless you prefer to fall out among your selves.' They did fall out among themselves, and to some purpose ; nor were they long in doing so. When the war began, most of the officers, like the majority of the Parliament, were men who only desired to curb the power of the Bishops and fix some bounds to the prerogative of the King. Could this much be secured, they would have welcomed a peace that set Charles, whom they still regarded as something semi-sacred, once more upon the throne. But four years of strife had brought forward men of fiercer temper and wilder hopes, who felt no special awe for King or Parliament, priest or presbyter. These ardent spirits, Independents, Sectaries, Levellers, Anabaptists and the rest, were the heart and soul of the New Model, and it is no wonder that their growing predominance was viewed with great distrust by many, indeed one may say by all, of the Presbyterian party.

# CHAPTER II.

### THE IRISH TROUBLES.

THE Presbyterian majority in the Houses dreaded the strength of their own army, and the war in England being over, thought it desirable to get rid of their dangerous servants as soon as possible, and so be left undisturbed to treat after their own slow and solemn fashion with the King, who was now in the hands of their own commissioners at Newark. A way to do this suggested itself to them. Ireland was still unpacified, and the massacre of the Protestants in 1641 was still unavenged. To defeat Charles on English soil had been the first necessity, and this most pressing need had pushed the Irish question into the background for the time being, although it was from Ireland that the spark had originally come which lit the whole civil conflagration. Now the subject need be postponed no longer, and the Irish war really might be a distinct help to the perplexities of the Parliament.

If they could disband part of the army, the remainder might be safely bestowed in Ireland, and if they could give the Irish command to their own faithful friend, brave pious old Skippon, they would provide a possible rival to Cromwell, who was already suspected to be the silent, watchful, moving spirit of the troublesome military 'adjutators' or agents elected by the soldiers.

But the New Model Army had not the least intention

of being put quietly by out of the way, and allowing the iron yoke of Presbyterianism to be imposed upon them thus. It would be an error to say that they were men who fought for toleration pure and simple. 'If by liberty of conscience,' wrote Cromwell to the Governor of Ross on a memorable occasion, 'you mean a liberty to exercise the Mass, I judge it best to use plain dealing and to let you know where the Parliament of England have power, that will not be allowed of.' Religious toleration, which is now the very root of western civilisation, had then barely dawned upon Europe. Only from the poor despised and persecuted sect of the Baptists was heard the plea for absolute liberty of conscience. At Amsterdam in 1611 they had declared, 'The magistrate is not to meddle with religion or matters of conscience, nor compel men to this or that form of religion, because Christ is the King and Lawgiver of the Church and Conscience.' To the Presbyterian such a sentiment was anathema; the Independents, though less intolerant, had no such noble ideal before them. But practical necessity constrained them. A party made up of jarring sects must set up some sort of toleration if it is to remain a party at all. The Independents demanded mutual toleration for themselves and the Presbyterians, on the basis of a common action to suppress Episcopacy and Romanism. Would the Presbyterians of the House of Commons agree to this? The Army closed in on London to see this question settled as they desired. The power of the sword lay with them. The Presbyterians had a majority in the House, and with them lay the right to legislate, so far as they had any right to legislate at all without a King. Which would carry the day?

Meantime Charles dallied with both parties. 'I am

not without hope,' he wrote, 'that I shall be able to draw either the Presbyterians or the Independents to side with me for extirpating one another, so that I shall be really King again.' He declined the suggestion of the Presbyterians to establish their form of worship and suppress everyone else. 'What will become of us,' said one of them, 'now that the King has rejected our proposals?' 'What would have become of us,' retorted an Independent, 'if he had accepted them?'

The Army was full of suspicions and fears. It could trust few, but it knew and trusted the men who had led its prayer-meetings and won its victories, and without those leaders it refused to go to Ireland. Ireland truly needed 'settlement,' the reports from there describing 'a huge blot, and indiscriminate blackness[1],' but the 'Ironsides' had fought for the settlement of England, and that must be attended to first. They were beginning to see that Cromwell was the only man whom they could trust to settle anything anywhere, and at present Cromwell had no time for Ireland.

Early in March 1647 the Houses voted that 12,000 men should be employed in Ireland under Skippon and Massey: promptly in answer came the mutiny of regiment after regiment, and the Army ended by declaring Massey to be a traitor. But the Irish affairs were pressing, and some troops must be sent. The New Model would not go, so the Houses were forced to send those who would. Officers who were well affected to the Parliament, and trusted to it for the work of reconstructing the government, volunteered their services and went obediently to the Irish wars, and many of them succeeded in inducing their regiments to do the same. Even in the New Model itself

[1] Carlyle.

the Parliament had some backers. Colonel Fortescue presented an address to Fairfax protesting against the Army overawing the Parliament, and of his own regiment about 400 or 500 men actually went to Ireland. On April 26 a letter to the Parliament says, 'All of six companies of Col. Fortescue's regiment marched, Adjutant Gray Colonel over them.' Colonel Hungerford too was reported with others on April 19 as ready to start, and four regiments of Norfolk men volunteered to go. After the Restoration of Charles II a distinction was always drawn between the Parliamentary officers who went to Ireland before 1649 and those who accompanied Cromwell thither in that year. Those who went before 1649 were technically supposed to be serving the King and Parliament, even though the King was at the time a fugitive or a prisoner.

On June 19, 1647, the Parliament ordered 'That Colonel Townesend and his regiment be hereby required and commanded to be shipped and transported into Ireland for the service of the Kingdom [1].' In accordance with this order, Colonel Townesend marched his regiment to the coast and there took ship. In the minute-book of the Parliamentary committee for Dorset previously referred to we find that the collectors of the British Assessment for the following year were ordered to allow to those liable to it—

'All such charges as they have been at in the quartering of Colonell Jephsons regiment and Lieutenant Colonell Townsend his regiment in their march to the place of their embarquing for Ireland, as they shall make appear by ticket under the hands of some officer of the said regiments respectively ... provided that the said allowance exceeds not 12 pence for one horse and 6 pence for one man for the 24 hours.'

[1] Commons' Journals, 1647.

## THE IRISH TROUBLES.

It is not mentioned what the place of their embarking was, but it was most likely Lyme itself, or possibly Bridport. Ten miles north of Bridport, and a little to the east of Lyme, there is a village called Corscombe, and 100 men of Colonel Townesend's regiment were quartered there, as we learn from the same authority, for nine days before starting.

So while the Army lay coiled round London, demanding the expulsion of the eleven members of the Presbyterian party in the House whom they declared to be traitors, and rejoicing in Cornet Joyce's *coup-de-main* which had brought the King into their power, Colonel Townesend and his men were tossing on the waves of the Irish Sea on their way to reinforce the ragged and starving army of Lord Inchiquin, which represented the power of the English Parliament in Munster.

It was indeed a most distracted country to which they were sailing. For if at this moment Englishmen were divided into three parties, unhappy Ireland was being devastated by five or six.

First were the old Irish, or natural Irish as they were called, Celtic in blood and to a large extent in language, Roman Catholics to a man; they had most of them risen in rebellion in 1641, and they were now a powerful organisation with an army of their own in the field. They very earnestly repudiated the accusation of complicity in the massacres which had thrilled England with horror at the outbreak of the rebellion; the accounts, they said, had been very much exaggerated, and such outrages as unfortunately had occurred were only due to roving guerilla bands and not to the true leaders of the movement for national independence. They were guided at this time by an Italian

Archbishop, Rinucini, who had been sent over as papal Nuncio to compose some of the differences that agitated the country, but who proved to be a very firebrand. The general of their army was Owen Roe O'Neil, 'Red Owen,' a prudent and experienced soldier who had held high commands in the Imperial and Spanish wars. His ideas were clear. 'God knows I hate and detest all English parties alike' were his words, and his object was to make Ireland an independent Romanist State under the protection of one of the Catholic powers of the continent, probably Spain.

Secondly there were the Anglo-Irish, or English Irish as they were called, a very different set of men. They were descended from the Lords of the Pale and the Anglo-Norman conquerors of Ireland. The Reformation had never taken hold of Ireland as it did of England, and for the most part they were Roman Catholics still; but they professed entire loyalty to Charles, and demanded only toleration for their religion and security for their estates, which latter had been much endangered by Strafford's late reign of 'thorough.' By this time, however, the tyranny of the Lords Justices in Dublin (who represented there the English Government) had wellnigh driven them to desperation. They sent petition after petition to the King for relief; but the King was now a prisoner, and they decided that their only hope was to join their co-religionists, the followers of the Nuncio. Both these parties therefore combined to establish a Provisional Government, carried on by a Confederate Council at Kilkenny, and the Anglo-Irish general, Preston, and his army received orders to co-operate with Owen Roe. Thus for the time being they were united, but the truce between them was a hollow one, for the followers of Rinucini looked with great suspicion upon their new allies, who still nursed hopes of help from an English King and were provokingly moderate in their demands for concessions.

Thirdly, up in the North were the Ulster Presbyterians, closely allied with their Scotch brethren, and fighting very much for their own hand under Munroe.

Fourthly were the true Royalists, headed by the King's Lieutenant-general, the gallant and chivalrous Earl of Ormonde. The head of the noble family of Butler, he possessed large estates in Ireland, but had been brought up as a Protestant in England, and had been admitted to the Irish Privy Council by Strafford himself at the age of twenty-four. He owned a splendid castle of black marble at Kilkenny, and in this his enemies, the rebels' Confederate Council, were now holding their sessions, while he was cooped up by their armies in Dublin with a handful of starving and mutinous troops, thwarted by the Lord Justices and troubled by contradictory orders from the King; for Ormonde was too honest a man to be entirely trusted by Charles, whose favourite dream as we know was to recruit an Irish army for his English wars from among these very rebels. The King sent him one set of orders in public, and contradicted them in private through the Queen's secretary, Digby, until Ormonde found his position intolerable.

To these four we must add a fifth, the party of the English Parliament. The Parliament had no such grip on Ireland as it had on England, but its interests were represented in Dublin in great measure by the Lords Justices, who ever since the beginning of the rebellion had occupied themselves in thwarting Ormonde's endeavours to suppress it, hoping to keep his army so busy that no men could be spared from it to reinforce the King in England, and hoping too, it is hinted, that the wider the rebellion spread, the richer would be the harvest of confiscations that would follow on its suppression.

Perhaps we may even enumerate a sixth, for Lord Inchiquin in Munster was fighting very much for his own hand. Since his abandonment of the King in 1644 he had been reckoned as an adherent of the Parliament, but neither party trusted the other very far. Inchiquin entirely declined to put himself into their power or to obey their orders except so far as suited his own purposes, while the Houses on their part stinted him of supplies, and this very spring, in April 1647, sent over Lord Lisle and his brother Algernon Sidney to displace Inchiquin and give his command to his former friend Broghill. Inchiquin declined to give way and, his army being faithful to him, they had no power to enforce their commission to displace him, and Broghill for once returned unsuccessful to denounce his ex-convert as a traitor. Luckily for Inchiquin the Houses were too busy with accusations of their own members and fears of their own army at home to attend much just then to such a far-away place as Munster, and Inchiquin did his best to restore their confidence by hammering away at the rebels as hard as he could during the summer.

Charles's party in Dublin had by this time become a vanishing quantity. Ormonde found himself compelled to relinquish his position there to one party or another. Nothing would induce him to yield to the rebels, so he chose to surrender his post to the English Parliament. The Houses had no one in Ireland that they trusted enough to receive it, so they sent a faithful and energetic soldier, Colonel Michael Jones, with fresh troops to Dublin, where he landed in June, and Ormonde formally handed over the capital and retired to France.

The stoppage of supplies to Munster reduced Inchiquin to great straits; his men were even compelled to subsist on any wild roots they could dig up. Thrown thus on his own resources he made a vigorous effort to supply their needs, and after he had successfully stormed Cahir, the fertile county of Tipperary lay open to his famished troops, so that actually, as the water-mills were destroyed, they had more corn than they could consume, and were obliged to burn £2000 worth! His next great success was the storm of Cashel. He summoned the inhabitants of the town, offering to give them leave to depart on paying a heavy contribution, but as the magnificent ecclesiastical buildings that crown the Rock of Cashel had been newly fortified, the garrison rejected his offer and retired into the Cathedral. Inchiquin stormed the Rock, put three thousand to the sword, and slew the priests under the very altar. In August he overran Kerry, taking booty right up to the gates of Limerick, but avoiding the strong places, on account, he said, of the difficulty of transport for his artillery. He took care to keep the Parliament informed of these successes, and as a result reinforcements were sent to him freely.

But how loose his own allegiance to Parliament sat on him and his officers we may gather from the following letter printed in the *Moderate Intelligencer*, Aug. 26. The writer, dating from Cork, says:—

'Our condition here is strange; the Officers of War under Lord Inchiquin were no sooner returned hither from Field but they began to contrive a way of quarrel with the Parliament of England, the pretence being want of pay, discharge from service and such like, but the true reason conceived was to put somewhat in the scale against the Army in England and Parliament as it then stood, as they apprehended having the Army a rod over them.'

We should remember that the army had occupied London the first week in August; a number of horse were encamped in Hyde Park; troops were stationed round the House and on every avenue leading to it, so that by military force the Independents had now made themselves masters of the situation.

The writer goes on:—

'And that the design may not be thought in the least to countenance or accommodate the Rebels, it is declared that they resolve to go on against them with as great vigour as before, but yet they declare to the world that for the causes aforesaid they will not admit of any alteration in Government Martiall until their arrears are paid them, both what is due in England and Ireland, and until the Parliament of England be again free: these are the main pieces of the declaration which is large. At first the Lord President (Inchiquin) seemed not to have knowledge or hand in it, yet the Officers laboured in it and invited the other forces of that Kingdome in Parliament pay to the same, and were in hopes of a generall concurrence. But since then the Lord Inchiquin hath engaged to send the said Declaration unto Parliament in England.'

Possibly Inchiquin was at the bottom of it all, as the writer, evidently no friend of his, plainly hints; but it is just possible too that he may have been playing the part of the French demagogue when he observed of his mob, 'Of course I must follow them. Am I not their leader?' Anyhow, this war-correspondent of the seventeenth century continues:—

'We are here about 7000 Horse and Foot, and having secured our garrison can march about 5000 into the field, which, had we a mind, might not only block up but take townes, no enemy appearing: but we follow the old way in England, get a town or castle or two and then come home and stay half a yeare before we go out again, making a little work go a long way. The regiments of my Lord Lisle, Sir Hardresse Waller, and Sir Arthur Loftus are given away by the Lord President. One Knighted by his Majesty for his good service done at the taking of Leicester (? Sir Robert Sterling) is made Colonel of Horse and chief Commissioner of the Horse in Munster, and it must not be wondered at that many such are put in places of command.'

Plain speaking, truly! we need not wonder that the writer remained anonymous.

One can easily imagine the savage sarcasms of the Royalist newspaper writers over the dissensions of their enemies. These unlicensed prints made fun of both factions. *Mercurius Melancholicus* for Sept. 11 begins with verse:—

'To the Presbyterians
Your light is almost out; it was not fire
From God's own Altar taken, but his ire:
What Heaven doth plant shall to perfection grow:
If you be such, oh then! why droop ye so?

To the Independents.
Think not because ye are percht upon the throne
You are cocke-sure of all, that all's your owne:
The game's not lost as yet, but there I'll sticke,
An English game may have an Irish tricke.'

Charles's dream of an Irish trick to turn the game in his favour had found a lodging in the brains of his followers. *Mercurius* goes on to banter the Parliament with what he insinuates are but victories on paper.

'Newes, joyful newes from Ireland: the renowned Inchiquin has banged Oneale to some tune: all that the Rogues and Kernes can boast of is, That one payre of heeles is worth two payre of hands, and had not the woods sheltered their retreat 'tis thought this battel had struck a bargain to a Munsterian conquest.'

Alluding to a despatch of Inchiquin's after a battle near Limerick on his Kerry raid. Then he turns up his eyes and snuffles with the sanctimonious affectation he attributes to the saints,—

'To a resolved spirit, perills are but enterludes: let us not thwart those high designs, those happy events, with selfe ends, sinister reaches and domestic squabbles!'

These Royalist papers, surreptitiously printed and passed from hand to hand, are of course poorly off for news. They abound in ribaldry, and are untrustworthy to the last degree. They are not to be put at all in the same category as a paper like the *Moderate Intelligencer*, a weekly which is in many respects quite on a par with a high-class newspaper of the present day. But one can get a good deal of amusement out of their flouts and jeers at their conquerors, and sometimes rumours find a voice in them which the Puritan journals are less in a hurry to print. *Mercurius Melancholicus* evidently has hopes of Inchiquin's army, for next week he says,—

'They talke of a Scotch invitation made to the Lord Inchiquin and to Col. Jones governor of Dublin to join with the Blew Bonnets in Ulster (i.e. Munroe and his Scots) against the Army in England. Perchance they might have thrived among the Rebels better, for birds of a feather willingly flocke together: Scots and Irish make one monster, and it is a hundred to one but they will come together.'

The invitation may have come from the other side, for presently the *Moderate Intelligencer* proclaims that Jones has arrested a servant of Colonel Sterling, Inchi-

## THE IRISH TROUBLES.

quin's major-general, for making this identical proposition to Munroe in Ulster and 'General Levin'[1] in Scotland, and that the House has ordered Inchiquin to send Sterling over under arrest, and Puritan *Mercurius Anti-Pragmaticus* calls Sterling—

'A perfidious Scot who would have blown up all Ireland, but the Highest prevented his trecherous design from taking effect. And so, O thou that rulest Behemoth, confound all their plots and devices that now are very active to engage the two nations of England and Scotland in a new and bloody war.'

It was into this weltering chaos of parties at crosspurposes that Colonel Townesend (he was made full Colonel now) saw himself plunged as soon as he landed in Ireland, and it was this army of Inchiquin's, already hesitating in its allegiance, to which he found himself attached. The exact date and place of his landing we do not know; the most probable supposition is that it was at Cork in August. At all events strong reinforcements under Colonels Gray, Needham, and Temple, reached Inchiquin in September, and Colonel Townesend arrived then, if not earlier, at his destination. He had not long to wait for active service. The desecration of the cathedral at Cashel and the slaughter of the priests had roused the Nuncio, Rinucini, to fury. He denounced Lord Taaff and Lord Muskerry as traitors for having abandoned the defence of that holy spot, and declared that they were secretly in league with Inchiquin. Lord Muskerry was on the Supreme Council at Kilkenny, and his duties there did not allow him to take the field; but Lord Taaff, who was the general of the Council's army in Munster, was stung by these taunts, and the feeling they aroused, into moving his

[1] The Earl of Leven.

army in search of Inchiquin in spite of the inclement season. Inchiquin had already distributed his forces into their winter quarters, and seems to have been disinclined to go to meet his foe: he held a council of war to decide whether to call out the men from their garrisons or not, and it is said by some that it was only the urgency of the English officers, headed by Colonel Temple, that resolved him to fight. He is reported to have expressed his dissatisfaction with the Army-party in England, and to have even received overtures from the Irish. He had, however, excuse enough for not wishing to take the field in November apart from such considerations. The damp climate was telling severely upon the troops from England in their destitute condition. A letter written to the Parliament from his camp certainly does not mince matters.

'We long,' it runs, 'to hear from England that this poor Kingdom may have relief in its starving condition. 'Twould make your soul bleed to see the poor soldiers march out with never a whole rag to their backs nor shoes to their feet, feeble and faint for want of what should suffice nature; and yet they are as valiant as any in the world and showed themselves so in the battle, tho' kept eight or nine days in the Field when all our bread was spent and the battle was to be struck; never poor wretches more willingly went on, yea those that were sickish skipt for joy.'

It is true that the remonstrance of Inchiquin's officers had reached London, Sept. 18, and on Sept. 20 the Parliament had ordered seven thousand suits of clothes, shoes, and stockings, for Inchiquin. They also sent Colonel James Temple and Mr. Challoner to him 'to transact the business of the Houses with him.' This jam-and-senna combination affords *Mercurius Melancholicus* a fine subject for his gibes.

'The Commons,' says he, 'voted that 7000 suits of clothes, shoes, and stockings should be sent the Lord Inchiquin in Munster. This is not the first time they have voted what they never intended to send. Alas! Inchiquin is a Presbyterian (just such an one as my Lord of Manchester was) and if he receive no more comfort than he is like to have from a Westminster vote, his heeles may quickly cool for want of shoes, and he look as threadbare as a Scotch Laird in sackcloth upon the Stool of Repentance. But if Inchiquin will be converted (to Independency), that is turn round like a weather-cock with all winds, then 'tis probable he may thrive. And therefore he had best prepare his stomach for wholesome Counsell for the House hath ordered Col. Temple and Mr. Chaloner (one that said not long since in Parliament that the best Scot in the world was not worth whistling after) to go over to Munster and feele his Pulses whether there be any possibility of banishing the Scottish uncleane spirit and possessing him with seven worse.'

The officers who had brought over the 'Remonstrance' were committed to the custody of the Serjeant-at-Arms of the House of Commons to be proceeded against as the Houses should see good. They confessed themselves in fault and submitted; upon which the Commons graciously ordered a committee to be appointed to bring in an Ordinance for their Indemnity.

But the shoes did not come! It is said that the only anxiety that could ever keep the Duke of Wellington awake at night was thinking of the state of his soldiers' shoes. Lord Inchiquin might sleep sound enough; his men had none at all. At all events, ragged and barefoot as they were, in response to Lord Taaff's advance, he advanced with them to Mallow to meet him. The two armies encountered one another at Knocknones, a few miles west of Mallow, and there the battle was fought which for a time decided the fate of Munster.

# CHAPTER III.

### THE BATTLE OF KNOCKNONES.

THERE are various accounts of the battle in the newspapers of the time and in certain contemporary letters which were published in pamphlet form. Of these, the best and fullest is one preserved in the British Museum, which we propose to print entire, both for the quaint and graphic touches with which it describes the action, and because it alone gives the preliminary challenge and acceptance which passed between these two Irish noblemen of the seventeenth century previous to the encounter. Before beginning it, a few words on the tactics of the period and on the way in which the men were armed may not be amiss. Our authority is Major Walford, R.A., whose book, *The Parliamentary Generals of the Civil War*, contains an excellent summary of the art of war, as it was then practised.

The infantry were armed with pikes and musquets, the relative number of the pikemen and musqueteers being variable. The pikemen formed squares and the musqueteers fired on the enemy from their flanks, taking refuge within the squares of pikemen when assailed by cavalry. The horse were all armed with the sword, and carried in addition either a short carbine or a pair of pistols. The order of battle was generally formed in three lines, named respectively the main battle, the battle of succour, and the rear battle. The guns were posted between the battalions of the first line. The cavalry was divided pretty equally between the right and left wings, and about half on each wing was kept in reserve. On the whole it was considered that the force which stood on the defensive had a great advantage, as the attacking force was liable to get out of order in moving forward, and so expose itself to a counter attack. Small bodies of troops, styled 'forlorn hopes' and composed mainly of musqueteers, were pushed to the front by the defence as the enemy advanced, in order to delay and confuse his movements by their fire. The guns also played upon the advance with the same object, while the advancing party's guns could not return the fire until their own line was halted. The cavalry on each wing usually began by having a little separate battle to themselves, and the victors in it were then at leisure to fall upon the flanks and rear of their enemy's foot. As long as the squares of pikemen remained intact they were comparatively safe from the horse, but if they once were broken the footmen were at the mercy of the cavalry, who 'had the execution of them,' as the phrase was, while daylight lasted.

In the battle of Knocknones Colonel Townesend commanded the main battle[1], Colonel Blunt the right wing of foot, Colonel Gray the left. The 'forlorn hope' of foot was under Lieut.-Colonel Crispe. Inchiquin's own regiment of horse and Sir William Bridges' were on the left wing. Broghill's, Temple's, and Jephson's regiments of horse formed the right wing under Colonel Temple, having Captain Southwell and Captain Randolf

[1] *Moderate Intelligencer*, Dec. 16-23. *Newspapers*, 1647, British Museum.

as a reserve. The guns, six field-pieces, were posted on the left wing. Lord Taaff had no artillery with him, though he tried to make Inchiquin believe that he had. His troops outnumbered Inchiquin's almost two to one, but they were mostly armed with pikes, his supply of firearms being small, while the proportion of musqueteers in Inchiquin's foot was very high. The best troops in Taaff's army were a body of veteran Highlanders, armed with the musket and claymore, and led by Sir Alexander Macdonnell, the redoubtable Colkitto. A man of gigantic stature, he wielded his formidable sword equally well with either hand, which gained for him the nickname of Colkitto or the left-handed. He had fought like a hero of romance all through Montrose's wonderful campaign in the Western Highlands of Scotland, and had brought, after the disaster which befel Montrose at Philiphaugh, a regiment of staunch partisans from the Highlands to help in the Irish War. What fate had in store here for him and his 'Redshanks' let the narrative which follows tell.

A Perfect Narrative of the Battle of Knocknones by an Officer of the Parliament's Army present and acting at the fight. Directed to an Honourable Member of the House of Commons.

It was now a season as unapt for action to the naked English as opportune for the Irish, better inured and accommodated to the hardships of that country, when the Lord Taff, General for the Irish, advanced towards the English quarters with a designe to block up or distress them in their garrisons, wherein it being discerned that hee might prevalently proceed to their destruction if a seasonable opposition were not given; it was at a Council of Warre, summoned by the President, long debated whether to issue forth of our garrisons to encounter this approaching torrent or not, and at length, after an earnest endeavour of divers to the contrary, resolved to be more consistent with our safeties to make head against the rebels in the field, than to suffer them to come within our quarters, and so disable us either to join together in an offensive, or subsist together in a defensive posture. In pursuance of which resolution the Army (being by the general vote and the President's orders drawne together at Moyallo [1]) marched on the twelfth of this Instant [2] (after a due discharge of those pious invocations and exercises of addresses to the Divine Providence which the President had injoyned) to a place called Gariduff (in English Black-Gardens), the Rebels encamping at Knocknones within two miles of us; but the day so far spent as that it was not held fit to make any attempt then upon them. About the evening came a Trumpet from the Lord Taff with a letter to the President in these words,

MY LORD,

The delay of my not sending to you a returne of your last letter by your Trumpet was occasioned by my stay for my Artillery, which being come I tell your Lordship, that Captain Courtopp very much magnifying the excellency of your foot, I offered (more for recreation than with a suspicion that it might breake your army) that a thousand or two of mine should (when ever you made an indifferent appointment) fight with a like number of yours; which I am now ready to perform in this place, And if you please to draw the Remaine of your Army hither, I will look upon you, and certainly neither of our Parties will want the gallantry of seconding their ingaged friends. Our quarrell is to maintain the Kings Interests which all of us with the hazard of our lives will maintain against any opposition; And when I consider that by the destruction of your party I may be in the more unmolested condition to serve him, be certain your invitation to battle is acceptably received by me. I know that in your Lordships Army there are a great many gentlemen which have been very faithful to their King, and am sorry 'tis your Lordships practise to abuse them by continuing them in a

---

[1] Mallow.    [2] Nov. 1647.

service so destructive to his Majesties Rights. And pray my Lord do not delude them by distracting this Army who are unalterably and without any hope of particular benefit determined to loose themselves or restore (as much as in them lies) the King to his former greatnesse; this is truth, and it proceeds cordially from

Your Lordships servant,

Knocknones                                        TAAFF.
12 Novem. 27 (i. e. 47)

To which my Lord President returned,

MY LORD,
I have received your Letter by your Trumpeter, and your Lordship might before this have perceived that I was not ignorant where your Army lay, had not the approach of night scanted me of time to march up unto you; And being[1] you have performed as much as I desire in bringing your Army hither, I shall not desire you to loose any advantage you may have in numbers of men, being your Offer was only made for Recreation; You are pleased to say your quarrell is chiefly to preserve the Kings Interest, and because I believe it will little avail me to offer Reasons to convince you of the contrary, I shall defer the dispute until we meet in the morning, when I believe these Gentlemen whom yee suppose to be deluded by me will by Gods help use Rhetorick that will better conduce to that end, to which I shall refer your Lordship for satisfaction, being resolved to contribute therein to the endeavours of

Your servant,<br>INCHIQUIN.

This night we lodged in a wood which equally afforded both security and convenience unto the souldiers. The wood was to the Foot (Pray) and to the Horse (Prevaile) and this night some real appearance[2] was observed in the

---

[1] ? 'seeing.'

[2] A natural phenomenon easily interpreted as an omen. Cf. Milton, speaking of a comet that

'from his horrid hair
Shakes pestilence and war.'

## THE BATTLE OF KNOCKNONES.

nature of a meteor: early in the morning we began to prepare (the light giving us now a clear manifestation of what was to be done) the enemy was drawn up upon a hill about two myles off called Knocknones, which being of great advantage to them, the Lord President (if possible) to withdraw them from it sent this letter to the Rebels General.

My Lord,

Here is a very faire piece of ground betwixt your Lordships Army and ours on this side the brook; whither if you please to advance we will do the like; we do not so much doubt the gallantry of your resolution as to think you will not come but give you this notice to the end you may see we do stand upon no advantage of ground and are willing to dispute our quarrel upon indifferent terms; being confident that the justice of our cause will be this day made manifest by the Lord, and that your Lordships judgment will be rectified concerning

Your servant,

Novem. 13, 1647.  Inchiquin.

To which the Lord Taaff returned verbal answer that he was not so little a souldier as not to improve any advantage he had whether of ground or otherwise, which he doubted not the President would do in like case.

The reason as we learned afterwards by some of their men taken prisoners (besides the advantage of ground being a steep hill) why the Lord Taaff so pertinaciously stuck to that place was this.

There was a certaine old blinde Prophecie running amongst the Irish which, converted into English rymes like their old bard, speakes thus—

    Mac Donogh (future age shall see
    A man of thy posterity
    By whom the English Lord shall fall
    Bloud shall ascend to the legges small
    The place we Knocknones do call.

Which was by the Lord Taaff applyed to himself, for that hill whereon he stood was called Knocknones and his ancestors had the lands of Mack Donagh given by the Kings of

England in reward of their service performed against the Rebels here; their Lieutenant Generall sir Alexander M<sup>c</sup>Donnell, known vulgarly by the name of Colkitto, was unwilling to have the fight performed on that day[1] (upon a superstitious observation for that he was exceedingly afraid of Saturns malevolent influence, that day being to him criticall); the former name of the place was antiquated almost this last age, the name of it now being Englishmans hill, as it proved on this happy and successful day.

The Lord Taaff therefore resolving obstinately to adhere to his chosen ground, the Lord President calling a counsell of War to advise whether it were expedient to assault them on such a disadvantageous place (the wind friending them likewise and their numbers almost doubling ours), but the sense of our present condition quickly resolved this scruple, it being to no purpose to have advanced hitherto if wee should proceed no further, and for the success to put ourselves upon the mercy of God. It is not to be forgotten here that before the counsell the Lord President commanded that God should be sought by prayer for our direction in this needful time of trouble. The word given on our side was Victory, the mark a branch of new broome in our hats, wherewith our Quarters then abounded. The enemies mark was a strawen rope about their hats, their Word was God and St. Patrick, they having forgotten how lately their country Saint had failed them (for that was the word when we put them to the sword at Cashel), their numbers consisted as themselves gave out 9000 Foote and 1000 Horse, but by list found afterwards in the Lieutenant Generalls[2] pocket they were mustered in the field 7464 foot and 1076 horse besides Officers. Our Army was neere 4000 Foote and 1200 horse, the enemie ranging their battel in a plain front, all along the hill, that so they might engage all their force together, their foot was drawn into nine divisions of which the greater part by much was Pike, winged with three bodies of Horse on each side beside Reserves, our foot whose number was by half the lesse were marshalled into three divisions whereof

---

[1] Saturday, Nov. 13.      [2] Colkitto's.

two parts of three were muskets, the right and left wing of horse were made of 13 bodies of Horse, 7 on the right wing and six on the left (with their Reserves). Both Armies thus drawn up.

The Rebels held firmly (their first resolution) not to part with their station, but that we should either not fight at all or do it upon these unequall Terms, the wind was for the Rebels, the Lord President (whose Rival no man can be in this piece of glory, it being indeed in all mens judgments under God the gaining of the day on our side, thoroughly weighing their numbred ground and commodity of the place above us, all which he considered of too much moment that they might be to turn the scale in the Ballance of War, thought of a way of forcing them to that they would not willingly be drawn to, to leave the ground and discompose their present forme that so (we might have the advantage in that disorder) to assault them, and this he effected thus; He drew the left wing[1] of his battle from the ground wherein he at first placed them, making them to move into a place of fallow ground more leftward, as if he would get upon the enemies backs on that side, and commanded his right wing[2] to wave a little that way too, as if he went with all his force to assail them in that one place. The Rebells, careful enough to support their own designe, had a watchful eye upon all our motions, and by this last imagining they might be charged in the rear or surcharged with the multitudes of our men at one place, the train of the Lord Presidents plot immediately took: for they breaking from their first form parted with their stands: Likewise drawing most of their Forces to succour their right wing, by varying the scene of their ground we got these advantages. The wind was made an indifferent arbiter, the ascent of the hill not so steep, and onely the Sun was now a neuter to ripen the Fruit of this Design quite, which was now more than green. The Lord President commanded two pieces of Artillery to be drawn to

[1] Inchiquin's own regiment on the left of his 'battle.'
[2] Apparently Sir William Bridges' regiment of horse on the right of Inchiquin's 'battle,' but it may possibly mean Temple on the right of the whole army.

play on their right wing and if any disorder thereby hapned our Horse and Foot were in that nick to fall on: our right wing [1] having observed the left of theirs made thin with some confusion likewise with sending relief to their friends, had command to resume their first stations and to incline further to the right hand (as our left wing had done before to the left) as if they likewise intended to surprise the Rebels on the back; to prevent which the Rebells resolved immediately to fall on: to this end they advanced with their Horse before their Foot to charge; but that error being soon espied by ours, our shot were commanded presently to advance under the shelter of a Ditch that parted them and us, who poured such showers of hail upon them (that it proved a funerall peall to many) the rest retired foul and routed their own Foot. This their neighbours espying followed their example and so their main body of Foot and the left wing of Horse [2] ran clean away, and our Horse [3] followed after them in the chase: but God willing to mingle a little gall with the sweet cup he had before given us (that so we might be contented to receive everything at his hand) was pleased that part of the ground which was assigned for our left wing was not so convenient for horse but yet to be accepted (where there was no choice of better) but very defenceable by Foote by reason of some enclosure and ditches and a lane near adjacent; there the Lord President made the bounds of his Foot but they by their vallour (if not rashnesse rather) fancying to themselves some imaginary advantage pressed further and so clouded us a little with the smoake of their shot; that the right wing of the Rebells Army which was led by Sir Alexander Mack-Donnel, alias Colkitto, the Rebels Lieutenant Generall, on whom our guns playing fiercely (to prevent that danger and performe some notable service as he had promised with his Red-shankes) came thundering down without the least

---

[1] Apparently Temple's brigade on the right of the whole army, but it may mean Sir William Bridges on Inchiquin's right.

[2] Under Lord Taaff himself who is said to have pistolled several men with his own hand in trying to stop their flight.

[3] Temple's undoubtedly. Inchiquin himself seems to have ridden round the Irish rear and met him after routing Purcell.

sense of danger, even the rebels horse on the right wing[1] advancing with those foot were charged by their opposite horse[2] on our left wing and routed; who following hard upon them, the Rebels foot slipped in undiscerned of them upon our foot, whose forwardnesse, seeing the enemies horse routed, had left their defensive stage which they might with ease and safety have maintained, and rouling downe like a Torrent impetuously on our Foote routed our forlorn hope[3], by which means our foot[4] being outnumbered the Enemy began to have the execution of them; possest two of our guns and one of them being loaded discharged it against us, and so tearing down all before them got to our waggons and there fell a plundering; had it not been for this disaster without doubt we had bought a most perfect and glorious victory at the easiest rate that might be without the losse as is imagined of ten men, but this cost some fifty of our common men their lives, and divers of our galantest Commanders not being able to stay their men nor willing to run along with them, there gloriously sacrificed their lives rather chusing to die though almost deserted of all than to give the least ground back to so barbarous and cruel Rebels. The Lord President was but newly parted from the left wing being on the right where he joyfully saw a Victory on the nick of gaining by the total discomfiture of that part of the enemy; but looking towards our left wing there his eyes were presented with the rueful spectacle of his mens slaughter and the Rebells overturning all before them even to our wagons, he immediately posted down some regiments of foot[5], and a troop or two of horse which had been there for Reserves[6] and had not come upon the charge: These coming down fell upon the Rebels in their return from our Baggage where they made their lives pay the price of their insolent attempt by putting the greatest part of them to the sword, amongst whom fell Sir

[1] Under Colonel Purcell.
[2] Inchiquin's horse.
[3] Under Lieutenant-Colonel Crispe who was captured.
[4] Colonel Gray's. He was killed at the guns.
[5] Colonel Townesend's and Colonel Blunt's.
[6] Captain Southwell's and Captain Randolf's.

Alexander Mack Donnell[1] and his Lieutenant Colonel. And thus by Gods help and the wisdom and vallour of our General, Commanders and Souldiers, a glorious victory was gained over the Rebels, the chase was followed every way by our Foote and Horse, but Horse especially, for they were too light for our footmen all over the Countrey, till night hindered the further prosecution, when a retreat being sounded for that time the Lord President and his Officers in the field with their Souldiers gave thanks to God for his extraordinary great mercy and deliverance. The slaughter was not made an end with that day, for the next day our Horse ranged the Countrey and found divers, and the foot hunted the woods and bogs and by that means found many of the enemy which were put to the sword upon the place.

The storm fell sore upon their foot, the Countrey who should know best report five thousand to be slaine, there could not be less than four thousand, we recovered neere 6000 Armes, 38 Collours of Foote, with some Cornets of Horse, wee also recovered their Waggons and all their Ammunition, took the Lord Taaff's their Generalls tent, field bed, and Cabinet wherein are papers of Concernment, importing much of this service of Ireland, which is to be delivered into the House. In it was likewise found his commission from the Supreame Councell for being Generall of the Forces of Munster; so that by the losse of his Army he wants Men to command and of his Commission, power to command men: On our part were slain in that unhappy rout of our left wing some noble and gallant Officers, Sir William Bridges Colonell of Horse, Colonell Gray, Major Browne, Sir Robert Travers the Judge Advocate was killed at our Baggage, a Captaine or two, Reformados, and some other Officers of inferior rank, when the sword had sufficiently quenched his thirst of bloud, then in a cooler vaine mercy began to take place and these Persons undermentioned were taken prisoners:—Colonel Randal Mack Donnel, Lieut. Col. Mack Namarra, Major John Fealane and about seventy officers more whose names are given in a list appended.

Divers other Captaines and Officers were made prisoners

[1] Killed, it is said, by Major Purdon of Broghill's regiment.

## THE BATTLE OF KNOCKNONES.

who remaining yet in the Souldiers hands unbrought in could not be inrold in this list, on our part were taken prisoner Lieutenand Colonell Crispe, who is now released and with us for an Officer of theirs of like quality, besides one Lieutenant more, here to give you just account what every Officer and Souldier performed (except that small party which unfortunately fled) would swell this relation too much, and inquire the actors modesty, who desire the glory should be ascribed to God, themselves being but employed as instruments. For the Officers, and amongst the forwardest of them Colonell Temple who had seen them performe this dayes service, would have thought them worthy of a better reward, then having conquered all their enemies abroad, to go home and be conquered themselves by their owne wants, each Souldier honoured God by his vallour, and none dishonoured themselves. The Lord President has not yet made an end of his victory, for he is prosecuting it vigorously by reducing all the Countrey into Contribution, where he marches notwithstanding the violence of the weather, and the practises of some to draw the Souldier to a mutinous crying out, Home, Home, it being now a deepe snow and his men almost naked, that so the Province may be subdued and the Rebels disabled to draw suddenly to a head againe, which if it please the Divine Providence to assist us with seasonable supplies, we shall use all possible and effectuall meanes to prevent.

A brief of the slain and taken

| | |
|---|---:|
| Taken of the Enemies Horse | 200 |
| Slain of the Foot | 4000 |
| Officers taken Prisoners | 68 |
| Gentlemen of the Countrey | 6 |
| More Officers | 4 |
| Colours of Foot | 38 |
| Cornets of Horse | 3 |
| Of Ammunition, wagons | 4 |
| Of Armes | 6000 |

The Lieutenant Generall slain.

FINIS.

The above is a straightforward account of the battle by an eye-witness, a soldier himself, and is to be much preferred to descriptions of it written by non-military authors long afterwards. It may, however, be supplemented on a few points by other contemporary evidence. A letter from William More, written on the night after the battle, says—

'The dispute by parties lasted some two houres until at last the Rebels began to descend from the top of the hill and then the fight was very fierce but lasted not long for in half an hour they were routed and broken: no quarter was given to the Irish Rebels nor to the Redshanks. The Lord Inchiquin charged many of the quality of the enemy's party, amongst the rest one his Lordship pursued to a wood and there slew him, a confederate officer: and his Lordship did so cut the Rogues that he brake his sword into three pieces.'

Inchiquin's own words, in his report to the Speaker of the Commons, are—

'The dispute lasted not above half a quarter of an hour but the execution ended not in that day; for though we were killing till night as fast as we could yet we found two or three hundred next day in the woods as we were viewing the bodies, but could not possibly get any exact accompt of the number slain; for after I had an accompt of more than 2000 that the pursuing parties slew in their several walks, I was informed of many hundreds that were slain in divers other places, so as our men believe there were not less than 5000 slain; but I do not think it possible there should be above 3000, because the dispute lasted not at all; and that except the three regiments of Foot that came on with Sir Alexander Mack Donnell the rest made the best use they could of their heels to the woods and bogs towards Kanturk, Newmarket and Lyscarrol; yet we cut 200 of their horsemen.'

The 'butcher's bill' was complete. 'Homo homini lupus.' No wonder Ireland swarmed with wolves, when man provided such feasts for creatures not more savage than himself.

The report in the *Moderate Intelligencer* for Dec. 16-23, from which we took the names of the divisional commanders in the order of battle, says that the rout of Colkitto's Redshanks was effected by Captains Southwell and Randolf

'To which Townsend and Blunt gave good help . . . the gainers of this happy victory, under God, appear in the relation of the fight; more need not be said in their commendation; it is usual to give by name commendation to those who do gallantly, therefore none will take it ill.'

'But 'twas a famous victory.' At Buttevant still stands a ruined Franciscan Priory, in whose crypt is piled a great heap of mouldering human bones, which are believed to be the relics of those who fell at Knocknones. The mighty frame of Colkitto and his valiant arm impressed the imaginations of the people. Under the name of MacAllisdrum, the memory of the gigantic Sir Alexander MacDonnell lingered long among the Irish peasantry. Down to the middle of the following century a 'very odd kind of Irish music' was well known in Munster as the MacAllisdrum's March: it was a wild kind of rhapsody in his praise, and was so much esteemed that it was played by the Irish at all their Feasts [1].

NOTE.—For some account of Knocknones from the other side, the curious may consult the *Aphorismical Discovery*, an anonymous MS. printed by Mr. J. T. Gilbert in his *Contemporary Hist. of Ireland*, 1641-1652. It gives an insight into the frantic quarrels of the confederates among themselves.

[1] Smith's *History of Cork*.

# CHAPTER IV.

## PLOT AND COUNTERPLOT AND THE SURRENDER OF CORK.

Proud of his success Inchiquin hastened to send off a messenger, Captain Piggott, with despatches to announce it to the Houses. They received the news with effusion, ordered a thanksgiving for it to be celebrated all over the country, voted £50 to the lucky Captain Piggott as a gratuity, £10,000 for the Munster army out of the first moneys for Ireland £1,000 as a present for Inchiquin himself and a special letter of thanks, passing likewise that Ordinance of Indemnity for those who acted in the former disturbances there. At the same time there was a report made to the House of the Merchant Adventurers' consent to £5000 more being advanced [1].

*Mercurius Pragmaticus* makes very merry over the whole business:—

'And it is very needful now that the citizens should refund, else what sign will there be of great thankfulnesse to God for Inchiquin's great victory in Ireland, which the Houses give them to understand is one main step to the recovery of the old adventurers upon Irish lands; and therefore appointed them a day of thanksgiving in hope to be invited to dinner and then to break the business to them; but the citizens say they are quite weary of such bold and sturdy beggars as will have victuals and money too.'

[1] *Perfect Occurrences*, Nov., Dec. *Newspapers*, 1647. British Museum.

We must remember that the city was decidedly Presbyterian, and not at all inclined to overmuch confidence in this New Model of Parliament where Independency was rampant, and, of course, Pragmaticus does his best to foment discord between the two. Also, that the very day of Knocknones, when Inchiquin's cavalry were riding down the wretched kernes, Charles himself was riding blindly southward, having fled from Hampton Court, a fugitive not knowing where to look for safety, seeking it at last in the Isle of Wight, which he was never to leave again save as a close prisoner. Also that a very dangerous 'Levelling party' had now risen in the army, and that Monday, Nov. 15, had seen Cromwell face this alarming movement at the mutinous rendezvous in Corkbush Field between Hertford and Ware, and trample it out for the time not without shedding of blood. Cromwell knew well the necessity of keeping up the army in England, for its work was not yet done, but he was resolute to keep it in hand. Pragmaticus, however, goes on to hint that the Irish war was but a sham, an unreal excuse for maintaining an army at all.

'So then it is supposed, though the Houses in a frolic have ordered £10,000 for Inchiquin's army with £1000 for Inchiquin himself, yet the Devill a penny are they like to have, and so their heeles may cool for all a Westminster vote which seldom conveys any comfort into Ireland because that Warre must be kept on foot still, the better to countenance the keeping up of forces here, and thus they must be content with an ordinance of Indemnity for their former mutinies.'

The everlasting indemnity and still no shoes! 'Thank you for nothing' the Munster army might well rejoin. Chasing barefoot through the snow after the wretched fugitives of Knocknones might be necessary to ensure their own safety, but was not calculated to warm their hearts towards the Parliament that had set them the task. 'More naked than the very Indians' is one description given of their state at this period, yet they kept up the campaign. Lord Taaff was busy raising a fresh army, and they dared not relax their efforts.

'Our Commanders-in-chief in Ireland are all in the field,' says the *Moderate Intelligencer*, in February, 1648, 'notwithstanding those necessities that surround them, Hunger, Nakedness, and want of pay, sharper than the swords of their enemies: the truth is the extremities of the very officers are intolerable. The Lord Inchiquin hath taken a castle of my Lord Ormondes within 8 miles of Kilkenny.'

If their extremities were intolerable Parliament at least could not plead ignorance of them. Early in 1648 Inchiquin's officers joined in a Declaration of Remonstrance to Parliament on their treatment[1] This Declaration sets forth very plainly the shocking state in which the soldiers of the Munster army had been left for want of supplies. To abandon them to cold, hunger, and nakedness, was but a poor return for the blood they had shed so freely in the Parliament's service. The clothes promised them before winter had never come, and of the £10,000 but a bare £2,700, and of that only £1,500 was destined to procure them food. Their enemies were more threatening than ever, and for lack of supplies they were unable to defend themselves. If, therefore, the Parliament did not mean totally to abandon them to their fate, let them either have supplies enough sent them to enable them to feed and defend themselves, or else let shipping be sent to

---

[1] Borlase, who gives the full text of the Remonstrance.

fetch them off to England. And failing either of these things, they asserted that there was nothing left for them to do but to make such terms as they could with the rebels.

Assuredly this was plain speaking. It is never pleasant to be told by those who have fought for you that you have treated them so ill that they are ready to abandon your service. The Parliament was very naturally angry, and many of the subscribers were sent for to England and committed to prison; they apologised however, and were soon released, and an act of Indemnity for them passed. But the work was done: when you have exposed your life for masters who leave you to starve, it does not conciliate you to be clapped into prison for remonstrating; Inchiquin had got his officers thoroughly dissatisfied with the Parliament. The first name in the list of those who subscribed to the Remonstrance is that of Colonel Richard Townesend.

There can be no reasonable doubt that this Declaration was a move of Inchiquin's in the game he had now made up his mind to play. For he had by this time decided to break off entirely with the Army party in England, whose grip on the Parliament was daily tightening. He deeply distrusted the form their ideas were taking. Even in England there were growing fears of the fanaticism of the 'levellers[1],' and Inchiquin was clear that a 'commonwealth of saints' was not fit for a gentleman to live in, and was not pleased to think every victory he won might be bringing the day nearer when plain McMurrough O'Brien, no longer Lord Inchiquin, would have to rub shoulders with any

[1] See Cromwell's letter to Colonel R. Hammond: 'This fear of levellers that they would destroy nobility.' Carlyle.

ploughman or cobbler who was 'moved to give his testimony' on the management of all things spiritual and temporal.

But would the officers who had joined him from England share his views? The very fact that they had come to Ireland when they did showed they had little in common with the dominant party in the English Army, while now they had not much cause for loyalty to the neglectful English Parliament. Most of them belonged to the party which for a year past had been negotiating for the restoration of the King on condition of the establishment of Presbytery, and some, like the D'Oyleys, were Royalist gentlemen who had been pardoned by the Parliament on condition of going to the Irish wars.

But the balance of power having shifted from the Houses to the Army the Government was no longer the same that had sent them over. Did they still then owe it fidelity? England was drifting wildly towards some unknown goal. Among the new powers that had sprung up the Crown only was unchanged. Might not the King have learned wisdom from adversity, and if they supported him might they not crush this wild Independent party and guide England back to her old constitutional course? Was not this the duty of every patriotic English Protestant?

All that winter, 1647-8, the negotiations between the King, the Parliament and the Scots' Commissioners had dragged on. The Army, under its able leaders, Cromwell and Ireton, now proposed moderate and hopeful grounds for accommodation, but the King clung to his infatuated belief that he could play all parties off against each other, and gave no real heed to their proposals.

For the time it seemed as if his policy would succeed: the Scots concluded a Secret Treaty with Charles, which bound them to send him an army, and the mere hope of these Scotch reinforcements made the Royalist party spring to life again everywhere.

In February Wales rose, then followed Cornwall and Devon; there were riots in London, and in May the men of Kent were up in arms. The second civil war had begun.

The more moderate party of the Irish Confederates, weary of the violence of the Nuncio, determined to break with him and join the King's party. Accordingly they sent Lord Muskerry and Geoffry Brown, Lord Ormonde's legal adviser, over to France with secret instructions signed by their generals, Preston and Taaff, to negotiate with the Queen. Fortunately for her cause Ormonde had taken refuge in Paris, and his wise advice induced her to return a prudent and gracious answer to their proposals. The Presbyterian Scots of Ulster were now inclining, like their brethren of Great Britain, to the side of the King, the officers of the Parliament's Dublin garrison were wavering, and even Broghill's name was mentioned among the allies [1].

At the end of February, Bishop George Synge [2], who had left Dublin when it was given up to the Parliament, arrived at Cork with dispatches from Lord Ormonde, and on receiving them Inchiquin sent off an officer to Scotland to assure himself of support in that country, and received the full approbation of the Scots Parliament, who actually agreed to his making an alliance with the Romanists at Kilkenny!

By the 3rd of April Inchiquin was sure that most of his officers would support him, and he sent for

---

[1] Leland's *Hist. of Ireland*, iii. 323.      [2] See notes on chapter vi.

certain 'surly parliamentarians'[1] into the presence chamber of the castle at Mallow and spoke openly to them, reminding them that the Independents had forced the Parliament to break the Oath of Allegiance which required his Majesty to be secured on the throne, and were now threatening the whole constituted order of government and society in England. 'I hope before Michaelmas,' said he, 'to see them flat on their backs[2].' On parade next day he harangued the rest of his troops, and almost all were ready to follow him.

Still there were a few 'surly parliamentarians' who were not to be turned round so easily. They held that the popish queen, Henrietta Maria, was at the bottom of all the troubles of the kingdom, and they were not to be flattered by the gracious messages she might send through Bishop Synge and the Duke of Ormonde. Were they, at the bidding of a French woman, to offer the right hand of fellowship to the papist Taaff and forget all that

> 'The Hand of God had wrought
> For the Houses and the Word'?

Several of them, Sir William Fenton, Colonel Phair, Capt. Fenton and some others, made a desperate plot to seize the seaport of Youghal and so keep open the communication with England, from whence they hoped for a ship with supplies. But Inchiquin was on the alert and promptly imprisoned them in different castles, where they remained till the following autumn, when they were exchanged for Lord Inchiquin's son, who had been detained a hostage in England[3].

---

[1] Prendergast, *Cromwellian Settlement*.
[2] *Moderate Intelligencer*, April 13, 1648.
[3] Borlase. Lord Inchiquin's son was sent to the Tower in October. Inchiquin to Ormonde, Nov. 14, 1648, mentions the landing of his son at Castle Haven, Co. Cork.

Lord Broghill, who always felt a jealousy of Inchiquin, was extremely indignant at the imprisonment of these gentlemen, who were his relatives and particular friends. As he believed that Inchiquin had arrested them from private dislike, not from public motives, he seriously thought of breaking off negotiations with the adherents of Ormonde and joining Jones the Parliamentary commander at Dublin[1]. But whether from dislike of the Independents, or from finding the army not yet ripe for revolt, he thought better of it, and allowed a chilly reconciliation to be patched up between himself and Lord Inchiquin.

To the Royalist journals it seemed that at last the good time was really coming when Charles should have his own again. The Scottish Presbyterians were raising an army of forty thousand men under the Duke of Hamilton, to come and put down the English sectaries; Colonel Poyer's rising in Wales was thriving apace; and now the Munster army had declared itself. *Pragmaticus* for April 11 is very cock-a-whoop, and informs the Houses—

'That it is high time to unvote those wild and peremptory conclusions against kingly power. For the Lord Inchiquin likewise holds the same resolution with the Welsh, and hath given the high and mighty STATES to understand in plain terms that he will stand for the king, and bids a figg for their supplies and their orders and ordinances [they had just treated Munster to yet another Ordinance of Indemnity], and says he scornes to own the thing at Westminster for a Parliament, because it is a Beast ridden by troopers and fit for nothing but to be baited on holydays by the London Apprentices.'

Parliament promptly voted Inchiquin to be a 'Rebel and a Traitor.'

[1] Carte's *Life of Ormonde.*

Inchiquin having now definitely broken with Parliament, hastened to make a cessation with the Lord Taaff, on the terms that Taaff was to have Limerick, Clare, and Tipperary to support his army, while Inchiquin's share was to be Cork, Kerry, and Waterford. It was signed on May 20. The Nuncio, a bitter enemy to Taaff, was furious at it, and breathing forth excommunication and interdict against all who should accept this unholy compact, he fled to the camp of his only friend Owen Roe; and so frantic was his hatred of the Moderates whom Taaff represented, that he actually made common cause with Jones the Parliamentary governor of Dublin. But that move did him little good, for Lord Inchiquin sent Major D'Oyley with 500 horse to reinforce Taaff's army, and ere long O'Neil had to retreat to Ulster, and D'Oyley and Taaff drove the Nuncio to Galway, where they held him closely besieged. The hopes of the leader of the Munster army rose high. For a moment it seemed as if he was yet destined to crush the great Independent party and aid in re-establishing the Royal authority in England. It was only for a moment. Inchiquin's new allies were anything but cordial, and his officers began to see that they had gained little by their change of sides. However neglectful of them the English Parliament might have been, England was still their own country and it was bitter to side with the Irish against her. A letter in the *Moderate Intelligencer* for June 29, dated from aboard the 'Lion' at Kinsale, and doubtless written by one of the escaped officers who kept up communication with his comrades of the Munster army, shows how some at least of them felt about it already:—

'The sad effects which usually follow revolts are fallen upon the Province of Munster. The Lord Inchiquin and his officers we are credibly informed are sick of the agreement with the Rebels, insomuch that a line of one hair would bring them back to the Parliament.'

He alleges that Inchiquin had recalled the 500 horse under D'Oyley and had marched his Foot into Limerick in search of supplies which were refused him by his new allies. The necessities of his troops were greater than ever, and they were afraid to separate into small parties in search of what they needed for fear these new allies should turn upon them suddenly and, joining with Owen Roe again, cut them off utterly.

Their discontents indeed were great, and any hopes that they entertained of relief from a Presbyterian victory in England were speedily dashed to the ground. The Scots under Hamilton crossed the border in July just as Cromwell had driven Poyer to surrender at Pembroke, and so had stamped out the Welsh rising. Marching rapidly to the north, Cromwell fell upon them at Preston and smote them hip and thigh for three long August days, from Langridge Chapel all the way to Warrington. That crushing defeat ended the second civil war at one blow. The leaders of the various risings paid the penalty. Fairfax at Colchester shot Sir George Lisle and Sir Charles Lucas after a military trial. Poyer suffered the same fate a little later on, and the Duke of Hamilton was beheaded in Palace Yard. Inchiquin must have felt his own head loose upon his shoulders. He was really at a standstill. A report under date Dublin, Sept. 4, says—

'The Lord Inchiquin acts nothing, neither the Lord Taaff that we know of, neither against one another nor the Rebels who are still at difference, Preston making several attempts upon Owen Roe and he again upon Preston, the first (Owen Roe) being Irish naturall and the other English Irish:

after ages will wonder when they read of such a posture as this,'

Whatever Inchiquin's personal feelings may have been he saw that it was too late for him to draw back. He and Taaff are said in default of money to pay their forces to have let most of their men go to the plough, retaining with them only about 600, rather as a bodyguard than as an army, and with these they joined Preston in besieging Fort Faulkland, and there defeated an attempt of Owen Roe's army to relieve it, with heavy loss. Moreover, Ormonde landed at Cork in September, bringing some supplies to allay their armies' discontent, bringing also many promises; and for some time it seemed as if Inchiquin's personal popularity would prevent the discontent from coming to an outbreak.

But, on November the 8th, Colonel Edward D'Oyley[1] came to him at Castle Lyons, where he was staying with Colonel Jack Barry[2], and told him that the disaffection of the officers arose from a fear that all those who disliked the treaty which Ormonde was negotiating with the Irish would soon share the prisons of Fenton and Phair. If his Lordship would only sign a paper assuring the officers of their personal freedom they would, if the treaty succeeded, quietly leave the service; but if the treaty should be broken off, as treaties had occasionally so ended, they would continue in the army with all faithfulness.

Lord Inchiquin and Colonel D'Oyley were perfectly agreed in distrusting each other, and Inchiquin saw the danger of signing an unconditional amnesty which would cover all possible future misdemeanours. He temporised, and said he would ride to Cork and address the officers and do his best to satisfy them,

[1] Carte's *Ormonde*, book v. p. 45.  [2] See chapter viii. for Barry.

intending, as he wrote to Lord Ormonde, to flatter the mutineers with the hope that the treaty would be wholly waived, so that when the army was quieted and the heads of this faction secured, the treaty could be carried out in safety. Colonel D'Oyley protested that he was only the mouthpiece of others, and was himself perfectly satisfied of his Lordship's intentions, and was ready to attend him to Cork; and so went out to his horse. But when Lord Inchiquin followed, Colonel D'Oyley was not to be found. He had galloped off to his own troop at Limerick and started at their head for Dublin, to join his fortunes with those of Jones' garrison. Inchiquin did his best to keep D'Oyley's example from being followed, and wrote the following letter to his lifeguard at Kilkenny:—

'Fellow-souldiers, I doubt not but you have notice of a revolted body of horse officers who are labouring to betray this noble army into the hands of the Independents, and quite to extinguish that small spark of hope that is left for his Majesty's restitution, without which, as we can never hope for a freedom of parliament, (for no king no Parliament) so we can never expect if we come once under their power but they will keep us in perpetual bondage to an Independent tyranny. And being apprehensive that some of the late revolted officers have too great influence upon your captain and lieutenant I have thought fit to place in their rooms ——, captain, and ——, lieutenant, whom I shall desire you to observe and obey as your officers, to whose care I do commend you, assuring further unto you that the pretences of those revolted officers are of all things most false and unjust; for that as we never intended to engage against Jones, so upon my credit there is no conclusion nor likelihood of a conclusion for peace with the Irish until every person interested be satisfied. And so not doubting of your constancy and good affection I remain your loving friend—Inchiquin.

'Cork, 10 November, 1648. Addressed to my very loving friends the gentlemen souldiers of my lifeguard at Kilkenny.'

Was ever mutiny more gently soothed? 'We never intended to engage against Jones,' so how false and unjust of Major D'Oyley it is to pretend that in resisting O'Neal we are fighting Jones and to gallop off to Dublin to join him. The Munster army must have been in a very ticklish condition when Inchiquin thought it necessary to roar so gently. D'Oyley's defection came to nothing however after all on this occasion, for Ormonde was too quick for him and sent a body of Irish horse to bar his way. D'Oyley had to turn and retrace his steps to Cork, and as Inchiquin was not sure of the temper of his troops he was obliged to receive the Colonel's apologies graciously and to promise indemnity and leave to depart to the discontented officers.

It is difficult to disentangle the events of this autumn; the fears and dissatisfactions of the Munster army ebbed and flowed. Ormonde was in daily dread of its making submission to the Parliament and 'too prevalent party in England.' He was not even sure of his own safety; 'if we can keep our own persons free,' he wrote; adding 'that he especially feared some of the Presbyterian party in the army, who had advised the troops to make declarations against the Independents, and might now endeavour to make the revolt of the army the price of their own reconciliation.'

The coalition which Ormonde had built up with so much care seemed crumbling like sand between his fingers. The Munster army was inclined to desert him bodily, while the Irish did not trust his promises. On November 14 he writes that 'noe arguments' would make them believe in his fair dealing till they saw the officers who had interrupted the settlement removed from a possibility of doing so any more, and 'in one way or other secured.'

But, although they knew that a rope was round their necks, the officers were not to be silenced: shortly after the suppression of the mutiny Colonel Townesend and Major Charles D'Oyley wrote to the English war committee which sat at Derby House, proposing to surrender the towns of Munster, on condition of indemnity and receiving part of the arrears due. They said they were acting on behalf of Lord Inchiquin himself, and that he with his own hand had approved and interlined the conditions in several places [1]. The Derby House Committee in answer sent over Colonel Temple with authority to treat. His letter to Lord Inchiquin is preserved at Kinsale [2]:—

'Kinsale Harbour, 7 Dec. 1648.
Aboard the Elizabeth Frigate.

'In answer to the proposition subscribed by Colonel Townesend and Major D'Oyley (in the name of the army of Munster) I have instructions from Derby House to treat with your Lordship and these officers and desire you command me to wait on you.

'I propose that some hostage be sent on board for my safety, any one of six I shall nominate to your Lordship, but if you approve not I desire Mr. Bettesworth to come aboard and view my instructions, for whose safe return I shall enlarge myself to your Lordship, beseeching you that during the treaty neither the Elizabeth nor Dragon frigates may have any annoyance.'

But while Colonel Temple had been on his way to Ireland, things had changed in Munster. Possibly

[1] Cox. It is difficult to fix the date of this letter. Borlase seems to imply that it was about July or August, but looking at the course of events this seems impossible, and it was not answered till December.
[2] Caulfield, *Annals of Kinsale.*

Inchiquin had never authorised the officers to write to Derby House, possibly too he may have chosen to do it through them so that he might disavow them if he felt inclined; certain it is that the Prince of Wales' secretary, Sir Richard Fanshawe, had arrived in Cork about November 17 bringing promises, supplies and money, and news that the fleet which had revolted to the Royal side would soon anchor in Kinsale harbour, under the command of the young Duke of York. Before this flattering breeze from Court, round veered the Munster weathercock. Perhaps there were whispers of an Earl's coronet that would decorate Baron Inchiquin when the King should enjoy his own again, for in a contemporary letter Inchiquin is compared to a panther who springs from side to side after the bait till he falls into the trap.

Fanshawe knew very well how to bait his trap, but he knew also how easily his game might elude him. 'I shall not be at full rest,' he wrote, 'till I see those frigates gone [1].'

Inchiquin himself wrote to Ormonde in the lofty tone of a general who has had a little trouble with some mutinous officers:—

'I have already committed Lieut.-Col. D'Oyley to safe custody and have given the enclosed account of my reasons for doing so to a council of war; Colonel Townesend being at the same time out of my reach, so that I have not secured his person, but taken an effectual course for it [2].'

Carte in his Life of Ormonde says that Colonel Townesend was deprived of his employment at this time, and, not caring to risk a court martial, fled to England with Colonel Temple. Others believe he was taken and

---

[1] Caulfield's *Kinsale*.      [2] Carte MSS., Bodl. Lib. A. 12.

imprisoned, but that he and D'Oyley were only treated with this severity in order to impose on Sir Richard Fanshawe and make him believe in Inchiquin's abhorrence of their negotiations with England, and were released and restored to favour when Sir Richard left [1].

At any rate, the few who were loyal to England were silenced, outward peace was restored, and Ormonde was able to carry on his negotiations with the Confederate Council in his own castle of Kilkenny, surrounded with all the pomp and affection due to the representative of royalty [2]. The King indeed had publicly directed him not to make any treaty with the Irish; but as at the same time a private message commanded him to obey the Queen in all things, Ormonde proceeded to negotiate a treaty that was so favourable to the Irish pretensions that even the officers who had remained faithful to Inchiquin were thunderstruck, and Sir Charles Coote said the news aroused such anger in England as to give the last blow to any hope of an accommodation. *Pride's Purge* had swept all waverers out of the House of Commons, and the Army was obeyed when it demanded that the King should be brought to justice. On the 30th of January, 1649, his head fell on the scaffold before the palace of Whitehall.

Horror at the King's death united all Irish parties at once, and Ormonde proclaimed Charles II as King at Cork and Kinsale; and the Nuncio finding his power completely gone, fled to France, whence he was soon recalled to Italy, and there, being severely censured by the Pope for his mismanagement and violence, he is said to have died of vexation.

[1] John Sealy Townshend, MSS. Memoir.
[2] Leland, *Ireland*, iii. 332.

For several months we hear nothing further of Colonel Townesend. Carte says—

'He returned after the King's murder pretending an utter abhorrence of that act and of the proceedings of the Independents, and to be so engaged in matters with the Royalists in that Kingdom as to be forced to skulk in private whilst he was there, and to have come over again to Ireland to venture his life in the same cause with his Lordship. He was in reality sent over by Cromwell as a spy [1] to corrupt the Munster army and send him intelligence, Lieut. Col. Piggot and Robert Gookin being likewise employed to the same purpose. Townsend was upon his fair pretences restored to his command and drew in others to join his revolt.'

It is necessary to allow for the strong bias of Carte (a Romanist and a Jacobite), who can see no good in those who were opponents of his hero the Duke of Ormonde, but as Colonel Townesend always appears as an open opponent of the alliance with the Irish he hardly deserves the name of 'secret spy.'

Long afterwards, when Cromwell's friends were getting their rewards, Colonel Phair [2] gave the names of the men who 'stayed in Inchiquin's army to serve the English interest' or who had paroles from the North to come to Munster to collect their ransom as a 'disguise for their employment' there. They were Captain Eames, Lieut. Foulkes, and Captain Robert Townsend [3]. If Colonel Townesend had been one of them he would

---

[1] The four spies sent over by Cromwell were Captain Robert Gookin, Colonel R. Townsend, Lieutenant-Colonel William Piggott, Captain St. John Broderick; Carte MSS. lix. 35 a, Bodl. Lib.

[2] See Depositions made in 1652; *Council Book of Cork*, reprinted in the *Gentleman's Magazine*.

[3] See Caulfield's *Council Book of Cork*, Appendix D, list taken from Carte MSS. lix. p. 35 a. This Robert Townsend may very possibly have been a descendant of Sir Robert Townshend of Chester. Many of that branch of the family were named Robert.

have claimed his reward at the same time. Possibly Carte confused him with Captain Robert Townsend, of whom nothing more is known. Carte in his lists compiled for the use of the Duke of Ormonde does not include Colonel Townesend among the officers who betrayed the towns of Munster, but numbers him with the 'Principal Actors in the revolt of Cork.'

But Carte's suggestion is interesting. He tells us what Colonel Townesend's spoken opinions were, and they were exactly those of the moderate Presbyterian party, which Ormonde had especially feared would carry the Munster army back from the Irish to the English side. Colonel Townesend was a soldier of the Parliament, and he could hardly admire the Independents who had just turned half of that Parliament out of doors [1]. He had begun his career in the Presbyterian Army which was nominally fighting for 'King and Parliament'; he had served in Cornwall under Fairfax, whose command was given him by the Parliament, 'being then unseparated from the Royal Interest [2]', and whose wife, the sister-in-law of pious Sir Roger Townshend, spoke the feelings of the whole Presbyterian party when she protested at the King's trial, 'that not one half of the people of England approved of what was being done.' The loyalty to the Parliament which had made Colonel Townesend risk his life and liberty must have received a severe blow by the death of the King.

The death of the King had united Ireland more completely than all Ormonde's diplomacy. Ulster presbyterians, Irish nunciotists, moderates from Kilkenny, cavaliers from France, and parliamentarians from Munster, all joined at last under the royal standard, and for

[1] *Pride's Purge.*  [2] See *Dict. Nat. Biog.*, art. Fairfax.

a short time the blessing, the inestimable blessing, of peace reigned over the country.

Ireland at peace is a land which has many charms, and Lady Fanshawe, the wife of the clever Secretary to the young King, found life so pleasant at Youghal that she writes, 'We began to think of taking up our abode there during the war; for the country was seeming quiet and fertile, and all provisions cheap.'

Some of the officers began to take up land and settle, at least one owned a farm[1]; and Colonel Townesend had a house somewhere in the country[2], and was already familiar with Castlehaven[3], where he afterwards settled down. It is believed that his second son Bryan was born in 1648 at Kinsale, where Colonel Townesend may have been living on garrison duty.

His name is not among those officers who accompanied Lord Inchiquin in his dash to the North, when he almost gained possession of the last foothold of the English in Dublin, although his friends Colonels Gifford and D'Oyley were at the defeat of Rathfarnham in September, where after a gallant stand Colonel Gifford was taken prisoner by Jones.

At present we know nothing of Colonel Townesend during the beginning of the year 1649[4].

By August the levellers in the Army having had another very stern lesson given them in the executions at Burford, Cromwell had leisure to turn his sword

---

[1] See Depositions, 1652; *Cork Corp. Council Book.* Ed. Caulfield.
[2] Murphy, *Cromwell in Ireland.*
[3] 'I hear by Colonel Townesend that Castlehaven is come in;' *Cromwell's Letter to Lenthall,* from Ross.
[4] Caulfield, in his edition of the *Council Book of Youghall,* App. F. p. 601, mentions that the Council received letters from Ireland from Colonel Townsend and Lieutenant Ch. Coote, on Feb. 26, 1649. But the original entry (*Domes. S. P., Interreg.,* Rec. Office) gives Colonel Jones and Sir Ch. Coote.

against Ireland. Ireland was indeed united under Ormonde, but England was united under Lord General Cromwell. At last the party cries were silent, the question had become a national one[1], England against Ireland, and the soldiers of the Munster army saw they were ranged against their own country. They soon saw, also, that they were ranged on a side which was doomed. Cromwell landed in Dublin, and the massacres of Drogheda and Wexford showed that at last the Irish question was undertaken by a man who intended settlement. Victory after victory marked Cromwell's course. Death or submission were the alternatives offered to his opponents.

Broghill was again in Munster, having been gained over by Cromwell himself in a private interview, and was now using his persuasive tongue on behalf of his new friend. He was a man to whom Cromwell and Ireton listened; he succeeded in fascinating the stern Regicides, Gough and Whalley[2], and the stiffnecked Presbyterian ministers of Edinburgh[3]; what wonder if the perplexed Munster officers thought him the wisest leader in the land. If any one were so foolish as to hesitate 'I discoursed with him half an hour in private,' says the triumphant Broghill, 'and left him fully satisfied that it was a national quarrel[4].'

The debates and anxieties among the Munster officers had begun anew as soon as Cromwell landed in Dublin. Captain Peter Carew held several secret meetings in Cork with men whom he knew to be well affected towards England, to see what could be done towards 'bringing over the city.' Some of these officers had been made prisoners by the English army, and had

---

[1] Cox.     [2] *Memoirs of the Boyles*, Budgell.     [3] Bailley.
[4] *Letter from Cork*, Nov. 22, Tract 203, Lib. Royal Irish Acad. Dublin.

been converted from the errors of their royalist ways so thoroughly, that when they returned to Munster to collect their ransoms or negotiate for exchange, they were really messengers charged to gain over adherents to the Cromwellian cause[1].

Their project was successful. Inchiquin saw officer after officer desert to Cromwell and even the Irish inclining to submit, and he began to fear for the safety of the sea-ports of the south, which supplied provisions to the whole island. The important port of Youghal was now occupied by Sir Percy Smith and a garrison of the Munster army, Inchiquin thought it wise to add to the defenders some friends of his own, Colonel Wogan and others,—Carte calls them 'Cavaliers,' but the garrison seems to have looked on them as Irish rebels. Cork he knew was too strong a place for the malcontents to attempt, Waterford was in the hands of the Irish, and Prince Rupert's fleet lay in Kinsale harbour although Blake and Deane prevented his doing more than protect that one port.

Cromwell was now on his march towards the south, and Sir Percy Smith determined, with the help of three officers, Colonels Townesend, Gifford and Warden[2], to have Youghal ready to receive the conqueror. He even hoped to seize Lord Inchiquin himself and end the Munster complications with one blow, and should he not succeed so far, Inchiquin's troops would at any rate be diverted from relieving Wexford, which was now threatened by the English army.

Inchiquin was at this time staying with Colonel Jack Barry[3], at Castle Lyons. Colonel Barry had married the widowed Countess of Barrymore, Lord Broghill's

---

[1] See Colonel Robert Phair's depositions, *Council Book of Cork*, Caulfield.
[2] Carte.     [3] See chapter viii. Barrymore.

sister, and although himself a Romanist, he kept on good terms with his protestant brother-in-law, who generally succeeded in getting any information he needed from Colonel Barry.

Long afterwards Colonel Townesend's eldest son married Lady Barrymore's granddaughter, but now there was no talk of friendship and weddings. An officer who had been asked to join in this conspiracy rode hard to Castle Lyons[1] and warned Lord Inchiquin, who promptly arrested the three Colonels and threw them into prison. But he seems to have reckoned without their powerful confederate Sir Percy Smith, who at once retaliated by imprisoning Lord Inchiquin's friends, Colonel Wogan and the other 'cavaliers,' and stood on his defence. It is hardly possible to reconcile the conflicting accounts of this incident. Some authorities think Smith rescued his friends with a high hand[2], others say he came to terms on finding that the rest of the Munster army was not ripe for revolt[3], saying, if Lord Inchiquin would grant an indemnity and release the three Colonels and remove Colonel Wogan and his confederates from the town, he, Sir Percy, would be delighted to be rid of them. Inchiquin was anxious to be off to Wexford, 'the disorder the revolt of Youghal breeds among us, and our great want of money,' wrote Ormonde, 'are terrible impediments to any action.' Inchiquin consented to the exchange of officers, and it is said[4], 'never discovered how many had been engaged in the plot,' for it was even re-

---

[1] Ormonde to Clanrickard, Oct. 9, Carte MSS. Vol. 25, No. 418.
[2] John Sealy Townshend, MSS. *Memoir.*
[3] Murphy, *Cromwell in Ireland*, and Carte's *Life of Ormonde.*
[4] Carte's *Life of Ormonde.*

ported[1] afterwards that Sir Percy himself had had no share in the revolt, 'he wished well to it, but could not act for reasons he would not declare.'

But the three Colonels were no sooner at liberty than they made another attempt[2]. Foulke had been sent from Dublin as one of Cromwell's secret agents, and Colonel Townesend and Colonel Warden made an appointment to meet him and Major Farmer with a party of horse at Tallow, and then march together to help their friends to secure Youghal. But once more Inchiquin got wind of the plot, a man named Johnson betrayed it to him, and instead of the friendly horse soldiers at Tallow, the conspirators were met by a party of Inchiquin's men. Warden and Gifford were taken at once, Townesend escaped into the country and was apprehended next morning at his own house, by Lieut. Francis Bettridge. Foulke and Farmer managed to hide in 'the stump of an old castle' till Cromwell's approach made it safe to 'take a cot and go down by water to Youghal.'

How little the formal deposition tells of the secret meetings, the flight through the dark country, the terror of Colonel Townesend's young wife when her husband returned with the words 'betrayed again,' the surprise at dawn, the summons to surrender, the hopeless farewell! For this time there were no cavalier hostages at Youghal to secure the lives of Inchiquin's

---

[1] Capt. Graham's deposition, *Carte Papers*, v. 66, p. 237. Bod. Lib.

[2] Major Jasper Farmer's deposition. It seems that this must have been a separate second plot, as the three Colonels were known by Cromwell to be imprisoned 'for the business of Youghal,' and he also says, 'they ventured their lives twice or thrice.' Or perhaps Sir Percy Smith had only rescued some of the Conspirators, leaving the three principals to their fate. When Youghal finally surrendered to Cromwell, Johnson and Sir Percy Smith were both imprisoned, which looks as if both were looked on as alike unfriendly to the parliamentary side.

prisoners, or perhaps Sir Percy had abandoned their cause; the records of those confused and anxious days only tell that all three were promptly carried to Cork, and they knew their peril was extreme.

Inchiquin would probably try them all by Court Martial and shoot them on the spot, as Laugharne and other parliamentarians had been shot at Kinsale the year before. Yet would the discontented troops quietly allow their officers to be executed now that Cromwell's victorious march was drawing near and the storm of Cork was imminent?

On the night of October 16th, Captain Myhill came to the three prisoners, and broke to them the news that next morning they were to be separated and sent to different castles. At these tidings, Colonel Townesend's deposition says, 'they were very much troubled, believing that this was with intent to have them executed speedily.' Some other officers then came in and declared they were undone and would be slaves to the Irish unless the three colonels would stand by them. The prisoners replied that if their friends would but fetch a sword and pistol for each of them, they would live and die with them. Lieutenant Granger brought them three 'rapyers,' which Colonel Townesend clapped under the bolster of his bed till all was ready, for Colonel Gifford, instead of remaining with them, had gone out of the north gate to Mr. Bettridge's and there kept secret[1] The others did not wait long for him, the guards soon perceived them coming downstairs, and cried out, 'We are for you too,' and thence they marched to the main guard, who declared with them, crying, 'Out with all Irish[2]'; 'and so,' says Colonel

[1] Deposition, Lieutenant P. Granger, aged 28, Feb. 1654, *Council Book of Cork*, Caulfield, App. B.     [2] Admiral Deane's *Letter to the Speaker*.

Townesend, 'they secured the city and fort for the parliament of England and the then Lord Lieutenant of Ireland.' Colonel Ryves[1] and Captain Myhill took the port, and Colonel Gifford claimed to have secured the governor, Colonel Stirling, 'who,' says a contemporary news letter, 'had passed the last eight years in a dream, and never wakened till those rude fellows presumed to do it[2].'

Lady Fanshawe, poor thing, was in Cork at this time, and tells her side of the story.

'I was in my bed when Cork revolted. My husband was gone on business to Kinsale. It was the beginning of November. At midnight I heard the great guns go off, and thereupon I called up my family to rise. Hearing lamentable shrieks of men, women, and children, I asked at the window the cause. They told me they were all Irish, stripped and wounded and turned out of the town. That Colonel Jeffries with some others had possessed themselves of the town for Cromwell.'

Probably Jeffries is put in mistake for Gifford, whose name is often spelt Jefford. He behaved with great courtesy to Lady Fanshawe, and gave her a pass to leave the town in safety.

On the 23rd of October 'The Protestant army of Munster now in Corke' drew up a Resolution[3] to send to Cromwell pleading, in excuse for their treaty with the Irish, that they had been 'under a mediate authority, seduced by the power and subtilty' of Lord Inchiquin to become slaves to the Irish. The first signature is Richard Townesend. The next problem was to carry this resolution to Cromwell, who was now before Ross, a walled town, which Taaf was holding with a strong

---

[1] Or Reeves, see chapter vii.
[2] *Irish Penny Magazine*, 106, Dub. 1833.
[3] Box 62, Tract 28 in Haliday Collect. Royal Irish Academy.

## THE SURRENDER OF CORK.

force[1]. Inchiquin had been there, but left it to make a vain attempt to regain Cork[2], and on the 19th, Lord Taaf, seeing the stern preparations to storm, preferred to escape the fate of the defenders of Drogheda and Wexford, and accepted Cromwell's terms. He marched away with his Irish troops, but the few hundred English of the Munster army who had been with him gladly joined the forces of their countrymen[3].

Cromwell was comfortably quartered in Ross when he heard that the capital of Munster had surrendered, and that Colonel Townesend was coming to bring him the submission of the city, but was hindered by a fort at the mouth of the harbour. Accordingly he sent General Blake in Captain Mildmay's frigate, the 'Nonsuch,' to fetch him, and the 'Ginney' frigate sailed with them. They passed the fort at the harbour mouth in safety, in spite of several shot which were fired at them, and as soon as they reached Cork, Colonel Townesend came aboard and was welcomed by Blake and the captains of the frigates. Gifford and Warden had been asked to take a hundred horse to assist Youghal, which had once more revolted against Inchiquin, and had now imprisoned both Sir Percy Smith and 'one Johnson who had formerly betrayed them, and for that treachery was of a Lieutenant made by Inchiquin a Colonell of Horse[4].' Blake with Townesend on board repassed the fort at the harbour mouth, and the 'Nonsuch' returned eastward along the coast. The two old comrades of the defence of Lyme must have had many memories to recall and many tales of

---

[1] Carlyle's *Cromwell*.
[2] Col. Ryve's *Deposition*; *Cromwell in Ireland*, Denis Murphy, pp. 201–203.
[3] Carlyle's *Cromwell*, p. 314.
[4] Letter from one on board the 'Ginney,' *A Briefe Relation*, Nov. 13–20.

their adventures since, to relate to one another as they sailed along, and Townesend doubtless explained the trials and perplexities of the Munster army, and the very difficult time through which he and his brother officers had just passed. He does not seem to have found his old friend an unsympathetic listener, for shortly after this time Blake wrote, 'I look upon it as an extraordinary and very seasonable mercy of God in stirring up and uniting so many resolute spirits to a work of so great consequence.'

Off Dungarvan, the 'Nonsuch' met the 'Garland' frigate with a transport having on board Colonel Phair and 500 foot destined for Cork. The wind which was favourable to the 'Nonsuch,' was foul for them, and learning from Colonel Townesend that Youghal had also declared for the Parliament, they steered for that place. Colonel Gifford, Colonel Warden and Major Purdon ('who,' says Cromwell[1], 'with Colonel Townesend, have been very active instruments for the return both of Cork and Youghal to their obedience, having some of them adventured their lives twice or thrice to effect it') came off to meet them, bringing with them the Mayor of the town; they were at first inclined to offer some propositions to Cromwell, but Lord Broghill, who was on board, assured them it would be more to their honour and advantage to make no conditions. As usual, he gained his point, and then landed with Phair and Sir William Fenton, and was received, in his own words, 'with all the real demonstrations of gladness an overjoyed people were capable of.' From Youghal Phair marched to Cork with 300 men, while Colonel Townesend and the other officers went on to carry the address of the city of Cork and resolutions

[1] Carlyle, *Cromwell*, 318, in the letter to Lenthall previously quoted.

of the garrison to Ross, which they reached on the 13th of November [1].

The surrender of Cork and Youghal was indeed a 'seasonable mercy.' The English army was suffering severely from exposure and the damp climate, which even Ormonde used to say 'retained a greater part of the original curse than the rest of the whole creation!' It was a matter of great importance to obtain such a large reinforcement of seasoned troops and comfortable winter quarters for the wearied army, which else would have had to be shipped back to England. In the words of Colonel Deane [2]:

'Thus it hath pleased God of his infinite goodness to help when men were most weak after the taking of Ross and besieging of Duncannon what with sickness and (leaving men in) garrisons my Lord Lieutenant was very unable to attempt anything further upon the enemy without recruits.'

'I hear,' said Cromwell, 'by Colonel Townesend that Baltimore, Castle Haven and other places of hard names are come in.' Munster had submitted. The Lord General established his headquarters at Youghal, and made progresses to Cork, Kinsale, Bandon, Skibbereen and other towns in the province. Colonel Townesend and Colonel Gifford were appointed to command the two regiments formed out of the Cork garrison, the horse being under Lord Broghill, with Warden and Purdon as his Majors [3].

The next year, 1650, the hollow truce between Ormonde and his Irish allies was broken, the Bishops declared Ormonde and his followers to be 'imps of

---

[1] See Cromwell's answer, dated Nov. 13th.
[2] *Letter from Colonel Deane to the Speaker*, printed for Robert Ibbitson dwelling in Smithfield, 1639, pp. 61-68. British Museum.
[3] Cromwell's reply to the letter of the soldiers of the garrison of Cork, 'Youghal.' *Youghal Council Book*, Caulfield, App. A.

Satan,' and pronounced sentence of excommunication against all who favoured them. In December, Ormonde, Inchiquin and the surviving Royalist leaders retired to France in despair. Broghill persuaded the Lord General to permit Lady Ormonde to reside on her Kilkenny estate and the Parliament to grant terms to Clanrickard, who died in London of a broken heart. Limerick and Galway capitulated, and Ireland was conquered.

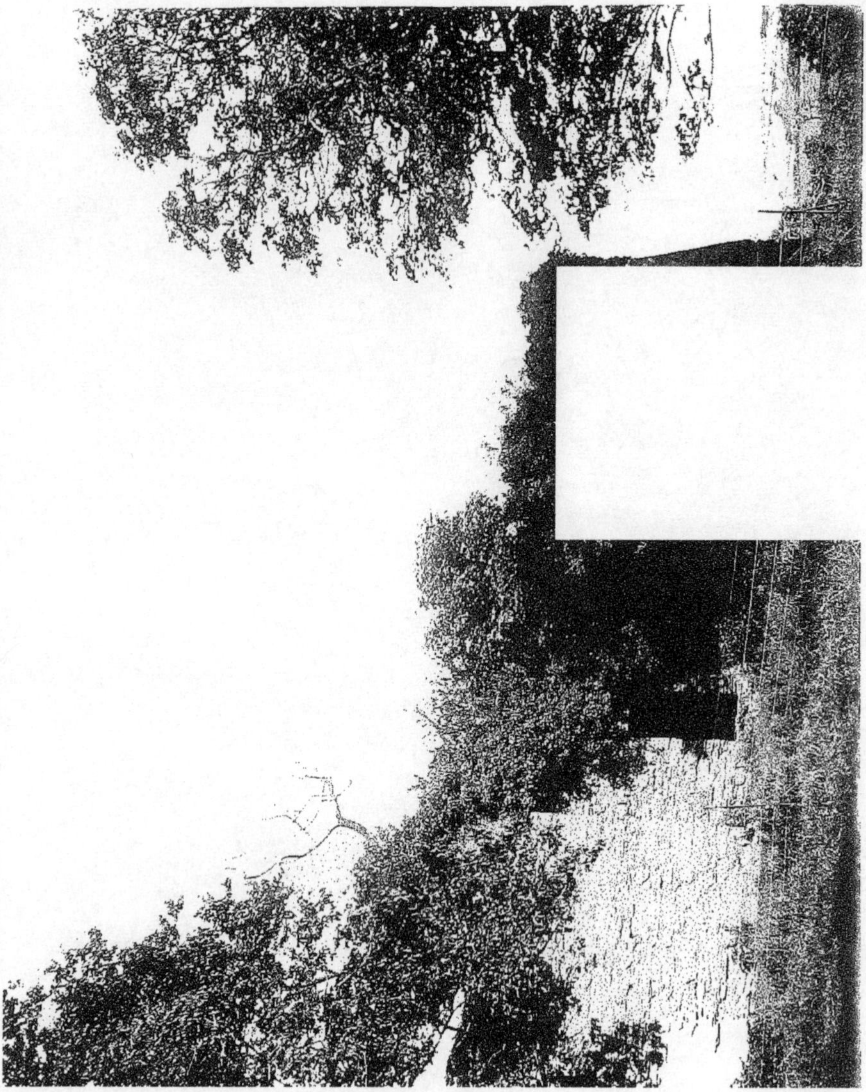

## CHAPTER V.

### SETTLING DOWN.

An entirely new chapter of Irish history had begun. After the chaos of the ten years' war the whole country had to be re-arranged. Some English settlers had been dispossessed during the rebellion, and now demanded to have their estates restored; adventurers who had advanced money for the expenses of the war expected to be compensated by grants of forfeited land; soldiers were to be allotted portions in place of their arrears of pay; much land lay waste and deserted, its original owners having vanished during the ten years' bloodshed. The natives who had taken part in the rebellion of 1641 were to be hunted down, and deprived of all their property; the other Irish were to be allowed indeed to exist, but most of them had to exchange the fertile pastures of the east for the barren wilderness of Connaught, and were removed thither under the direction of commissioners, one of whom was Colonel Edward D'Oyley. He may have recognised some of his old brothers in arms of Taaf's army[1] among the hapless fugitives to whom their stern conquerors gave the choice of 'Hell or Connaught,' but they were after

[1] See p. 70.

all only sharing the same fate of the conquered that had robbed Colonel D'Oyley's own family of land and wealth[1].

It is said that Cromwell remembered that Edward D'Oyley had once been a Royalist, and therefore never thoroughly trusted him: he was made governor of Jamaica; but although it is to his good conduct alone that we owe the possession of that colony, he received no other reward than the approbation of his own conscience[2]. Even to Jamaica the faces and voices of the conquered Irish followed him, for the merchants of Bristol drove a prosperous trade by shipping off the widows and orphans of the war into shameful slavery in the Western plantation[3]. Colonel D'Oyley returned later on to England, and died in Westminster in 1674.

Among the adventurers who had advanced money to the amount of £300 is one Giles Townsend, whose name was found by John Sealy Townsend among the Dublin records; and a Thomas Townsend was a dispossessed English settler, whose title was not affirmed till after the restoration[4]. He had owned much land in Kilkenny and Tipperary, and it appears that the adventurers and soldiers, finding it in the hands of the Irish insurgents, had voted it to be forfeited. If this Thomas were a relation of Colonel Richard Townesend, his sufferings during the rebellion may have been a reason for his kinsman to volunteer in the avenging army of 1647. There were certainly Townsends settled in

[1] The magnificent manor house, Greenland House, the residence of his elder brother John, was 'beaten about the ears of the garrison.' Whitelock.
[2] Long's *History of Jamaica*.
[3] Between 6000 and 7000 were transported, chiefly unmarried women and boys. Walpole, *Hist. Kingdom of Ireland*, 213.
[4] *Exchequer Records*, Dublin, Roll 7, Skin 68. He was of Card Castle.

## SETTLING DOWN.

County Cork before that year. Richard Townsend of the parish of Kinneigh, in 1630 became administrator to the will of his father-in-law, Francis Bennett, and the records of the Irish Court of Exchequer gave the name of a Miss Elizabeth Townsend, and the Court of Claims of an Edward Townsend. The will is also in existence of Thomas Townsend of Murragh 1636, and a Grace Townsend, daughter of Matthias Anstis of Bandon, has not been identified yet. She must have been a person of some position, as her second husband left a legacy to the poor of that town [1].

Carte says that Colonel Townesend had brothers in Ireland, and that a numerous family of the name resided in County Cork before the rebellion, who were probably his relatives; but no authority is given for this statement, which is contradicted by the constant family tradition, except that of Mrs. Edward Synge Townshend (born in 1742), who believed Colonel Richard's grandfather to have been the first settler.

But it seems very improbable that these Townsends were connected with the family at Castle Townsend, for it has always been marked by such strong family feeling, and has kept up traditional kinship so carefully, that it could scarcely have been ignorant of cousins living but a few miles off. Also some of the members of the family have been so long-lived that traditions have had a great chance of being remembered, and they handed down no tradition of an Irish origin to the family.

To return to the seventeenth century, Lord Clarendon says that Cromwell was anxious to disband [2] the Munster

---

[1] Bennett's *History of Bandon*.
[2] Cromwell cashiered Jones' regiments on his arrival in Dublin, 1649. Borlace.

army and get rid of it quietly, knowing that it had served the Parliament too long to be cordially on his side. Indeed it barely escaped the fate of the Presbyterians of the North of Ireland and of the many who found it difficult to prove their 'constant good affection' to the Commonwealth of England, as any one who had even paid a forced contribution to a papist or royalist officer was held to have shown no *constant* good affection! However, the Munster army was graciously pardoned, and even[1] applauded for having given timely help in 1649, although they had been guilty of a temporary defection in 1648.

The army was disbanded and paid off gradually as the Court of Claims could allot the claim, which was granted in satisfaction of arrears of pay. In February, 1654, many of those engaged in the 'bringing over of Cork' made their depositions[2], describing the whole event. Among others was Colonel Richard Townesend, described as now resident in Castlehaven, aged 36, so he seems to have settled in the West immediately after the rendering of the city, if not earlier. His name appears in no list of those to whom land was given in payment of arrears, so it is probable that he bought it. There were plenty of estates for sale just then, many of the soldiers gambled away their rights before receiving the shares, others gladly sold, wishing to return to England, or being in immediate need of money; and some of the original owners[3], when they regained their lands, did not care to live in the country under its new conditions.

Colonel Townesend seems to have left the army as

---

[1] *Ordinances of Cromwell*, 1654.
[2] See *Council Book of Cork*.
[3] Petitions to Court of Claims. John Sealy Townshend.

soon as he could with honour, for he was not present at a council of war held in Cork, Dec. 1654. It is said[1] that this was the reason that he had to buy land instead of being granted a lot by Cromwell.

Many men who preferred the more vivid life of towns and sought chances for satisfying their ambition would not have felt tempted to settle among the bogs and forests, the wild wolves and wilder Irish; but those who were weary of the strife of parties and sects in England and saw the calm that settled down over conquered Ireland, gladly turned from politics to make grass grow and cornfields wave, where the oak woods slope down to the lovely bays of West Carbery.

Monk had tried to leave the army and settle in Ireland; Lady Fanshawe had described the pleasures and conveniences of life in County Cork, so that even if Colonel Townesend had no relatives already in the country, he was far from being singular among his contemporaries in wishing to become a Munster landowner. He was a young man to retire from military life, which he must have liked, or he would hardly have volunteered for service in Ireland, when so many officers took the opportunity of leaving the army in 1647. But his commander Fairfax had left the army while yet a young man and full of ambition. He was thirty-eight, and Colonel Townesend was thirty-six. Fairfax's own poem on country life may represent the feeling of many another officer weary of the 'civil jar.'

> O how I love these solitudes
> And places silent as the night,
> There where no thronging multitudes
> Disturb with noise their sweet delight!

[1] John Sealy Townshend, who also says he saw the deeds of Colonel Townesend's purchases of claims and titles in the Records of the Court of Claims in the Customs House, Dublin. (Letter, dated 1846.)

> Oh how mine eyes are pleased to see
> Oaks that such spreading branches bear,
> Which from old Time's nativity
> And the envy of many a year
> Are still green, beautiful and fair
> As in the world's first day they were :[1]

How unlike all this is to the blood-thirst of those who would 'wade through slaughter to a throne!' The typical English man of action, having done his duty in the field, desires above all earthly things the simple life of a country gentleman, and Colonel Townesend followed no unworthy example when he chose to settle down as a landowner in West Carbery.

Though he had served in the campaigns against the Irish he seems to have been on friendly terms with all his neighbours, the Irishman Cornelius O'Driscoll, who gave his name to one of the Colonel's sons, the dispossessed McCartie Reagh, and the Romanist Copinger, descendant of the grim old tyrant who, tradition says, hanged men to the gables of his great mansion at Copinger's Court. So friendly were the Copingers to the Townesends that one of the Copinger's, Domenic, actually married Colonel Townesend's daughter Dorothea[2].

There were other neighbours too: Colonel Thomas Becher was a very great man, descended from a De Bridgecourt who followed Queen Philippa from Hainault, and now ruled over his estates and commanded a garrison of soldiers at his castle on Shirkin Island, opposite Baltimore; and round 'Protestant Bandon' dwelt the sons of Elizabethan settlers who kept up their English faith, Hulls and Synges; many of the 'forty-nine' officers also settled here, Sweet and

---

[1] *Great Lord Fairfax*, C. Markham, p. 352, Appendix.
[2] See chap. viii.

Arnop and Gifford, and became burgesses of the little town of Clonakilty where their faded signatures may still be seen in the Council book[1]. Most of the neighbouring gentry seem to have become burgesses and taken their turns in being Sovereign or Mayor. One wonders if the gentlemen ever talked politics after the meetings were over, or if such subjects were too dangerous to be mentioned.

The Earl of Carbery in 1650 was Richard Vaughan, who married Lady Alice Egerton the heroine of Comus, and the philosopher Robert Boyle was son of the Earl of Cork, so some echoes from the world of science and poetry may have penetrated the western wilds along with the news-letters bearing the tidings of Cromwell's victories in Scotland.

Castlehaven Castle was the nearest mansion to Colonel Townesend's estates, but its owner, Lord Castlehaven, had been one of the chief leaders of the Irish in the late war, and now Colonel Salmon held the Castle for the English Parliament. Colonel Salmon had been very active[2] in organising the chase of the Algerine rovers, who had burnt and sacked Baltimore not twenty years before, but the news was carried to Castlehaven too late and none of the unhappy captives were rescued. The Cromwellian settlers held their land with a stronger hand, and we hear of no more 'pirate galleys warping down.'

During the allotment of lands for payment of arrears Sir William Petty was commissioned to make a survey in which those who received lands were set down by regiments and which was therefore known as the Down survey. In this early account of the county, Castle-

---

[1] In the possession of Rev. J. H. Townsend of Tunbridge Wells.
[2] Caulfield, *Annals of Kinsale*.

haven and the old burying-ground by the well of St. Barrahane are accurately described. Many a Townsend has been laid in that burying-ground, and the grove of ancient ash-trees still shades the Holy Well, but of the 'two English-built houses' mentioned in the survey, there only remain the ruins of the Castle from which the Haven takes its name. It was originally a fortress of the Driscolls, and had been the scene of many a hard-fought engagement. Here the Spaniard landed two thousand men to reinforce Red Hugh O'Donnel at Kinsale, and their entrenchments are still visible on Galleon Point, and here Red Hugh bid farewell for ever to his country after his defeat in 1602.

The following year, 1603, there was a notable sea-fight in the Haven, when Sir Richard Levison defeated the Spanish admiral, and the Spaniards, English, and Irish, all had a sort of scramble for the Castle which finally fell into the hands of the English.

But this fighting was half a century back, and only the cannon shot in the walls of the Castle remained to show that Colonel Townesend was not the first soldier who had come to Castlehaven.

No dwelling-house is shown in the survey near the present Castle Townshend, a long mile up the bay. The land is described as for the most part profitable, but some rocky and boggy, and vessels of 500 tons can ride safely within the harbour.

The Castle of Rahine[1] stands on the opposite side of the bay; the lands around had been ravaged in 1649, and it is probable that the castle was bombarded in that year by some ships from the harbour. It formed part of Colonel Townesend's estates, but[2] a

---
[1] Donovan, *Sketches in Carbery*, 161.
[2] Note by Judge Fitz-Henry Townshend.

## SETTLING DOWN.

Townshend heiress carried that portion of the property to the Becher family. Here Colonel Townesend seems to have lived quietly for the next few years, reclaiming land and building the little fortress whose ruins still look out over the bay.

From the description given in Lord Orrery's state letters, we gather that the gentry of West Carbery had plenty of work in keeping down the 'Woodkerns' who infested the wild forest country. The saying still survives 'Beyond the Leap[1], beyond the law,' and the only law could be that of the stronger hand. Probably Colonel Townesend had stout hearts by his side, for the English soldiers of '49' gladly settled round the officers they trusted. But it must have been a lonely life for the scattered English settlers; communication by land must have been difficult, where moorland and bogs alternated with forest-covered hills, and the chief tidings we have of Castle Townshend for the next few years come from the sea. In February, 1654, the haven was visited by a ship of war, the 'Little Charity[2].' Captain Robert Haytubbe reported to the Admiral that he had been obliged through stress of weather and lack of horsemeat to bear up towards Ireland and put in to Castlehaven. 'Finding no relief here, he sent his steward to the Victualler at Kinsale for a supply, but he was ordered not to furnish any ship not listed to attend that coast. Addressed Colonel Phaer, Governor of Cork, who caused Colonel Townesend to furnish horsemeat.'

Probably the devastations of the long war had made hay and corn scarce, but it is satisfactory to know that at last the bonds of red tape relaxed and allowed

---

[1] A gorge a few miles east of Castle Townshend.
[2] *Collect. State Papers*, Domes. Ser., A.D. 1654, p. 433.

Colonel Townesend to supply the poor horses with provender. It would be interesting to follow the fortunes of the 'Little Charity' and know whether she bore out the promises of her name under Blake at Cadiz that year, or carried greetings from his kinsman to Colonel D'Oyley in Jamaica, where Penn's squadron was then cruising.

Although the beautiful bays and labyrinth of islands that fringe West Carbery were convenient shelters for wind-bound vessels, they might also be lurking places for more dangerous visitors. No one knew when the privateers of Prince Rupert, or slavers from Algiers, or ships of war of France or Spain or Holland, might make a dash on the coast, so several English ships were kept 'plying' between the Land's End and Kinsale, to guard against the roving enemy. Rich prizes often fell into the hands of these coastguards, and when most unknown ships were enemies, it is no wonder that sometimes a mistake was made and a friendly ship was plundered.

A letter from Colonel Townesend which was forwarded to the Lord General Fleetwood in April 1654, shows his hot anger at such a mistake. He writes to Colonel Phaire, the Governor of Cork, about a ship which had been driven by stress of weather to take refuge in Timoleague (Courtmacsherry) bay. She carried twenty-four guns, and was richly laden with elephants' teeth, leopard skins, and gold ore. As it was uncertain to what country she belonged, Colonel Phaire directed Colonel Townesend and Captain Robert Gookin to take possession of the ship and examine the captain. His answer is as follows [1]:—

---

[1] Phaire to Fleetwood, Add. MSS. Brit. Mus., f. 168. Colonel Richard Townsend, Add. MSS., Brit. Mus. 22, 546, f. 172.

'Sir,

'According to your order we sent for the officers and seamen in the Patience of Courland and find upon examination that the shipp belongeth to the Duke of that country of which the King of Poland is Protector. During the time of examination, and after we had taken the vessel and secured the seamen and officers on shore, three or four ffrigatts came and boarded her, and although we sent them an accompt of our power and proceedings, the captain of the Nicodemus forced the ship to sayle and returned us no other answer but we were fooles: Sir, unless there be more discovered than yet is evident to us, the vessel is not prize, for neither the King of Poland or Duke of Courland are enemyes to the Commonwealth of England and besides that they are Protestants. The violence they have offered by plundering I doubt they are not able to repayre: The merchants chest is worth twenty thousand pounds: The Masters three or four thousand pounds: Wee indeed were very careful that noo wrong might be done and therefore suffered not the soldiers to go aboard the shipp whilst the men were on shoar: But Liv$^t$. Codd siezed the shipp yesterday before witnesses and all the officers and men secured on shore, wee could not proceede in the examinacion soo farre as we intended, because of the trouble of the Man of Warr, the ship is by them most unworthily plundered: Wee doo therefore desire you to send to the governor of Kinsale that those Captaines may be secured for certainly the goods between decks were worth sixty thousand pounds and will be proved so. Pray consider of it and take care that the officers may be possessed of their shipp and the plundering Cap$^{ts}$ secured: I am resolved to attend your further orders at Kinsale for rather than such an unworthy action shall pass unpunished I will prosecute the business at Dublin myselfe.

I am yo$^r$ servant,

Rob$^t$ Gookine,

& I am both friend & servant,

Rich. Townsend.'

At first it seems the ships were very proud of their exploit. Captain Cowes of the 'Cat Pink'[1] reported to the Admiral that the 'Nicodemus' with his assistance had taken a ship richly laden, which he hears by Captain Gookin, Commander of 'Timilege Castle,' is from Guinea, and belongs to the Duke of Courland.

But Colonel Townesend's protests were heard, and on the third of July Captain Robinson of the 'Greyhound' writes[2] 'that the information sent against him as to staying a ship near Kinsale was premature, she was discharged when found to belong to the Duke of Courland, and the Master and Merchant satisfied the Lord General, as also Captain Gookin and Colonel Townson (*sic*) that they had not been wronged.'

All's well that ends well, but it is to be hoped the Captain of the 'Nicodemus' apologised for his strong language!

In the spring of 1656 Colonel Richard Townesend of Castletown, alias Castlehaven, 'obtained leave from the Sovereign of Kinsale, who acted as admiral of the south-western coast of Cork, to raise two sunken guns out of the channel of Castlehaven and what more may be found there as wreck of the sea[2].'

The next year, 1657[3], Henry Cromwell, the wise and kindly Lord Lieutenant, made a progress to Cork, and from thence visited all the harbours upon the western coast as far as Bandon, so very possibly he inspected Castlehaven.

But no sooner was the country sinking into calm, than the Restoration revived all the land questions and the rivalry between parties. Ireland had been quiet

---

[1] Domes. State Papers, May 7, 1654.
[2] *Annals of Kinsale,* Caulfield (Council book extracts), p. 23.
[3] *Memoirs of Oliver Cromwell,* II. 542.

as a conquered country is quiet, one party was triumphant, the other crushed,—now all sides started into new life. Those who had lost their properties through their loyalty to the King, naturally expected to regain them; the large number of men who had purchased forfeited lands, or received estates in return for money 'adventured' or advanced, were indignant at being robbed of their new possessions; while the original Irish owners of the country had some hopes that as the English were falling out with each other, they might come by their own again. The work of setting out land and deciding the arrears of soldiers' pay under the Commonwealth was not finished, and here were new commissions to alter all that had been done!

The King[1] had returned accompanied by a crowd of officers who had faithfully served him till June 1649, when they were driven from Ireland by Cromwell. These were known as the '49 officers.' They must not be confused with those who had been 'active in the rendition' of Munster to Cromwell, who had been given lands under the name of '49 arrears.' The sworn depositions of these 'active' gentlemen were used against them at the Restoration to bar their claims, and their '49 arrears' were handed by the Act of Settlement to the '49 officers' whom they had turned out of Munster. How Colonel Townesend and some of his friends managed to escape this fate is still a mystery, but he continued to possess his lands while Jephson and others were driven to rebellion by the forfeiture. All these conflicting demands were brought before two Courts of Claims. The first began to hear cases in 1663, and was principally occupied in deciding on the guilt or innocency of those who had property

[1] *Report on Carte Papers*, Bod. Lib., p. 146.

in Ireland at the time of the Rebellion in 1641. Among the Munster gentlemen who received 'decrees of Innocency' were some of the names of Galway, Fleming, Becher, and French, whom we meet later on intermarrying with the Townsend family.

In order to reconcile the claims of these 'Innocents' with those of the '49 officers,' and to provide for the immense grants to favourites with which Charles II proceeded to complicate matters, a Bill was prepared by Ormonde proposing that adventurers, soldiers, and those deriving from them, should resign one-third of the lands enjoyed by them on the 7th of May 1659[1]. This Bill was passed in 1665, and a new Court of Claims sat in 1666 to issue patents and certificates of what lands each man was entitled to[2].

The ancestors of most of the landowners in Cork received these certificates; Beamish, Becher, Cox, Folliott, Fleming, Hull, Hungerford, Jefford, Hodder, Owen, Riche, Foulke, French and Herbert are among them. Jeremy Donovan received a patent for land named Keamore, which he had purchased from Colonel Townesend, and Colonel Townesend received one for land purchased from Lord Kingston, named Ohe or Millane, and for his grants in Carbery[3].

It is difficult to know exactly what grants mean in this case. James, Duke of York, received 'grants' in eighteen counties, so the word cannot always mean

[1] See Appendix D. for Colonel Townesend's third of the lands of Drummenagh.

[2] Some of these certificates are in the Remembrancer's Office of the Dublin Court of Exchequer, the rest in the Rolls Office of the Court of Chancery. The ones relating to Colonel Townesend are Roll 30 and Roll 4, skin 16, 68, 88, 94, 66 in the Exchange Office. Katherine Barry, Roll 16, skin 46; Elizabeth Townshend, Roll 21, skin 29. (J. Sealy Townshend—to whom the above account of the Court of Claims is due.)

[3] *Report of Comms. of Public Records*, 1821-1829.

'soldiers' lots.' Yet Lord Orrery long after spoke of Colonel Townesend's estates as 'lots,' and he had made his depositions in Cork with the others when the soldiers' lots were being divided, and claimed his lands, as did Gifford and Warden, as a 'soldier serving in Ireland in the Commonwealth period[1].'

The first patent to Colonel Townesend is dated 18th Charles II, enrolled August 1666, the second patent, the 20th Charles II, enrolled August 15, 1668, the third is dated August 12, 1679, and enrolled Feb. 4, 1680. It is believed that the flattering terms of these patents, with their grants of free chase and free warren, were due to Colonel Townesend's connection with Lord Clarendon and the Duke of York, through his wife Hildegardis Hyde[2].

Among the '49' officers who were settled in Co. Cork were Noblett Dunscombe, Captain John Sweet, Nicolas and Robert Corker, and several Copingers, and also, wonderful to say, Lord Broghill! He certainly had fought previous to 1649, and now that he was in favour at court and had been created Earl of Orrery, it was not desirable to inquire too closely how long he had fought on each side! As well as the estates now assured to him Colonel Townesend purchased large quantities of land from time to time[3].

The Irish parliament met again, for the first time since Cromwell had united it with England, in Chichester House, Dublin, in May 1661. It was strictly composed of the English settlers, 'men of the new interest' as they were called. Colonel Townesend sat as a member for Baltimore, but, in spite of the interest

---

[1] *Records of Ireland*, vol. 1816-1820, p. 249, Gilbert.
[2] See Appendix to this Chapter for abstract of patent.
[3] See List of lands in Appendix to this Chapter.

he must have felt in the action of the Parliament on the land question, he did not often appear there, and was actually fined for non-attendance.

One of the grandest sights which introduced the new order of things in Ireland was the consecration of twelve bishops in St. Patrick's Cathedral. One of these was Edward Synge, Bishop of Limerick, whose daughter Mary afterwards married Colonel Townesend's second son and heir by survival, Bryan. It appears that St. Patrick's had become much dilapidated during the commotions and heresies of the Civil Wars, and those whose orthodoxy was doubtful were glad to raise a subscription towards the restoration of the cathedral and of their own good characters. Jones, Bishop of Clogher, had actually joined the army of Cromwell as scoutmaster, and was very active in this matter, and the Primate writes in 1660 'the army in Ireland will suffer none to build or repair St. Patrick's Church in Dublin but themselves[1].'

For a while Colonel Townesend seems to have been content to build a small fort to hold his lands at Castletownsend, and resided at Kilbrittan Castle, a very splendid pile overlooking Courtmacsherry Bay, which had been forfeited by the head of the McCarthies for his participation in the Rebellion of 1641. McCarthie Reagh naturally considered himself still the rightful owner of the land, which had only been wrested from him by the English arms, but the chivalrous courtesy of the new comer so won upon the chieftain that in his will he bequeathed to 'Colonel Dick Townesend, M.P.' all his rights on his vast territories. The will has been seen by many people who are yet alive, and was examined by the late Timothy McCarthy

[1] *Report on Carte Papers*, Bod. Lib., p. 36.

Downing, M.P. for Co. Cork. It is said that most of the dispossessed Irish gentry carried their title deeds with them when driven from their homes, hoping that a turn of fortune might yet bring them back to their own, continuing to devise and settle the lands, and charge them with jointures as though their rights were still tangible; so it is interesting to know that a certain part of Colonel Townesend's estates were held not only by grant or purchase, but directly from the native owner. In Colonel Townesend's patent the 8000 acres forming the Manor of Bridge Town are called his 'lawful inheritance.' The Historical Pedigree of the McCarthys[1] makes no mention of this will. The McCarthy Reagh at this date was Charles, who married Ellen, daughter of Lord Muskerry, so the tradition that he married Mary Townshend cannot be correct, but his grandfather, Donal Pipi, had done his best to abolish the law of inheritance by Tanistry, so Charles may have felt he had the right to will his property away from his own family.

At Kilbrittan Castle Colonel Townesend's sixth son Philip was born in 1664. Some people think that Colonel Townesend's first wife Hildigardis died soon after the birth of Bryan, as the rest of the family were much younger, and in 1666 a lease was signed by Richard Townesend and Mary his wife. But as no descendants of Colonel Townesend's younger sons survived, no information concerning their mother has been preserved.

The ruins of Colonel Townesend's first dwelling of Castle Townshend still exist, though several sieges have left but shattered remains[2]. It seems to have

[1] By Daniel McCarthy Glas., Exeter, 168.
[2] Judge Fitz-Henry Townshend, and Miss Hickson.

consisted of a dwelling-house and small courtyard all comprised in a square enclosure with a bastion at each angle, pierced with loopholes for musketry and some embrasures for small cannon. It was built on a well-chosen site of some strength. The dwelling-house consisted of two stories, the upper one overlooking the harbour. The lower one must have been lighted from the court, on the outer side of which was a parapet for defending the wall. It seems to have been hastily built, as the stones are small and not well put together.

A larger mansion appears to have been built before long, which was valued at £40,000, when destroyed in the troubles of 1690. At one of these dwellings, tradition[1] says, Colonel Townesend's eldest daughter Hildigard died, and was buried in the ancient graveyard on Horse Island at the entrance to Castlehaven. There is a large stone now covered by the earth of the mound or fence which surrounds the burial-place, which was said to mark her grave. It bears no trace of inscription on any part which is visible[2].

At Castle Townshend was born in 1665 Colonel Townesend's seventh son, William, and the next year there must have been gay doings, for John, the eldest son, brought home his girl-bride, Lady Catherine Barry, daughter of the Earl of Barrymore and great-niece of Lord Broghill.

But that very year a French ship sailed up the Kenmare river, and rumours of an invasion grew more rife. The Romanist clergy had held a convention in June, and it was expected that they would ask the King to pardon their share in the rebellion of 1641,

---

[1] John Sealy Townshend heard this from Mrs. Becher.
[2] Judge Fitz-Henry Townshend.

CASTLE TOWNSHEND

but a sturdy bishop[1] said they were aware of no crime of which they had been guilty, and needed no pardon. This boldness showed pretty plainly that they had powerful allies behind them, and preparations were hastened on to repel the threatened invasion from France. The national alarm was increased by a plot which Lord Orrery discovered among the remains of the old republican party, who hoped to regain their lots of land and restore the old Long Parliament; so that between fears of 'fanatics' on the one hand and of Irish rebels and French soldiers on the other, the Lord Lieutenant Ormonde hardly knew whom to trust, and Orrery hastened from place to place in Munster, repairing fortifications, watching suspected traitors, raising troops, and debating which English protestants might be trusted with arms. He says in his letters to Ormonde that he was so weak in his feet that he was scarce able to go, but he could ride in a coach or on horseback; and he rode to good purpose.

At Bandon he had an interview with the principal gentry, which he reported to Lord Ormonde. But the Lord Lieutenant was suspicious of the old Parliament men settled in the west, and their claims to his confidence had to be urged again and again. Orrery's own words tell the story best. He writes to the Duke of Ormonde from Charleville, June 15, 1666[2]

'I would be glad to know if the French intend to invade Ireland, whether it be with the body of an army or only 4000 or 5000 men to join with the discontented natives. I beseech your grace let me not be tied to make the militia troops but fifty, for some gentlemen will raise me eighty, some ninety, some seventy, some sixty horse in a troop, and if we limit them all to fifty all these horse will be lost, for they will not

---

[1] Bennett.   [2] *State Letters*, p. 154.

serve in militias but under those they love well. My Lord Barrimore's Company is all in Innisshirkin and Crookhaven.

'I humbly acquaint your grace that I believe if the French invade us or the Irish rise, there are very few English (that are not damnable fanatics indeed), who will not oppose either. The chief men in the West of the country besides Mr. Richard Hull and Cornet Emanuel More are Col. John Giffard (*sic*) and Col. Richard Townesend, Lieut.-Col. William Arnop, and Capt. Robert Gooking. Giffard is a stout man and a good officer and very poor; Arnop is somewhat crazed; Townesend and Gooking rich, and men of good brains, and they have been with me to protest their loyalty and offer their services. All they have in the world depends on their new titles and I do believe they would fight heartily against the French or Irish. But I would not offer them for any employments in the militia till first I had known your Graces pleasure concerning them. They are able to make above three hundred horse and four hundred foot in the West. Giffard and Townesend are fit to command foot. Moore is a good horse soldier and an honest man.

'June 22, 1666. We can do nothing without arms, the English generally having been disarmed three years ago. The militia arms which are distributed shall be kept in safe places and in the officers' hands, but the arms for the town militias I humbly conceive may be in the townsmen's hands. Your Grace finds in the enclosed list that Col. Townesend and Col. Giffard are prepared for a foot company each, which I am humbly of opinion may safely be allowed considering they live both in West Carbery where their lots are and where only they can raise these two foot companies, and they only fit to defend those wild places in which are great crowds of illaffected Irish, which these two will best keep in awe, so that thereby they may do much good and can do no hurt, and self interest binds them to defend their own stakes. Besides being recommended by the country it would be some cause of trouble to be laid aside in so inconsiderable a thing in itself, and which may be of good use in that wild country which no army forces can mind.'

At last Orrery got his way, and the companies of militia were formed. No regiments were raised, and the rank of Colonel was not conferred on any of the gentry, but 300 horse and 400 foot were ready to fight for their country. Lord Orrery being Chief Commander, the first troop of cavalry was commanded by Major Anthony Woodbiffe, Lieutenant Emanuel Moore, Cornet Frances Armitage, Quarter-Master R. Harris. The second troop, Captain Robert Gooking, Lieutenant G. Syms, Cornet J. Langton, Quarter-Master W. Baldwin. Third troop, Captain R. Hull, Lieutenant T. Becher, Cornet Bryan Townesend, Quarter-Master Edward Townesend, while Colonel Richard Townesend, Colonel John Giffard, Captain John Freake, were all captains of foot, and Mr. Francis Beamish, ensign.

My Lord Barrimore was guarding Sherkin Island and Crookhaven, and it seemed likely that John Townesend and his bride had gone to Kilbrittan Castle, as he is called in the pedigree John of Timoleague. Colonel Townesend and his elder unmarried sons were away with their troops, when a band of armed Irish saw their opportunity and dashed down upon Castletown. The Colonel's wife fled — but fortunately there were friends at hand; Cornelius O'Donovan was one of the native chieftains whose friendship had been gained by the English family, and he welcomed the fugitives to his home. Some authorities call him O'Donovan and others O'Driscol, but however this may be, his christian name was Cornelius, and when Colonel Townesend's eighth son was born beneath his hospitable roof, the grateful parents named the child Cornelius[1].

The next trouble that threatened Munster came from

[1] See *Memoir of Cornelius Townshend*, chap. viii.

England not from France. The English commons appeared to envy the prosperity of their fellow-subjects in Ireland[1]. The importation of cattle from the rich pastures of the Emerald Isle had always been looked on with jealousy, and in 1665 a bill was passed prohibiting their introduction to England. The Duke of Ormonde seeing the people impoverished, the army mutinous for want of pay, and the Romanists and republicans both busy with plots, acted with caution and vigilance. The difficulties under which he laboured may be guessed when even the Irish contribution of 30,000 beeves (all they had to offer) to the sufferers from the Fire of London was ungratefully represented to be an endeavour to defeat the act prohibiting the export of Irish cattle.

During the debate on that bill the profligate Buckingham echoed the cheap sneer so often used against the sister Island, 'None could oppose this bill,' he exclaimed, 'save those who had Irish estates or Irish understandings.' He was promptly challenged by the gallant Ossory, Lord Ormonde's son, but Buckingham's blade was busy with less reputable quarrels and he preferred to have his challenger sent to the Tower.

The turns of Fortune's wheel raised Romanist and Protestant alternately in Ireland, and those who were down were low indeed. As far as the cynical carelessness of Charles II let him favour any form of religion, he preferred that of his patron Louis of France, which his brother and heir, the Duke of York, had openly embraced. It was felt too at Court that the aid of the Irish Romanists might be valuable in counteracting the influence of Shaftesbury, who was the open enemy of the Duke of York, and even put

[1] Leland, *History of Ireland*, iii. 442.

forward Monmouth as a desirable protestant heir to the Crown.

So in 1670, when Ormonde was replaced by Berkeley, a marked degree of favour was shown to the Romanists; the Chief Secretary expressed a wish that high mass might soon be celebrated in Christ Church Cathedral; an attempt was made to introduce Romanists into the Corporation of Dublin, and a petition was drawn up praying the King to revise the Act of Settlement on which the possessions of all Protestant landowners depended. The country was filled with alarm, and even the English Parliament was aroused. Berkeley was removed, and Essex was sent to Ireland as a harmless Viceroy who might try to please all parties; but he found it hardly possible to steer his way among the conflicting interests that disturbed the country, and compared it in one of his letters to a deer flung to the mercies of a pack of hounds.

Then came the wild 'No Popery' scare roused by Titus Oates' romance of a 'popish plot,' and the Protestant side came uppermost again. The terrors of the country had to be pacified by the marriage of Mary, eldest daughter of the Duke of York, to the Protestant champion, William of Orange, and the King, although defeated in his plans for the time, was consoled by a fresh secret treaty and more subsidies from France. The English agitations were reflected in Ireland; it was hard to find any ruler for it who could be trusted. One April day the aged Duke of Ormonde was seen at Court. 'Yonder comes Ormonde,' said the King, 'I have done all in my power to disoblige him, but he will remain loyal, I must even employ him again, and he is the fittest person to govern Ireland.' So in 1677 Ormonde returned to Dublin, and although he had no belief in the wild stories of plots and French invasion, he was forced by public opinion to adopt exceedingly severe measures against the Roman Catholics.

During these years of tumult nothing of note occurred at Castle Townshend. In 1671 Colonel Townshend[1] was High Sheriff for the County and was present at Council meetings at Clonakilty; in 1674 John and Cornelius Townesend's names are entered in the Council book, and in 1675 John was sovereign.

Many of the Colonel's contemporaries were dropping from his side; a man of sixty was an old man in those days. Edward Synge, Bishop of Cork, died 1678, the silver-tongued Orrery in 1679, and the chivalrous Ossory in 1690. About 1681 Bryan Townesend married Mary Synge, daughter of the late Bishop of Cork.

In 1682 land was mortgaged by Colonel Townesend, and the following year he borrowed another £400. This may have been to buy more land, as his sons stood surety with him, and the estate of Derry, Rosscarbery, is said to have been bought in 1686, but probably the shadows of the coming troubles were plain enough to warn the Protestant gentry to strengthen their fortifications and have ready money in hand. The fear that landowners felt for the safety of their estates was soon justified, and even the McCarthy Reagh's will did not secure all Colonel Townshend's lands. In the 'Commission of Grace' it was enacted that by 'virtue of a fine of £20 by our well beloved subject Jeremy Cartie, Esq. . . . we do give, grant, bargain, sell and confirm to the said Jeremy Cartie all the Castles, towns, villages, &c. in spite of all acts of Settlement and especially of The Act of Settlement,' and so Garrantony Reagh was lost to the Townshends.

[1] Spelt thus by Lodge, *Lib. Mun.*

This Jeremy Cartie was youngest son of Tadvig an Duna Ist, known as 'the festive,' who had feasted away most of his possessions.

That same year, 1685, King Charles the Second died, and the storm that had been gathering broke over the Protestants of Ireland. At Bandon[1] Sir Edward Moore was charged with high treason, and Edward Riggs was accused of saying that if he could not live quietly in Ireland he would go to England. They were acquitted, but no gentry were safe from the charges of informers, the Protestant militia was disbanded and disarmed, leaving the dwellers in the wilder parts of the country at the mercy of the roving bands of freebooters who were beginning to infest the country.

It was soon seen that King James intended to favour the Romanists, and only the Romanists; an agitation was set on foot to repeal the Act of Settlement, and it was hinted to the Protestants that they would be wise to make terms and surrender a third of their estates before letting matters come to extremities. The Viceroy Clarendon was told that the King's servant ought to be of the King's religion, and the Romanist Tyrconnell replaced him as Lord Lieutenant. It is said that the King, knowing that his legal successors, Mary and William of Orange, would alter all his system of government, determined to make Ireland into a safe refuge for his Romanist subjects after his death. The Protestant burgesses of towns were warned that they must not fill their corporation with men of their own creed, and any post of honour now became a post of danger. The account of the meeting of burgesses of Clonakilty tells its own tale[2].

[1] Bennett, *History of Bandon*.
[2] *Council Book of Clonakilty*.

'October 18, 1685. Thomas Becher[1] chosen to be sovereign and refused to serve and was unanimously ordered to be disfranchised and struck off the roll. Col. Richard Townesend was unanimously chosen for the year ensuing and immediately sworn accordingly, and all his ensigns of authority delivered to him.'

In his life of sixty-seven years he had lived through many changes, and if civil war were coming again upon that 'most distressful country,' it would be well to have a man of experience to head the Protestants of the little town.

Old men still told of the ghastly murder of the sovereign of Clonakilty by the rebels of 1641, and a new Irish massacre was expected daily by the terrified settlers in West Carbery. Only two or three years before, the revocation of the Edict of Nantes had filled English and Irish towns with fugitives, who wrung the hearts of their hearers by their stories of the persecution commanded by the Most Christian King of France, the ally and counsellor of the King who now reigned in England. No wonder that a hurried exodus took place among the Protestants of Ireland[2]. Some crossed the channel in open boats, others crowded on board the ships in Dublin harbour, shrieking that the Irish were upon them.

Among those who left Co. Cork were[3] the Bernards, Richard Cox, Joseph Daunt, Percy Freke, Robert and Vincent Gooking, Sir Samuel Moore, Edward Riggs, George Synge, and Thomas Becher. It is plain why the latter had declined to be kept in Clonakilty to overlook market dues and regulate tolls. There was more congenial work in the North of Ireland, where

---

[1] See Becher Pedigree Table 5 a.
[2] Leland.
[3] Bennett's *Bandon*.

he soon after is found with many of the other fugitives, fighting under the banners of William of Orange. Bryan Townesend also left the country and placed his wife and three little ones in safety and then joined the Northern army.

John Hull, who had followed Colonel Townesend as sovereign of Clonakilty, was replaced by a McCarthy; Catholic sheriffs were at the head of every county. The Protestant gentry who did not emigrate or join the army in the North, drew together into the larger country[1] houses, and remained upon their guard with loop-holed walls and barricaded windows. At Castle Townshend, the Colonel 'girt on his old sword, and went to man the wall.'

Smith, in his history of Co. Cork, gives a graphic record of the perils of one member of Colonel Townesend's family, Catherine, who had lately married William, son and heir of William Gun of Rattoo, Co. Kerry. There is a tradition that she and her husband were in some place which was besieged by the enemy, and was reduced to surrender. Terms were made, and the women were allowed to leave, carrying their valuables, but Catherine said that she did not wish to bring anything with her but her gun, and this being permitted, the well-grown young lady appeared, carrying her husband, Mr. Gun, on her back. So the story runs, and if it is not true it ought to be![2] But Smith's story is unimpeachable, and runs as follows:—

'Sir Thomas Southwell with several other gentlemen of Co. Cork when the Protestants were disarmed in 1688, being unwilling to give up their horses and arms, many of them having been robbed and plundered of their stock before, and

---

[1] Walpole.   [2] Smith's *History of Co. Cork*, 211.

justly suspecting that, as soon as their arms were gone, neither their lives nor the rest of their substance would be safe, assembled together with their servants and resolved to march to join Lord Kingston at Sligo for their common defence. Mr. Gun's spouse accompanied him disguised in man's apparel in that expedition, when though very young she behaved with undaunted courage superior to her sex. In this march they were met in the County of Galway by Mr. Power, the High Sheriff, attended by a posse, and a party of dragoons, to whom they surrendered themselves, being fatigued with a long march, upon articles of safety and liberty and indeed contrary to the advice of some of their party who were for fighting their way [1].'

Another writer [2] tells us that it was Catherine Gun who earnestly counselled her husband and his companions to 'fight and die honourably rather than trust to the mercy of a perfidious enemy.'

It was promised that passes should be given them and horses in exchange for their own (reserved for King James' service) to enable them to return home.

'Notwithstanding,' continues Smith, 'they were robbed and made prisoners, and though several of them had plentiful estates, yet nothing was allowed them to preserve their lives, except the charitable contributions of their fellow Protestants in different parts of the kingdom. At Galway they were brought to trial before Judge Martin, who persuaded them to plead guilty, assuring them of the King's mercy, who was then just landed. But the judge soon after passing sentence of death on these gentlemen, they with much ado and a sum of money procured a reprieve which they were forced to renew from time to time. And thus they continued in close imprisonment, being removed from jail to jail till the general deliverance by His Majesty's victory

---

[1] Smith's *History of Kerry*, p. 59.
[2] Miss Hickson, *Old Kerry Records*.

at the Boyne, all which time they were not only in a starving condition, but once had a summons sent them, whether in jest or earnest, to prepare for execution, by the Earl of Clanrickard, who came to Galway about the beginning of November 1689. His Lordship being a new convert thinking it allowable to put a jest upon them as a testimony of his zeal against heretics.'

Catherine Gun and her husband returned in safety to Rattoo; there she lived to a very great age (she was alive in 1774 when Smith wrote), and died, leaving behind her two sons, Francis and Townshend, and three daughters, Rebecca, Sarah, and Catherine.

But to return to the stormy time when Catherine Gun started on her adventurous journey. The birth to James of a son and heir was the death-blow to the hopes of the lovers of liberty, who had gained courage to bear the tyranny of his reign by looking forward to the changes that would come under his daughter Mary. James plunged blindly on in the path of destruction: blunder after blunder alienated his most loyal subjects, and when, on the 5th of November, 1688, William of Orange landed in Torbay not a man raised a hand to retain the last Stuart king on his throne. He fled to France, where he was received by Louis with the warmest hospitality, and some covert contempt: the King of England it was felt was rather too pious to be successful in the affairs of this world. But twenty-three vessels were placed at his disposal, and in the spring of 1689 he set sail from Brest, the King of France gaily assuring him as a farewell that he trusted never to see him again.

James landed at Kinsale on the 12th of March; the peasantry did their best to welcome him, and as laurels were not to be had, they made garlands of cabbage stalks in his honour[1]. He reached Dublin after a stately progress, and there busied himself in organising the affairs of his little kingdom, coining pewter money, placing fellows of his own religion in Trinity College, and presiding over a Parliament composed only of Romanists, who felt that their turn had come to revenge the Cromwellian Conquest. He reproved the French envoy, who calmly proposed a general massacre of the Protestants; but the Act of Settlement was revoked, and two thousand four hundred persons, men and women, nobility, clergy, and yeomen, were proscribed as traitors[2]. In this tremendous list are found the names of Bryan, Kingston, and Francis Townesend; probably John, the eldest of the family, was dead, and Horatio, a sailor, was not in Ireland. Dean Rowland Davis fled from Cork when King James entered it, and from the diary[3] which he kept during his wanderings we learn all that we know of the Townesend family during that gloomy spring. The fugitives in England seem to have born their exile with true Irish light-heartedness.

'April 28, 1690. Went with Mr. Horace Townesend and P. Crosbie to the Roebuck in the Haymarket and dined for 8d; after dinner we had a famous bout of wrestling between Danter, a shoemaker of Ireland, and one Barton, a printer, and I won a bottle of wine on the latter's head.'

Soon after Mr. Horace Townesend had the honour of commanding the vessel that conveyed Duke Schomburg to his command in Ireland; and when they landed at Bangor, Co. Down, the aged general presented him with his watch. But the war in Ireland dragged slowly on; the soldiers murmured that Schomburg

---

[1] Bennett's *Bandon*.     [2] Green, *Shorter History*, 672.
[3] Published by the Camden Society, edited by Caulfield.

was past his work; sickness broke out, provisions were wanting, and at last William, weary of English factions, determined to hand the reins of government in Great Britain to his wife, and himself assume the command in Ireland. Many of the fugitive gentry flocked to his head-quarters at Lisburn. Dean Davis records:—

'May 21, 1690. I went in the morning to the meeting-house at Dunmurray where the regiment met and I preached to them on 2 Cor. v. 20. After sermon I went with Captain South to his quarters where I met the Lieutenant-Colonel just come from Lisburn, and with him Sir Pury Cust and Captain Bryan Townshend. We dined there and spent the evening.'

It seems most likely that Bryan would remain with the army till the eventful 1st of July, when the victory of the Boyne decided the fate of Ireland and the Stuarts; but no further mention has been found of the Townesend family at the time, though their companion, Thomas Becher, was present at the battle, and his descendants still preserve the large silver watch which King William gave him after the victory.

It is needless to describe the heroic struggle at the Boyne and the pusillanimous conduct of James II who fled the field, and how the defeated Irish cried 'change kings and we will fight you over again.' After James' escape from Kinsale, Fortune's Wheel slowly but surely brought the Protestants uppermost, and it was their turn to plunder and oppress. When William had to return to England, leaving Ginkle in command, the season was growing too late for any extended campaign, but Marlborough made a brilliant and successful dash at Cork and Kinsale. Dean Davis was back in Cork, and says, 'I gave Scravenmore an account of the usefulness of the Cathedral, whereupon Lieut. Townesend was sent with men thither, and accordingly did good service.'

Smith in his history gives a more detailed account of the action:—

'Lieut.-Col. Scravenmore having passed the river and being quartered at Gill Abbey, not far from which stood the steeple of the Cathedral Church which looked into the (enemy's) fort, detached Lieut. Horatio Townshend, who getting two files of men to the top of the steeple[1] killed the Governor of the fort and did considerable execution. To remove this party, the Irish traversed two guns against the steeple and shook it exceedingly. Whereupon the men offered to go down, but the brave Townshend with invincible courage commanded those below to take away the ladder and continued in that post till the fort was surrendered next day.'

After the taking of Cork and Kinsale the armies went into winter quarters, half the country was in the hands of the English, while Limerick, Clare, Connaught, and Kerry, were occupied by the Irish. Trade revived near the towns, but parties of disbanded Jacobite soldiers and Irish rapparees burnt and raided along the border country even to the walls of Bandon.

In November, Story tells us [2],—

'Five hundred Irish under young Colonel Driscoll attempted to burn Castletown, the mansion house of Colonel Townshend in West Carbery. But they missed their aim and were so well received by him and his garrison, consisting of about 35 men that twelve of them dropt at the first volley, and upon a second attack Driscoll, Captain Tieg Donovan, Captain Croneen, and about 30 others were slain and so many others wounded that they were forced to retire with loss and shame. One, Captain Mac-Ronaine, with his drawn

---

[1] 'Laying boards across the beams for them to stand upon,' according to Story, *Wars of Ireland*, I. 741.
[2] Quoted in Smith's *Hist. Co. Cork*, II. 211.

sword endeavoured to hinder his men's retreat, but he being killed they got away; several of them had bundles of straw on their breasts to resist the shot, but notwithstanding 30 were slain on the spot.'

Castletown was again attacked by MacFineen O'Driscoll with 400 men, who, having slain five of the garrison of thirty-nine dragoons, compelled the rest to surrender. Colonel Culliford retook the Castle (greatly dilapidated by all these sieges), after killing ten and capturing ten of the Jacobite garrison. In the grounds till lately[1] (says Miss Hickson) stood an old sycamore known as Diarmed's tree, from a tradition that on it Colonel Townesend had hung one of the besiegers. A skeleton of a man was actually found when a large oak-tree that grew between the house and the sea was blown down, but nothing was found to prove if these were indeed the remains of Diarmid, or those of some other of the many victims of the wars in Munster.

It was in compensation for this destruction of Castle Townshend that government granted £40,000 to Colonel Townesend.

The next year King William offered very[2] favourable terms to the Irish, but they did not condescend to answer proposals which they believed were dictated by his fear and not by his generosity. They learned their error too late, when the massacre after Aughrim and the surrender of Limerick had left them at the feet of the English settlers and the Dublin Parliament.

A desultory frontier warfare had been going on in Carbery all the year 1691. In January[3], Lieutenant Arthur Bernard, with twenty of the East Carbery Horse and eighteen Bandon Militia, advanced into the enemy's country, drove a hundred and twenty of

---
[1] *Old Kerry Records.*  [2] Walpole.  [3] Bennett's *Bandon.*

O'Donovan's Irish regiment off the field, and brought in large booty. On the 11th of April the Irish assaulted Clonakilty, but were driven off. The next day they were more successful at Inniskean, which they stormed and burnt to the ground, with the exception of one house, in which a detachment of Collier's regiment took refuge and held out till relieved from Bandon by Governor Cox. In May we hear of Colonel Townesend making head against the enemy near his home.

'There was now,' says Story, 'a garrison of the militia in Castlehaven, one of those forts which the Irish delivered to the Spaniards in Queen Elizabeth's time, famous for the sea-fight in the Haven between Sir Richard Levison and Don Pedro de Zubiaur the Spanish Admiral, when the greatest part of the Spaniards were sunk or disabled. From hence Colonel Townsend sent a party of his men to scour the country; they met with a party of rapparees and killed one Regan their captain with Borg his lieutenant, and four more.'

In the following month Inniskean, which had been relieved, was garrisoned by a force of the Bandon Militia, a detachment of which, under 'the brave Townsend,' marched into the country around Bantry, where they did great execution, killing a hundred rapparees and bringing off large plunder. But even this did not discourage the enemy: in July they attacked Skibbereen, but here also they were routed by the militia under Colonel Becher. He also recaptured a Dutch ship from the Irish in Bantry Bay, when, besides those killed in the struggle, thirty of the enemy who leapt overboard were drowned before they could reach the shore.

At the battle of Aughrim (July 12, 1691) the Earl of

Meath's regiment was engaged and had five officers wounded. There was a Captain Townsend serving in this regiment shortly after, who may have been present on that fatal day for the Jacobite cause when the gallant St. Ruth fell. This Captain Townsend may have been either Bryan or Francis. We hear of him from Story, who says (Feb. 28, 1692),

'Captain Townsend of the Earl of Meath's regiment took eight or ten Frenchmen prisoners who had come ashore from a privateer in Castlehaven.'

This year, 1691, saw the winding up of the struggle in Ireland, when Limerick surrendered and twenty thousand Irishmen went over-seas to serve the King of France.

The romantic story of Horace Townesend wooing and wedding Colonel Becher's beautiful daughter will be found later on.

In 1792 Bryan Townesend was sovereign of Clonakilty, and Colonel Richard Townesend died, aged seventy-four. His will[1] was signed on June 24th 'being sick in body but in perfect sense and disposing memory.' He was buried in the old graveyard at Castlehaven; his tomb is still marked in the chancel of the ruined church, by a slab bearing the words 'This is the burial-place of the Townshends,' and the arms of the family.

A peaceful resting-place it looks, lulled by the ripples breaking on the strand of Castlehaven; involuntarily the words rise to one's mind 'So Thou bringest them to the haven where they would be.'

If any calm settled down over Ireland after Aughrim, it was for the Irish 'a calm of despair.' They were

---

[1] See Appendix to this Chapter.

brought very low. Dean Swift said they were only allowed to survive as hewers of wood and drawers of water. Their best and bravest were driven from the country, and carried their swords and talents into foreign service. Colonel Townesend's grandson, young James Coppinger, lost his estates of Lissapole and Rincolinsky, and his descendants had to settle far off in Britanny[1]. The Irish who remained were ground down by penal laws of such ferocity that they often defeated themselves. The gentry, it is said, frequently refused to recognise the Roman Catholic priests who passed them in disguise, and Colonel Townesend's successor Bryan aided many of his neighbours to save their lands from confiscation.

It is pleasant among the stories of intolerance and oppression, which make Irish history such grievous reading, to remember Samuel Townshend of Whitehall, the High Sheriff, who induced the parish priest and the protestant rector to combine with him to preserve the peace and safety of Aughadown amid the terrors of 1798, how Horace Townsend of Derry, 'the friend of the poor,' did the same for the neighbourhood of Clonakilty, how Samuel Townsend of Firmount was said to be[2] 'the favourite arbitrator of his poorer neighbours,' and to recollect the ten thousand pounds arrears which Maurice Fitzgerald Stephens Townshend remitted to his tenants. Fuller accounts of these descendants of Colonel Townesend will be found in the succeeding chapters.

No relics of Colonel Townesend survive unless it be his letter from Pendennis Castle[3], his signature in

---

[1] See Notes on Dorothea Townshend, Chap. viii.
[2] *Statist. Survey*, Co. Cork.
[3] Tanner MSS., Bodleian Library, Oxford.

the Council Book at Clonakilty and appended to various deeds and leases, and the Royal Pardons and Grants to him which are preserved among the deeds of Castle Townshend.

Judge Fitz-Henry Townshend has seen a ring that was formerly preserved at Castle Townshend, and was believed to have belonged to the founder of the family. It bore the arms of Townshend of Norfolk, azure a chevron ermine between three escallops argent, but being neither quartered nor impaled, they gave little real information.

The fires which have destroyed the successive mansions at Castle Townshend must have also destroyed many relics and papers, so it is difficult to find other evidence of the origin of the family than tradition. But unfailing tradition does represent Colonel Richard Townesend as descended from Roger Townshend of Raynham, Norfolk. He named his son Horatio, a name derived from the Fighting Veres, and borne by his contemporary the first Baron Townshend[1]. Bryan also bore a name that may have been derived from the same source. Bryan Fairfax was a well-known antiquary and writer, and as General Fairfax and Sir Roger Townshend married the Vere sisters, the name may have come into the family at that time. But it is not an unusual name, and a good authority, John Sealy Townshend, Master in Chancery, said it was derived from Bryan, Chief Justice of Common Pleas in England in 1484, of which Court a Sir Roger Townshend was also a Judge. John was also a family name among the Townshends of Norfolk.

But at present no Richard Townshend, born in 1618 or 1619, has been found in the pedigrees of the

[1] Viscount Rainham.

Norfolk family or among their relatives in Salop or Worcestershire.

Richard Townesend, son of John Townesend of Dichford, Co. Warwick (pleb.), matriculated at Hart Hall, Oxford, in 1637, aged 19. He is the only Richard Townesend of the right age who has been met with as yet.

There were burgesses of Warwick named Townsend, one of whom, Richard the son of John, matriculated at Oxford in 1601, and had a son John.

The name Richard occurs among the Townshends of Northampton, who founded one of the American branches of the family. Walter Townsend of Hinton, Co. Northampton, mentions his son Richard in a will dated 1630.

Several Richard Townshends emigrated to America from Gloucestershire in the seventeenth century, but they claimed no connection with the Townshends of Raynham. A Richard Townshend married Frances Gason at Brackinashe in Norfolk in 1618, and it is of course not impossible that he may have been the father of the subject of this memoir. It is not yet proved what connection this Richard Townshend had with the Townshends of Brackinashe, but if he belonged to their family he would through them be closely connected with the D'Oyleys. Thomas Townshend of Brackinashe married Anne D'Oyley of Shottisham, and his first cousin Dorothea Townshend of Testerton married Henry D'Oyley.

Among the wills of the Townshends of Devonshire are those of Richard, Samuel, and Dorothy, but no connection has yet been traced between this family and that in Co. Cork.

At one time there was an idea current in the family,

which found its way into one of the earlier editions of Burke's *Landed Gentry*, that Colonel Townesend had nine brothers instead of nine sons. John Sealy Townshend disposes of this theory in a letter dated March 9th, 1846. He says—

'My uncle John[1], now in his 82nd year (whose father was born in 1733 or so, and did not die till 1817, and was eminently versed—as my uncle John still is—in all that relates to the pedigree from Colonel Richard down), affirms that Cornelius and Francis were sons of Colonel Richard, and his affirmation concurs with Colonel Richard's will (which one would think ought to be deemed decisive). But I have in my power the infallible evidence of Chancery pleadings and Registered deeds. To detail these here would occupy more time and space than I can just now command, but I will give you chapter and verse under the hands and seals of Bryan and his son Richard and brother Philip.'

George Digby Daunt says—

'It appears very unlikely that the Colonel could have induced all his brothers, if he had any, to come to Ireland and settle there on his being ordered for active service, except it can be proved that his grandfather was the first settler.'

It has always been believed that Colonel Townesend's wife was Hildegardis Hyde, a near kinswoman of the great Lord Clarendon, and therefore of Queen Mary and Queen Anne. If the belief is correct, this connection may explain the safety of Colonel Townesend's life and lands through so many perilous times; and some relations of the Hydes did become enriched by forfeited lands. Thomas Keightly, Lord Justice, married Lord Clarendon's youngest daughter and was given grants of land from the forfeitures of 1688 as a portion for his daughter, Lady Katherine

---

[1] Master in Chancery. See ch. xi.

Keightly, 'who was a dependant on her late Majesty Queen Mary[1].'

Colonel Townesend seems also to have had a wife named Mary: more than one deed exists signed by Colonel Townesend and 'Mary his wife.' Some suggest that Hildegardis was too peculiar a name to be used in a Puritan family, and that she was therefore usually called Mary, both as being a common name and also that of her probable grandmother, Mary Langford, who married Henry Hyde of Purton. But John Sealy Townshend believes that Colonel Townesend really married a second time, Mary O'Brien. Lord Clarendon married Catherine O'Brien, daughter of Henry seventh Earl of Thomond; and her youngest brother Henry Horatio, Lord Ibraken, was a contemporary of Colonel Townesend's son Horatio, and served with him under Marlborough. An excellent genealogist, the late Mr. Denis O'Callaghan Fisher, thought it was clear that Colonel Townesend married twice, 1st, because family tradition makes all the present Townshends of Co. Cork descend from a lady named Hildegardis Hyde; 2nd, that Colonel Townesend was unquestionably at one period of his life married to a lady named Mary, whose surname had possibly been Kingston, as one of Colonel Townesend's younger sons was named Kingston, and others Philip and Cornelius, which are not Townshend family names.

A family named Kingston was settled near Bandon. Colonel Samuel Kingston, of Skeaf in East Carbery, died 1703, leaving a son James, who was admitted freeman of Clonakilty, 1710, John Townesend being sovereign; and in 1708 Bryan Townesend granted Garrendruig for 980 years to James Kingston on such

[1] Rep. Com. in Pub. Rec. v. 3. p. 40.

very favourable terms as to make it probable that it was some sort of family affair[1]. John, Baron Kingston, may have been a friend of Colonel Townesend and given his name to his son, as his regiment went to Ireland in 1647, at the same time as Colonel Townesend's, and Colonel Townesend purchased some Carbery land from him.

The members of the Townshend family have always shown their independence of character in the variety of ways they have spelt and still spell their name.

It seems at first to have been in Norfolk 'Atte Town's end,' and during the fifteenth and sixteenth centuries it was spelt in as many as twelve different ways—Townsend, Tounneyshende, Towneshende, &c. About 1500 it was most usually spelt Townsend, but in 1580 the chief family at Raynham resumed the use of the h.

The first members of the family in Ireland spelt their name Townesend, then Townsend became most common; but a few records have been found of all dates which use the h. The commission of Samuel Irwin, son of General Sam. Townsend, as ensign in the 1st Regiment of Footguards, is made out to S. I. Townsend, but four years later, in 1799, his Lieutenant's Commission spells the name Townshend; and in the year 1870 the head of the Irish branch, the Rev. Maurice Fitzgerald Stephens Townshend, after consulting with the Marquess Townshend as head of the family, induced the greater part of the Irish Townshends to spell their name uniformly with an h.

As no descendants of Colonel Townesend's younger sons exist, it is probable that no one cared to preserve the name of their mother, while Bryan's descendants

[1] Note by Cecil C. Woods, Esq., 1889.

have been proud to remember their ancestress Hildegardis Hyde.

Colonel Richard Townesend had the following children:—

JOHN. Died before his father. His descendants in the female line are represented by Townshend of Skirtagh, which see.

BRYAN. Ancestor of all the present family of Townshend in Ireland.

FRANCIS. Represented by the families of Stewart and Beamish.

HORATIO. Represented by the families of Daunt and Herbert.

KINGSTON. Died unmarried in Barbadoes. He is mentioned in his father's will and was proscribed as a traitor by James II.

PHILIP. Represented by Sir Henry Becher.

WILLIAM. b. 1665. Died unmarried. His will was proved 1711; it is sealed with the Townshend crest and bequeathed all he had to his nephew 'John Fitz-Bryan.'

CORNELIUS. Represented in the female line in the branches of Townshend of Derry and Donoughmore, which see. Also by Orpen of Ardtully, Kerry.

EDWARD. Probably died comparatively young, as he is not mentioned in Colonel Townesend's will; but in a schedule laid before the Court of Claims, 1665, he is mentioned as in possession of Keamore. He was quarter-master of militia in 1666. He may have been only a kinsman to the family at Castle Townshend.

HILDIGARDIS. Died young.

MARY. Said by Mrs. E. Synge Townshend to have married an Irish chieftain named O'Regan, by others to have married McCartie Reagh or Dr. H. Jones, Bishop of Meath. (Mrs. Mary McCartie Reagh received a pension of £100, Com. Journ. 1710.)

CATHERINE. Married William Gun of Rattoo, Co. Kerry, and left descendants.

A DAUGHTER. Married John Owen. See note on Chap. VIII.

DOROTHEA. Married Domenic Copinger and left descendants. See note on Chap. VIII.

The history of the descendants of Bryan Townshend will be first given as being head of the family, then that of Colonel Richard's and of Bryan's younger children.

## APPENDIX A.

WILL OF COLONEL RICHARD TOWNESEND, DATED JUNE 24, 1692. EXTRACTED FROM THE PREROGATIVE COURT OF ROSSCARBERY BY GEORGE DIGBY DAUNT.

'In the name of God. Amen. I Richard Townesend of Castle Townesend in the County of Cork, Esqr. being sick in body but in perfect sense and disposing memory, for which God be thanked, do make this my last will and testament in manner following. Viz. I give and bequeath my soul to God that gave it, hoping in a glorious resurrection through the merits of my Saviour. My body to the ground, to be decently buried in the Church of Castlehaven by my executors hereafter named. Item, I give and bequeath unto my grandson Richard Fitzjohn Townesend the house and lands of Bridgetown and my whole freehold in Coronea the house and lands of Curromteige and Lorrogo with the mills and salmon fishing, the ... and lands of Skeaf North Moreahine, Stuckeen, Gorrilomore, Dyrinedangan, Dromig, Lahirtidally, Lisanuhig, Drishanemore and fishing. My part of Cappaghmore, the ... and lands Redcaum Bargorum and Cooldoragh and Glaun Ikillean to him my said grandson during his natural life, and after his decease to the heirs male of his body lawfully begotten, and for want of such issue to my son Bryan Townesend and his heirs male, and for want of such the remainder to my son Francis and his heirs male, and for want of such to my son Horatio and his heirs male, and for want of such to my son Philip and his heirs male, and for want of such issue to my son William and his heirs male, and for want of such to my grandson John Fitzcornelius and his heirs male &c., and for want of such to the heirs general. The said estates to be nevertheless subject to the payment of £500, within five years after the date hereof by equal portions yearly to be paid to my granddaughter Susanna Townesend as well to be a marriage portion as in satisfaction of a debt due from me unto her, and whereas I have settled several lands on my son Bryan Townesend on his marriage if therefore my above named grandson Richard Fitzjohn shall sue implead or disturb my said son Bryan or his heirs by reason of any pretence of former gift grant or otherwise of any part of the whole of the lands settled as aforesaid and thereby dispossess him or them, it is my will that from the time of dispossession he or they enjoy the before bequeathed lands. I give the profits and issues of them to my executors the better to enable them to pay my debts and particularly those for which my sons are bound, and after satisfaction made of my debts it is my will that my son Philip and his heirs shall have them, and failing such the remainder to my son Bryan and his heirs and for want of such to my son Francis and so to descend as aforesaid.

'I appoint my sons Bryan and Philip my executors of this my last will and testament revoking all former wills and testaments, and I do hereby give my said executors to enable them with what before I have given to pay my debts and funeral charges, all my goods and chattels of what kind soever of which the lease made by Thomas Becher, Esq. of the Fairs and Markets of Skibbereen is a part. In witness whereof I have hereunto set my hand and seal this 24th June, 1692.

RICHARD TOWNESEND.

Being present
RICHARD TOWNSEND FITZJOHN.'

## APPENDIX B.

The following list of lands belonging to Colonel Townesend was made by John Sealy Townshend.

The lands named in Colonel Townesend's patents of 1668 are:

1. Ardglasse in Barony of Carberry, parish Kilcoe.
2. Ardgehan in Barony of Carberry.
3. Bargorum in Barony of Carberry.
4. Ballycahan in Barony of Carberry.
5. Bawnishal in Barony of Carberry, parish of Fanelobish.
6. Cooledurrogh in Barony of Carberry.
7. Dunbeacon.
8. Derryfunstone.
9. Enan alias Eoan.
10. Garrantonyreghy, Parish of Fanelobish (recovered by Jeremy Cartie under the Commission of Grace, 1684).
11. Gortbrack.
12. Killaderry (part of Glanteige).
13. Killcaughy.
14. Murrahine North.
15. Ratooth townland in Barony of Ratooth, Co. Meath.
16. Sleughteige, Barony Carbery.
17. Stackeen or Sprickeene.

In patent of 1666 are:

Ardgehan in Barony of Carberry.
Ballycahan.
Banishall.
Coolederry.

18. Carribegg.
19. Cluonleaugh.
20. Castle Ire.
21. Curramac Teige.
22. Cloughvolly.
23. Coroone alias Coronea, 'called by the name of Skubereene.'

## APPENDIX B. 137

24. Clonbanine in Barony Duhallow.
25. Drishane beg in Barony Carbery.
26. Dromig.
27. Derrindangan.
28. Drishane more.
    Enane alias Inane.
29. Fornaught.
30. Glanteige (part of Glanteige was granted John Eyres, Esqre. the owner, 246 acres, and in Sleughteige 9 acres, also land in Galway).
    Gortbracke.
31. Gortagolane.
32. Glounboage alias Clonbooge.
33. Island in Barony of Duhallow (in the Commons Journal called islands of Clonbairene, 401 acres, arrears of quit-rent were due for the years 1693-4-5, when Col. Richard and Richard Fitz-John were living).
34. Keamore (sold to Jeremy Donovan 1679, bought back by John Sealy Townshend, Master in Chancery).
35. Listurcane.
36. Lahir teedally.
37. Lissinugg.
38. Lurigo.
39. Loghcrott.
40. Rathnapoole.
    Sleighteige (save Farrindoligin, Farrinda, and Drishaneen).
    Stukine.
41. Skeagh.

By a registered deed of July 21, 1772, made between Bryan, his son Richard, and Philip Townsend, Col. Townesend also had the following lands which are in the copy of the patent in possession of T. Downes, Esq., of Skibbereen.

43. Fillenderry in Carbery.
44. Lisseenapin.
45. Ballycronane.
46. Coronea-gneeve.
47. Lissnaneane.

48. Cappamore.
49. Banelahan.
50. Cross Teas.
51. Yeokane.
52. Barnagordan.
53. Cahirsna.
54. Ardra.
55. Farangulla.
56. West Blood.
57. Laherdene.
58. Milane.

And from the Archbishop of Dublin.

59. Aghills.
60. Killcoe.
61. Myross.
62. Part of Drishane.
63. Part of Farrenda.

By the account of the collector of quit-rents the district of Baltimore, 1695, it seems Col. Townesend was also seized or possessed of:

66. Kinroshanra.
67. Carron.
68. Knockroone.

And John, probably his son, was seized of Drumalighy.

This property was in a large part purchased upon the restoration, and even after his first patents were granted.

It appears from a deed registered July 21, 1722, made between Colonel Townesend's son Bryan and *his* son Richard and the Rev. Philip Townsend that Colonel Townesend leased land from the Archbishop of Dublin (Michael Boyle), and the fairs and markets of Skibbereen from Colonel Thomas Becher[1].

---

[1] Probably Colonel Townesend only was granted the fairs and markets of Bridgetown, his part of Skibbereen, and so leased the right to the rest of the town from Colonel Becher.

By the same deed it appears that on Nov. 16, 1682, Colonel Townsend borrowed £400 from the Right Hon. Richard Earl of Cork, the Right Hon. George late Viscount Lanesborough, and the Right Hon. Lady Countess Dowager of Orrery, to whom, on that date, he mortgaged the lands of Corran Teige, Cooldonagh, Stuckeen, and Castle Ire, and he borrowed another £400 from Arthur Pomeroy, late Dean of Cork, and on June 1683 mortgaged to him Drishane-more. He incurred many other debts, no doubt in purchasing land in which his sons are joined as securities. See his last will and testament.

EXTRACTS FROM PATENT OF SKIBBEREEN MANOR, ALIAS BRIDGETOWN, ALIAS CORONEA, GRANTED TO COLONEL RICHARD TOWNESEND.

(From a copy in possession of T. Downes, Esq.)

'Charles the Second by the grace of God, &c., &c., whereas our trusty and welbeloved subject Richard Townesend, Esq. hath humbly represented unto us, that he is now in possession of ye undernamed Townlands, tenements and heredits, in his own right, as his lawful inheritance, viz. ye towns and lands of Bridgetown als Coronea licke, Drishanemore, Rhynecormac, Lahirdane, Ardagohane, Ballycahir als Ballicuchane, Gurtbrack, Enane, Castletown, and ye four ploughlands of Slughteige, Magragh, Tornagh, with the appurtenances, Garrybegg, Letterhinglass, Morromisholanane, Ranypole, Killaderry, Berneteownen, Blood and Ballynegallop, ye two ploughlands of Knocknaheely, Rahine, Ballycrohane, Ardra, Barryshull, Cahirgall, Castleire, Clonecah, als Clonedcahill, Listercaw, Shickeen, Cooledurah, Glanboige, Glankilleen, Ardglaw, Curragh meteige, with the appurtenances, Dereendangan, Drishanbegg, Lurgo als Lurigo, Smorane, Lissimihig, Lahertadally, Drummig, Cloghwoly, Gurtogowlane, Skeagh, Bargormane, Cahirsnagh, Meolune, Favingilly, Mihill, Scobaned, Downey, Dunbeacon, Derryfinistan, and Caherlikenny, containing in all 8000 acres or thereabouts, lying in the barony of Carbery . . . hath humbly prayed us in consideration of his loyalty and for the better improvement and settlement of his said estate to make ye said towns and lands into one entire manor to be knowne and called by ye name of ye manor of Bridgetown als Coronea . . . with ye advice and consent of our right trusty and right welbeloved cousin Arthur Earl of Essex our Lieutenant general and general governor of our kingdom of Ireland . . . also the lands Knocknagowna, Ballyroe, Yookane, Ryne de cassane.'

This patent gives permission to hold Court leats and baron and Frankplege and build a prison and have pounds, stocks and duckingstools and have rights to all quarries, mines and minerals and have fisheries fowlings and huntings of what game soever, and to enclose so many acres as they think fit, not exceeding eight hundred acres, into a park for deer and other beast of venery, and also free lycence and power henceforth and forever to have free warren, park, and chace, upon the said manor, and also to hold markets every Friday, and fairs 3rd of May and 3rd October, and appoint officers for the market.

Ninth day of June, 28th year of our reign (1677).

## APPENDIX C.

### Deposition of Colonel Townesend.

'Colonel Richard Townesend, now resident in Castle Haven, English Protestant. At the declaring of Cork for the Parliament of England Oct. 16, 1649, a prisoner in the said city, being duly sworn, saith: That about three days before the declaring of Cork, Captain Robert Myhill came to him, to acquaint this Examinant that the Lord Inchiquin had ordered Colonel Jefford should be sent to Bandon Bridge and Colonel Warden to the Fort of Cork, and this examinant to the fort of Kinsale next morning, upon which tidings this Examinant with his partners was very much troubled and did believe this separation was with intent to have them executed speedily. Whereupon Captain Myhill took Examinant aside and advised him to endeavour their continuance in the place where they were, and he believed it would be much to their security, and he thereupon acquainted him with an intention of several persons to secure the city and port of Cork and Castle of Shandon for the parliament of England and the then Lord Lieutenant. Given Feb. 16, 1654, by Colonel Townsend, aged 36.

'February 21, 1654. Colonel Richard Townesend further deposeth that Captain Joseph Cuff then a Lieutenant to Captain William Bryan, the Lord of Inchiquin's son, about four o'clock in the morning of that night the City of Cork declared for the Commonwealth, he, the said Examinant met said Joseph Cuff on the North bridge of Cork and after some conference with said Cuff this Examinant and Colonel Gifford agreed that said Cuff should go into Carbery where his troop lay and bring as many of them as he should engage to Cork for the better securing of the town; and the said Cuff did go and bring sixteen troopers well horst the next night after the town delivered.

'And that one Lieutenant George Water was by Examinant made acquainted with the design to secure Youghal for the Parliament, that he did joyfully consent and brought in four ... to the place appointed for meeting and the same night that Youghal was secured he was (by the treachery of one Johnson) taken prisoner with Examinant, Colonel Warden, and Colonel Jefford [1].'


## APPENDIX D.

### From Notes by Rev. Aubrey Townshend.

In October, 1859, T. Tuckey, Esq., of 10 South Mall, Cork, was in possession of a deed dated Jan. 1665, making over Drummeragh on the part of 'Coll. Richard Townesend

---

[1] Extract from Carte papers in *Council Book of Corporation of Cork*, Caulfield, Guildford, 1876. P. 1155. App. B.

of Castletowne[1]' to Captain Daniell O'Keiffe, and confirmed by Mary Townesend the married wife of the within named Richard Townesend, the fifteenth day of October, 1666.'

Also the following deed :—

'WHEREAS by Act of Parliament the soldiers and adventurers have lost one third of their lands let out for services and adventure in this his Majesty's kingdom of Ireland, and that therefor I have lost one third of my lands of Drummeragh and that for reasons best known to myself I have parted with my title to the rest to Captain Daniell O'Kiefe the former proprietor and accordingly conveyed my interest therein to him, I therefore hereby appoint you Teige O'Kyeffe to give him livery of seizin thereof with all convenient speed in manner and form usual in such cases and for your doing this shall be your sufficient warrant. Dated at Cork this second day of June, 1666.

RICHARD TOWNESEND.

Signed and sealed in the presence of us
MARY BAKER, JOHN MURPHY.'

[1] The house built by Colonel Townesend was known during his lifetime as Castletown. The name was gradually altered to Castle Townsend (now Castletownshend) to distinguish it from other Castletowns, Castletown Bere, Castletown Roche, &c.

MARY, DAUGHTER OF THE VERY REVEREND ED. SYNGE
BISHOP OF CORK, CLOYNE, AND ROSS

*Wife of Bryan Townsend of Castletownshend. Married 1681*

# CHAPTER VI.

### BRYAN TOWNSEND, WITH NOTES ON SYNGE.

IT is curious that although all the present family of Townshend in Ireland are descended from Bryan, and have cherished his name so devoutly, as to have almost forgotten his far more interesting father, Colonel Richard, the place and date of Bryan's birth are unknown. His last surviving son, Captain Philip, of Derry, used to say that his father was seventy years of age at the time his youngest son Horace was born in 1706. But it is improbable that this tradition is correct, as it would place Bryan's birth in 1636, when his father was but eighteen years of age. Mr. John Sealy Townshend has suggested that Bryan was born at Kinsale in 1648, but if he was so he must have been a cornet at the age of twelve, which seems improbable. He certainly was cornet of Militia in 1660, and afterwards commanded the frigate 'Swiftsure.' The events of his early years have been told in speaking of his father's life. He became a burgess of Clonakilty in 1678; his name in the Council Book is always spelt Bryan. About 1681 he married Mary Synge, daughter of the Bishop of Cork, Cloyne, and Ross [1], and in 1689 was proclaimed a traitor by James II's Irish Parliament. He took his wife and four children to England for safety [2] : and in

[1] See notes on this chapter.
[2] See T. C. D. MSS., list of protestant fugitives.

the record which mentions this fact his estates are described as worth £300 a year. He was at Schomburg's head-quarters shortly before the battle of the Boyne.

If the very handsome picture at Castletownshend which has always borne his name is truly the portrait of Bryan, it most probably was painted while he was a naval officer, as he wears his own hair and not the voluminous wig in which gentlemen on land used to enshroud themselves. The portrait at least gives a fair idea of a grandee of Munster, with the stately and half-melancholy dignity which some writers compare to that of a Spanish Hidalgo, while others complain of the 'insane pride of birth and position' engendered by living amongst a conquered people.

But proud though he might be, Bryan Townsend was no tyrannical representative of the ruling race. A contemporary writer says the proposals for a Union between England and Ireland had been so scornfully rejected by the English Government that there was 'scarcely an Englishman who had been seven years in the country and meant to remain there who did not become averse to England and something of an Irishman[1].' And although a member of the established church and the son-in-law of a bishop, Bryan became the chosen friend and protector of his Romanist neighbours.

He succeeded to the bulk of the Castletownshend estates on the death of his nephew Richard Fitz-John Townsend[2]. He represented the borough of Clonakilty in Parliament from 1695 to 1699, and when he came home from Dublin it was to assist his neighbours to evade the Act passed by the very House in which

---

[1] Walpole, *Hist. Kingdom of Ireland*, 349.
[2] Vid. Registered deed, dated 1722.

he had been sitting! But in truth the penal laws were so ferocious that they defeated themselves. No Romanist might possess arms, or send his child to be trained in his own religion, or bury his dead in the holy places of his faith, or relieve its priests, or even own a horse of more than £5 value! It is said that some low fellow meeting a Romanist gentleman driving a pair of valuable horses insolently tendered him £10 as their price. The owner got down from his carriage, and drawing a pistol shot both animals, and thus disappointed the greed of the informer.

The laws made it almost impossible for any but a Protestant to hold land, so many of the Carbery Romanists, especially the O'Heas and O'Donovans, trusting in Bryan's high character for integrity, gave their properties entirely into his hands, being obliged to do so without any written guarantee[1]. At one time he had under his care upwards of £80,000 worth of property which he defended at considerable cost to himself, and when it was safe to restore it to the real owners he did so with all the arrears that had accrued while he held it. This fact was ascertained by the research of the late John Sealy Townshend.

Many letters from Bryan to his wife are still in existence, written with great tenderness, but none of them have been available to copy. He must have been a man of strong feelings[2]: there is a tradition that he was so grieved by the early death of his son Bryan that he said he bequeathed a curse to any of his descendants who used the name. It is certainly curious that while Richard and Horatio are the commonest names in the family there have been but two Bryans, of whom one

---

[1] John Sealy Townshend's notes.
[2] Judge Fitzhenry Townshend.

died young and the other, who lived to old age, passed a singularly unfortunate life.

In 1692 Bryan was sovereign of Clonakilty, and again in 1693; in the entry he is called 'Coll. Bryan Townesend.' That year he and his son John (of Skirtagh) are entered as having signed the Protestant Oath, and in 1696 Bryan with the rest of the Association of Lords and Commoners signed the address welcoming William III as king[1]. In 1710 the last wolf in County Cork was killed near Kilcrea Abbey[2], it is believed by the hand of Bryan Townesend.

In 1717 Bryan signed the Council book of Clonakilty for the last time. His hand is feeble and uncertain, probably he had made an effort to be present when his two sons Samuel and Philip were sworn in as freemen. Judge Townshend says in his later years his understanding seems to have been much impaired by age or infirmity, and he gave up the management of his affairs to his eldest son Richard, whose affectionate letters to his father are still preserved. When he was an old man the family moved for a while to a house near the shore while the castle was being painted and papered. A violent storm came on, and a frigate lying at anchor was dashed against the house and actually broke the window of the old man's bedroom, from which accident he got a severe cold which ended his life[3].

He died in 1726, and is buried in the vault at Castlehaven beside his father. The descendants of Bryan Townesend kept up a warm family feeling, meeting for a yearly dinner of 'The Bryanite Club,' as they

---

[1] Smith's *History of Co. Cork.*
[2] Master Brooks told the Rev. Aubrey Townshend this story.
[3] John Sealy Townshend, through his daughter Mrs. Ed. Townshend.

called it, till they grew too many to sit round one table. 'Bryan trees' were made, and the various branches of the family were carefully recorded, so that its history is well known from his time; a great contrast to the scanty information preserved about his father, Colonel Richard. It has been suggested that the Tory principles generally adopted by the family caused them to neglect the records of their Roundhead ancestor; but apart from this, the many accidents that befell the house at Castle Townshend quite account for few very old family papers being preserved. Bryan Townsend's seal, bearing the arms of the Norfolk house of Townshend was preserved till lately at Castle Townshend, and Miss Townshend of Derry has his china teapot.

There is a tradition that he proved his kinship to good Queen Anne by once eating a whole leg of mutton, the Hyde family having been always noted for their healthy appetites! There are various Carbery sayings that seem to date from Bryan's time, such as 'Townsends must eat well, drink well, and sleep well, if they are to work well'; and 'There never was a Becher that couldn't ride, a Hungerford that couldn't shoot, or a Townshend that hadn't a good head'; and also 'There never was a Hungerford a rogue nor a Townsend a fool.'

The children of Bryan Townsend and his wife Mary were—

1. RICHARD of Castle Townshend.
2. EDWARD, born Sept. 17, 1685, and died unmarried.
3. BRYAN, born 1686, died unmarried.
4. JOHN of Skirtagh, born 26 May, 1691.
5. SAMUEL of Whitehall, born Sept. 23, 1692.
6. FRANCIS, born August 12, 1694, died unmarried.

7. WILLIAM, born April 20, 1699, died unmarried.
8. PHILIP of Derry, born August 13, 1700.
9. HORATIO of Donoughmore, born Sept. 1, 1706.
10. MARY, married Dr. John House, or Hough, of Castle Townshend, and had a daughter Mary who became Mrs. Nisbit.
11. KATHERINE, born Jan. 10, 1689-90, died unmarried.
12. HELENA, born Sept. 29, 1695, and married Very Rev. W. Meade of Balintober, Dean of Cork, grandson of Sir John Meade, and left descendants the Meades of Ballymartle and Ballintober.
13. BARBARA, born March 1696-7. Married in 1724 Thomas Hungerford, of Cahirmore, and left descendants, the Hungerfords of Cahirmore, near Ross.
14. There was also a BARBARA the eldest child, born March 1682-3, who died young.

In his will, Bryan Townsend says that he had already made provision for his younger children, whose portions his son Richard had paid or secured, besides having paid considerable debts in 1722; therefore he leaves all his property, real and personal, to his son Richard. Probate was granted of this will in 1727.

## NOTES ON THE SYNGE FAMILY.

The Synges descend from an ancient English line. Ware, in his *History of Ireland*, says their name was originally Millington, and was changed to Synge on account of the fine voices in the family.

George Synge was born at Bridgenorth, and educated at Balliol College, Oxford. He came to Ireland as a clergyman in the beginning of the reign of Charles the First, and was made Bishop of Cloyne 1638.

He acted as the Duke of Ormondé's agent during his negotiations with the Munster Army in 1648, and afterwards retired to England and died at Bridgenorth 1653.

His brother Edward, who had accompanied him to Ireland, was born at Bridgenorth, and educated at Drogheda and Trinity College, Dublin. He became a Doctor of Divinity, and held some ecclesiastical preferment in St. Patrick's Cathedral and also in Donegal, where he lived after Ormonde surrendered Dublin to the Parliament in 1647.

The English Parliamentary Commissioners proposed to the clergy to adopt the Presbyterian Directory of public worship instead of the Book of Common Prayer. The remonstrance of the clergy against this proposal was signed by Edward Synge, and by his persuasive letters to Dr. George, the Auditor-General, he obtained permission to use the Prayer-Book in his Donegal retirement up to the time of the Restoration. He then became Dean of Elphin, and was one of the twelve bishops consecrated at St. Patrick's on January 27, 1661, being then made Bishop of Limerick. Two years later he was translated to the bishopric of Cork, Cloyne, and Ross.

He died Dec. 22, 1678, leaving two sons, Samuel, born 1656, afterwards Dean of Kildare; Edward, Archbishop of Tuam; and a daughter Mary, who married Bryan Townsend, and is ancestress of all the present family of Townshend in Ireland.

Dean Samuel Synge married in 1878 Margaret, daughter of the Right Rev. Michael Boyle, Archbishop of Tuam. Their daughter Mary was first wife of her cousin Richard Townshend of Castle Townshend.

# CHAPTER VII.

CASTLE TOWNSHEND HOUSE, WITH NOTES ON SOMERVILLE AND TABLES OF THE FIRST HOUSE (I) AND SOMERVILLE (II).

RICHARD TOWNSHEND, of Castle Townshend, was born July 15, 1684, and succeeded to the estates on the death of his father Bryan, 1727.

It was at this period[1] that Dean Swift spent some time in West Carbery. He stayed at Myros, but is said to have written his poem *Carberiae Rupes* in a ruined tower at Castle Townshend, still known as Swift's Tower. It is also said that letters from the great Dean are still preserved at Castle Townshend, and that he named one of the houses in the village Laputa[2].

In 1706 Richard Townshend married his cousin Mary, daughter of the Very Rev. Samuel Synge, Dean of Kildare, and had two children, Samuel, who died in 1725, aged nineteen, and Mary, who in 1746 married the Rev. Thomas Daunt of Fahalea. She died of smallpox, 'brought in some new dresses from her Mantua maker.' When her husband died, he left directions that he should be buried in his wedding garment.

Richard Townshend married secondly Elizabeth, only daughter of Henry Becher of Creagh[3], settling

[1] G. Digby Daunt.
[2] Now Glen Barrahane, the seat of Sir J. J. Coghill, Bart.
[3] See Becher Notes in ch. viii.

RICHARD TOWNSHEND, OF CASTLE TOWNSHEND

*Born July* 15, 1684.   *Died* 1742

£300 a year on her as jointure. He died before his eldest son by Elizabeth came of age, and left her sole legatee and guardian to all the children. If she should die while they were young, his brothers, Samuel, Philip and Horatio, were appointed guardians. His will was proved Nov. 1742. His wife did not long survive him. Her will is dated 1746. It desires land to be held in trust to pay annuities for the education of her sons Henry and John, and portions for her daughters. She left six children:—

First, Richard, of Castle Townshend.

Secondly, John, of Shepperton, who married Mary, daughter of Jonas Morris Townshend, of Barley Hill, and Mary Townsend, of Skirtagh (Table IX). He was Commissioner of Excise and member of Parliament for Doneraile, 1797, and member for Clonakilty at the time of the Union, for which he voted. His portrait is at Drishane, a handsome decided-looking man, with regular features, heavy eyebrows and piercing eyes. His grandson, John Fitz-Henry Townshend, Judge of the Admiralty Courts, Dublin, is the oldest judge in the British Isles.

Thirdly, Henry, who was an officer in the Navy, and died unmarried, leaving his Irish estates to his nephew Richard, son of John of Shepperton.

Fourthly, Elizabeth, who married Captain Gwyn of Gower, Glamorgan, and Upham, Hants. She was a great beauty, and her descendant, General Sir Charles Shute, M.P., K.C.B., has a crayon portrait of her drawn by Sir Joshua Reynolds.

Fifthly, Helena, who married one of the Herberts of Kerry, the Rev. Arthur Herbert, of Cahirnan. He was afterwards Rector of Myros, and lived at Myros Wood, where he 'erected a very elegant and commodious house[1],' afterwards bought by Lord Kingston, who sold it in a few years time to John Sealy Townsend, Master in Chancery.

Sixthly, Harriet, who married the Rev. David Freeman, rector of Castle Haven. His tombstone is in the churchyard of Castle Townshend. He is said to have been of the ancient family of Freeman of Castle Cor.

The eldest of this family, Richard, was educated at Westminster. He must have been a singularly handsome and attractive man; for he is said by one family chronicler to have been the handsomest and most polished gentleman in Ireland, and when he contested the county Cork the electioneering nickname he went by was 'the Munster Peacock,' from his beauty and the slenderness of his long legs. He was admitted a freeman of the Corporation of Youghall in July, 1760, at the same time as his kinsmen, Edward, John, Captain Philip, and the Rev. Richard Townsend. He much improved the village of Castle Townshend, where he erected one of the first bolting mills seen in the barony[2], and 'such was the encouragement he gave for building, as well as the desire of being near a man beloved, admired and respected to a degree which only those who knew him can justly appreciate, that in a short time a new town arose.'

Although a little sunshine lit up Castle Townshend, these were dark days in Ireland, and there were numerous midnight outrages by Whiteboys, while absentee landlords, remorseless middlemen, and a starving peasantry made even Lord Chesterfield, then Lord Lieutenant, say, 'the poor people of Ireland are

---
[1] *Statistical Survey*, Co. Cork, ii, 338. Townsend.
[2] *Ibid*.

RICHARD TOWNSHEND, OF CASTLETOWNSHEND, M.P.
*Married Elizabeth Fitzgerald.* 1750

worse used than negroes by their masters.' The chief business of the Lord Lieutenant seemed to be to gain a majority in Parliament by any means, and the business of the opposition was to make the best terms possible for themselves before they permitted any bills to pass.

Richard Townshend was a staunch Tory, but no bait, not even that of a peerage, could induce him to vote blindly with his party. When Lord Townshend was Viceroy he wrote in 1767 to his 'kinsman of Castle Townshend' reproaching him with a difference in politics which went 'so far and no further and neither advanced himself nor his party.' A later Viceroy, Lord Buckinghamshire, says in a letter dated 1780,

'I had not contracted any absolute engagements of recommendations either to peerage or pension till difficulties arose. I must have been culpable in neglecting any possible means of securing a majority in the House of Commons. Mr. Townshend was particularly recommended to me by Lord Shannon for a seat in the Privy Council, and I have reason to believe his Lordship is extremely anxious for his success.'

Lord Shannon was son of Henry Boyle, first Earl of Shannon, the owner of sixteen Parliamentary seats and of vast patronage. He was one of the great powers who had to be propitiated before a hapless Viceroy could carry on his government.

By fair means or foul the Oligarchy which headed the Protestant gentry could be kept in good temper, but those who were too proud to be bribed and too strong to be bullied watched with anxiety in the days of the Georges how Irish trade was threatened with ever fresh disaster and the English settlements beyond the Atlantic were being driven to open revolt by similar oppression.

The attacks of pirates on the undefended coasts of Ireland had obliged the government to allow the nobility and gentry to raise bodies of volunteers for their defence, and these armed forces were not inclined to sit still in patience while the war ruined the linen trade and the export of provisions from Irish ports was made illegal in order that the Army in America should get its salt beef cheap! 'Talk not to me of peace,' cried Hussey Burgh, 'it is smothered war! England has sown her laws like dragons' teeth and they have sprung up armed men.'

There is a story that in 1780 an officer of the Guards asked a volunteer in a London coffee-house to what corps he belonged. He answered, to one of the Cork corps. 'Ah!' said the officer, 'you'll soon be disarmed.' 'Pray, sir,' answered the Cork boy, 'were you ever in America?' 'Yes.' 'And did you find it easy to disarm them?' 'No,' answered the officer, 'but it will be no difficult matter to settle *you*.' 'I hope,' answered the Irishman with an oath, 'that *you* will be one of those sent over to try the experiment!' The feeling grew so fierce in Ireland that Lord North was obliged to yield and permit the repeal of the trade restrictions; but it was felt that what one English Parliament had granted another might take back, and in 1780 Grattan moved 'that the King with the consent of the Lords and Commons of Ireland is the only power competent to enact laws to bind Ireland.' The volunteers, headed by Lord Charlemont, Flood, and Grattan, determined to secure the full expression of the public will in spite of any manipulation of the Houses of Parliament, and they passed resolutions in favour of legislative independence. These were echoed throughout the country. At the Spring Assizes of 1782 the

Grand Jury of Cork passed the following resolution:—

'Resolved that we think it necessary to declare no power has a right to make laws for this kingdom save only the King, Lords and Commons of Ireland, and that we will with our lives and fortunes maintain and defend the Irish Parliament in such a declaration of rights and in any measure they may think proper to defend it.

RICHARD TOWNSHEND,
Foreman.'

Richard Townshend was Colonel of Militia and Commissioner for the Revenue, Member for Co. Cork from 1759 to 1783, and High Sheriff in 1753. He maintained, it is said, 'a princely hospitality at Castle Townshend and had a commanding influence in the county[1].' Some echoes of those old festivities may be heard in the following extracts from the *Cork Remembrancer*[2] In November, 1766, a violent storm from the south-west, with thunder, broke over the west of County Cork, and on the 28th—

'His Highness the Prince of Monsereda, on his travels through Europe on board the Delight, was by contrary winds forced to put into Castle Townsend where he was treated with every mark of respect and distinction suitable to his dignity and received with the entertainments the place could afford.'

1769. 'A meeting of the Atlantic Society took place at Rahine Castle in the harbour of Castlehaven.'

But under the surface there were still smouldering the old fires of discontent and outrage. The next extract tells an oft-repeated story:—

'1777, Feb. 18. Richard Townsend, John Townsend, Samuel Jervoise[3], and Daniel Callaghan, Magistrates, with

---
[1] *Statistic Survey.*   [2] Tuckey.   [3] Probably of Braad.

several gentlemen of the county and their servants well mounted, set out at two in the morning to the Mountains above Bantry in the neighbourhood of Murdering Glin and Glannhannone where they apprehended several persons charged with cutting off the ears of a horse.'

The dwellers in the West had to hold themselves in readiness for the visits of less agreeable foreigners than the prince of Monsereda. In 1780 we hear that the 'Count D'Artois,' a French vessel of 74 guns, was taken off the harbour of Castle Townshend by Captain McBride, commander of H.M.S. 'Bienfaisant,' who was afterwards presented with the freedom of Cork city in a silver box [1].

Richard Townshend married in 1752 Elizabeth, only daughter and heiress by survival of John FitzGerald, 15th Knight of Kerry, by whom he had one son and one daughter. Elizabeth FitzGerald's only brother Maurice, 16th Knight of Kerry, had married his cousin Lady Anne Fitzmaurice, and died leaving no children, but even now he is remembered as 'the good Knight.' He left all the Desmond estates in Kerry to the son of his sister Elizabeth Townshend.

The Knights of Kerry descend from Maurice Fitz-Gerald, who accompanied Strongbow in his invasion of Ireland. He was son of Nesta, Princess of Wales, and ancestor of all the Geraldines of Desmond, of Leinster, and the Knights of Kerry, of Glyn and the White Knight.

To give a detailed account of the ancestors of Elizabeth Townshend would be to write the history of Ireland—yet as the revival of the Earldoms of Desmond and Thomond was offered as a bribe to her son, it may be well to note from whence the titles were derived.

[1] *Cork Council Book*, Caulfield.

ELIZABETH FITZGERALD

*Wife of Richard Townshend, of Castletownshend*

> 'Ye Geraldines, ye Geraldines, how royally ye reigned
> O'er Desmond broad, and rich Kildare, and English arts disdained;
> Your sword made knights, your banner waved, free was your bugle call
> By Glyn's green banks and Dingle's tide, from Barrow banks to Youghal[1].'

The last Earl of Desmond in the male line was the luckless 'Queen's Earl,' the godson of Queen Elizabeth, who was brought up in the Tower. The Queen allowed him to go back to his own people when he was grown up, but their rapture of welcome only lasted till they saw him enter a Protestant church: and he returned to England to die young and lonely, a disappointed man. James the First granted the Desmond title to the son of the Earl of Denbigh, who had no connection whatever with it, and the great Geraldine family was represented by the sister of the Queen's Earl, Katherine, who married the first Viscount Clare, brother to the Earl of Thomond.

> 'Of Desmond's blood, thro' woman's veins, passed on the exhausted tide.
> His title lives, a Saxon churl usurps the lion's hide[1].'

The grand-daughter of the Viscountess, Honora O'Brien, transmitted her Geraldine claims to the Earldoms of Desmond and Thomond to her descendants the Knights of Kerry; for the line of her only brother, the gallant leader of 'Clare's Dragoons,' died out, exiled in France. In 1674 Honora's son, Maurice Fitzgerald, Knight of Kerry, bore his Fitzgerald arms supported by the dragon and boar of Desmond. He fought on the side of James the Second at the battle of the Boyne: if the fortunes of the day had favoured the Stuarts it is possible that he might have died Earl of Desmond. He claimed a royal descent through his grandmother, Lady Katherine Fitzmaurice, a descendant through the Ormondes from Edward I. He retired

---

[1] Thomas Davis, *The Geraldines*.

into private life after the Revolution and married (June 30, 1713) Elizabeth Crosbie of Ardfert, sister of Maurice first Lord Brandon and aunt to the first Earl of Glandore, and lived at Rahanan Castle near Ventry. Elizabeth Crosbie was the first Protestant wife in the long line of this branch of Geraldines, who thenceforward conformed to the Church of England. Her wardrobe of yew, ten feet high, is still in the possession of a member of the Geraldine family, James O'Connor of Dingle. A wonderful description is extant of this Knight of Kerry as High Sheriff receiving the Judges, riding on an Arab horse caparisoned in velvet and gold, and followed by numberless pages and servants and thirty-five members of his own family. Unfortunately for the splendour of the procession the Judges' coach stuck fast in the mud, and the banquet that followed had to be cut short for fear that the rise of the flooded river should prevent their further progress. John, the eldest son of Maurice Fitzgerald and Elizabeth Crosbie, married Margaret, fifth daughter of the Right Hon. Joseph Deane, Lord Chief Baron of the Exchequer, and his wife Margaret Boyle, granddaughter of the Earl of Inchiquin and of the Earl of Orrery (Lord Broghill). John, Knight of Kerry, and Margaret Deane, had one only daughter Elizabeth, wife of Colonel Townshend; she was a very beautiful woman with the Fitzgerald blue eyes. Her portrait hangs at Castle Townshend, a slight, pale, distinguished-looking figure in a fur-trimmed gown.

The tomb of her father, John Fitzgerald, fifteenth Knight of Kerry, was rescued from destruction by a kinsman, James O'Connor, and has been restored, in 1892, by Mrs. Pierrepont Mundy and Mrs. Courteney Vernon, great-great-granddaughters of the Knight.

Richard Townshend died December 23, 1783, leaving one son, Richard Boyle Townshend, born in 1753. He was educated at Eton and Magdalen College, Oxford, and after taking his degree, made a trip to Spa in company with his father, Mr. St. Leger, afterwards Lord Doneraile, and Horace Townsend of Derry. The last-named published some recollections of this trip many years after in *Blackwood's Magazine*[1]. He describes his companions

'as a respectable and respected friend and relative much older than myself, to whom the waters had been ordered by his physician; his son, and a young man, heir to a title and what is still better a good estate. The Hon. Mr. S. was a great acquisition, for he had received part of his education in France, and was besides a well-tempered and agreeable companion. Young Mr. T. just left the University for which he had been prepared at Eton, and being a youth of polished mind and gentle manners, afforded ample assurance both of giving and receiving pleasure on such an excursion. His father had been conversant with the first ranks of society in Ireland, and was besides a man of sound judgment and amiable disposition.'

They certainly anticipated a very pleasant tour, but at the very outset it began with an adventure which nearly landed them in a French prison, for no sooner had they sailed from Waterford bound for Milford Haven, than they were chased by a French privateer. She gained on them and they gave themselves up for lost, when the wind dropped and both vessels were becalmed. Hereupon the privateersman got out their sweeps and continued the chase. The Irishmen did the same, and an exciting race ensued. The captain ordered that all who could should help to row, and the rest to serve round grog. Horace Townsend, a

[1] *Blackwood's Magazine*, Sept. 1827.

powerful man over six feet in height, gained great credit with the crew for his able assistance at the oars, while the other two 'obtained immortal honour by their alacrity and adroitness in compounding and handing about the grog.' Between the grog and the hard rowing they won the race, and favoured by night slipped back into Waterford, and two days after crossed safely to Hubbister. A week later they were in Ostend, and there their Irish servants fell in with some fellow-countrymen on the pier. The fellow-countrymen proved to be the crew of one Captain Kelly. Of course they foregathered. 'By Saint Patrick,' said one, 'we're all friends here, and we'll have a booze together and drink success to Ireland.'

'With these friends of Ireland,' says Townsend, 'they repaired to a public house, and in the course of conversation we learned that Captain Kelly was the master of a smart privateer, which turned out to be the very one that we had so narrowly escaped from a week before.' Kelly was only a rough sailor, but later on at Spa 'we chanced to meet the owner of the vessel himself, and he joked with me for robbing him of so rich a prize as our ransom by my rowing exertions. "However," said he, "I owe you some compensation for the uneasiness you must all have suffered, and if you return through France, I will give you letters to my friends which you may find of some use."'

When Richard Townshend died, 1783, his son succeeded to a troubled inheritance. He had already entered public life, and sat as member for the family borough of Dingle from 1781 to 1795. The first event in 1783 was the visit of a body of cavalry to Castle Townshend 'in quest of some insurgents, said to be meditating mischief against the inhabitants of that neighbourhood. After scouring the country they apprehended Denis Connel, alias Cockabendy, who was charged with sounding a horn to assemble a mob[1].'

That same year the Volunteers attempted to overawe the Dublin Parliament which had rejected Flood's Reform Bill, and it was only the moderation of Lord Charlemont that prevented the outbreak of civil war[2]. Rotten boroughs, vice and corruption among the ruling caste, Whiteboy outrages and starvation among the peasantry, decaying trade and blighted hopes for the middle classes—there was only one line for a high-spirited young man to take, and the young member for Dingle took it, and although he nominally belonged to the party of Pitt, he was as independent as his forefathers had been from the days of the Long Parliament.

Pitt was indeed anxious to improve the commercial relations between England and Ireland, but the influence of English manufacturers was too strong for him, and the propositions he laid before the House were such that Fox declared they entailed slavery on Ireland, and Dublin received them with a shout of indignation. Nothing daunted by this failure, the idea of the Union as the best means of checking Irish trade competition was still urged, but the more support the measure received in England, the wilder was the storm it aroused across the Channel. Not even the offer of an English peerage could bribe Richard Boyle Townshend to vote for such a Union. Long afterwards, Sir Robert Peel, when Chief Secretary, complained of the difficulty of conciliating Tories who were so powerful and so independent as the Townshend family. So Mr. Townshend lost the favour of his party and also

[1] Tuckey's *Cork Remembrancer*.   [2] Walpole's *Hist. of Ireland*, 408.

his borough of Dingle, which was disfranchised. The Government could not avoid compensating him for a loss which was an important gain to them, and he received £1500.

A new complication arose in England when King George's mental health failed and the question of a Regency was raised. Grattan had made a treaty with Fox, the ally of the Prince of Wales, who engaged if the Whigs came in to pass a bill to put a stop to the corruption of the Irish Parliament. Accordingly the Irish opposition actually determined to forestall the English Parliament in the choice of a Regent, and voted an address to the Prince. Mr. Townshend again displeased his party, and supported the right of Ireland to choose her own ruler.

To the confusion of the opposition, the King recovered, and the English Government determined that those who had combined against its authority should be crushed.

From this time matters grew steadily worse, the hopes raised by Grattan were frustrated, those by Fitz-William disavowed. There is nothing to tempt one to linger over public history.

In 1785 Richard Boyle Townshend was High Sheriff for County Cork, and stood for its seat in Parliament, but was defeated after a hard struggle. The previous year, May 16, 1784, he had married Henrietta Newenham of Maryborough, sister of Mrs. White of Glengariff[1]. Both these ladies were extremely beautiful: there is a spirited portrait of Mrs. Townshend at Castle Townsend which gives a vivid idea of her large grey eyes, dazzling complexion, and masses of brown curls.

---

[1] Their mother was Henrietta Vereker of Roxborough, Co. Limerick, of the family represented by Viscount Gort.

She wears a white cloth riding-habit faced with blue velvet, for though small and slight, a 'pocket Venus' in fact, she was a great horsewoman, and celebrated in Wiltshire hunting society for her daring riding. In 1785 their eldest son Richard Fitz-Gerald was born; and the next event that marks the course of life in Carbery was the alarm of a French invasion in 1796, when Mr. Townshend went to great expense to fortify Castlehaven against the enemy, and equipped a flotilla at his own expense; but the foggy weather veiled the harbour entrance and the French fleet passed on to Bantry, where the story goes no messenger could be trusted to carry the news to Cork, and Mrs. White herself rode on the errand, and a kinsman of Mr. Townshend's sailed with the despatches to England[1]. Then came the rebellion of 1791, the story of which is more fully told in the records of the Whitehall and Derry Houses[2]; and in 1800 the Irish Parliament met for the last time. It is needless to repeat the tale of corruption and disgrace which heralded the Union, but it is satisfactory to remember that Richard Boyle Townshend was one of the hundred members of the Lower House whom the Government were unable to bribe or coerce. A picture of the sitting of the last Irish House of Commons was painted by Hayter and Barraud, but the portrait in it of Richard Boyle Townshend was not considered to be a successful likeness. When the Government majority for the Union was known and the House adjourned, the Speaker walked out followed by forty-one members. The populace outside uncovered, and in deep silence accompanied them to the Speaker's house in Molesworth Street. On reaching it the Speaker turned round, bowed to the crowd,

---

[1] See chapter ix.     [2] See chapters x and xi.

entered his house, and the whole assemblage dispersed without uttering a word[1]. All was over.

Five sons and two daughters were born to Richard Boyle Townshend, but a heavy blow fell on him in 1805 when his eldest son died at Christ Church, Oxford, where he was entered as a fellow-commoner, and claimed the privileges of founder's kin for his royal descent through the Fitzmaurice line. Although he died in England his mother began to fear that Castle Townshend was not healthy and that the rooms were not high enough, so it was decided to raise them by lowering the floors. Unfortunately the lowering was done only too thoroughly, the foundations were shaken, and the great house, with its thirteen best bedrooms, was a ruin.

The family never lived much in Ireland again; the agent's house, which was converted into a residence for them, did not feel like home—they had a house in Montague Square, London, No. 8, and a hunting residence in Wiltshire, near their relative Lord Lansdowne at Bowood, and also at Hurdcott in Dorset when the younger sons were preparing for Westminster at Sherborne. Those who remember Richard Boyle Townshend when visiting his Irish home in 1826 describe his snow-white hair and deep sapphire eyes and delicate-featured face, and say how no one could resist the charm of his perfect manners of the old courtly school. He was a good classical scholar and also a sportsman; his memory was so retentive that he could quote Horace freely; he could also name every winner of the Derby without a pause. He kept a pack of harriers at the Barn, as the present home farm was then called. He died in Dublin in 1827.

[1] Walpole, *Hist. of Ireland*, 527.

He left four sons and two daughters. The eldest surviving son, John Townshend, who succeeded to the property, was, at the death of his father, Major in the 14th Light Dragoons. It is said that some of the exploits of Lever's Charles O'Malley in the Peninsula are taken from those of Major Townshend and his friends. His beautiful sister, Eliza, used to carve the victories of her brother's regiment on the old laurel-trees that grow round Bryan's fort.

John Townshend embarked on board the transport 'Benjamin and Mary' in December, 1808, as Lieutenant in the 14th Light Dragoons, in which regiment he remained more than forty years. His letters home were preserved with the greatest care by his mother, together with the contemporary newspapers and gazettes. John's letters are generally short and to the point, touching very lightly on the gallant actions that he performed, chiefly urging that all steps should be taken to aid his promotion, and asking for the Waverley Novels, and saying what clothes and remounts he required. He often called his father 'the Commander-in-Chief of the Bryanites.' More details are given in the merry letters written by his younger brothers Maurice and Boyle, who visited him in 1810 with their school and college friend the Marquis of Worcester (afterwards seventh Duke of Beaufort).

*John Townshend to his Mother.*

MY DEAREST MOTHER, BELEM, *Jan.* 1, 1809.

... Our first division marches on Saturday for the frontier but what we are to do no one knows. Sir D. Baird has joined General Moore but whether they have had any engagements we can't tell, for all our news comes from England. We live here excessively well—our breakfast which is coffee and eggs for about 4½ pence and dinner for about 2s. 7½d. and wine into the bargain. Tell Eliza I have seen but three parrots and four monkeys and they belong to the Prince of the Brazils but she shall have one if I can get one. The French have not left a single vestige of anything in the country that is valuable. Skibbereen of a wet day is a drawingroom in point of cleanliness to Lisbon.

*John Townsend to his Father.*

BELEM, *March* 3, 1809.

The news here is very bad indeed, from what we understand our troops suffered uncommonly at the battle of Corunna and that many more were lost than is accounted for in the papers. We had the Brest fleet off the bar the day before yesterday consisting of sixteen sail of the line and some Frigates and yesterday Sir J. Duckworth with 12 sail of the line took . . . from this river and went in pursuit of them and no doubt he will give a good account of them if he overtakes them. The army here march tomorrow for Bucellas and Torres Vedras where they are to take up a position that is remarkably strong in order to be in readiness for the French if they should come here again.

Your ever affectionate and dutiful son

JOHN TOWNSEND.

MY DEAREST FATHER, BRAGA, *May* 25, 1809.

I take the first opportunity of writing to you well knowing how anxious you must be concerning the ragged 14th after having read Sir Arthur Wellesley's dispatches concerning our giving the enemy a good drubbing.

We (the cavalry) met the enemy on the morning of the 10th about four o'clock and we skirmished with them and charged and a little play until about twelve when they retired. We took about 30 prisoners and 60 horses. On the eleventh the infantry went at it and drove them from a village called Gujon. On the 12th we forced the passage of the Douro under a very heavy fire of cannon and musketry and eventually succeeded in taking Oporto and about 16 pieces of cannon. I would have written to you by Fitzroy Stanhope but really I had not time, for the moment we crossed the river we dashed thro' the town and charged the enemy retiring in confusion towards Valonga and that evening I was on patrol all night in front of Oporto and the next day we marched following the enemy up thro' the mountains as far as . . . . . a frontier town about two miles from Gahera into which province we drove the enemy with the loss of 300 horses and a great quantity of plunder all their cannon and ammunition and 2000 men killed wounded and taken prisoners. I hope the people in England are satisfied, for it was the very same army (tho' not so numerous) that drove Sir J. Moore's army out of Spain commanded by Soult himself that we have beat first and then drove them out of Portugal. Our two squadrons of horse that you see mentioned in the papers of having behaved so well on the 12th, were our right squadron commanded by Hervey and our left by Buther in which I was. We lost about 29 men killed wounded and taken. Hervey has lost his right arm, very high, Knipe has been shot in the neck but doing very well, and Hawker slightly wounded in the lip and lost his horse, no other officers touched. We halt here for a few days to get our horses shod; we had a dreadful time of it from the 13th of May until the 23, nothing but incessant rain and all the time in the mountains . . . The poor mare is almost done up. Florist in fine order, a charming warhorse, I was on back from eleven o'clock one night until ½ past five the next afternoon, and neither he nor I had anything but some water which we got in a brook during that time.

*To his Mother.*
TALAVERA, *July* 25, 1809.

. . . Since we left Thomar we have not been under any other cover than what the woods afforded us. On Friday last we formed a junction with the Spanish Army under Cuesta, and on Saturday morning both armies advanced towards this place; about two leagues from hence we fell in with about 12,000 of the enemy who retired before us, and took up the position which we now occupy and were there joined by another corps of about 1000 men, the whole commanded by Victor in person. We halted the evening of Saturday about five miles from them and were to have attacked at daybreak but Cuesta refused and said he was not ready. On Monday we advanced an hour before day in high spirits, every individual determined to do his duty to the utmost, when we came to the Tagus which was to have been forded in front of all their cannon and in the centre of their lines by the British troops, they had walked off at about one in the morning, leaving us their encampment full of forage.

*To his Father.*
ELVAS, *August 29, 1809.*

You doubtless have seen by the papers of the battle that was fought at Talavera, and how nobly our army behaved during such trying circumstances. I had a severe fit of illness about a month ago so much so that I was delirious for two days but afterwards I got better but was reduced to nothing and even at the present time I am only a skeleton and on the sick list. . . . I am perfectly certain my illness was brought on by excessive fatigue and being deprived of wine and being two days without rations. Nothing but dry bread and water. Those privations at a time when we were undergoing the severest duty occasioned a great number to fall sick the very moment it relaxed.

*(Undated.)*
DEAR ELIZA,

I send you by Maurice a gold chain and another for Harriot. . . . Our friends the French are very civil, we have had no difference of opinion with them these three days, but expect one every morning. . . . I am quite ragged and out at elbows and knees, there is no inhabited place within ten leagues of this that you can buy anything wearable. I suppose if you are to go to Ireland this winter there will be no bearing you, you will be queens of the ring at Castle T. and Glengariff.

Val de Coelha, one league in front of Almeida, *July* 4, 1810.

My dear Mother,

... By the newspapers I see the beautiful Misses Townsend were at Court and that their dresses were only to be surpassed by their beauty. The enemy have been canonading Cuidad Roderigo these ten days, it still holds out most gallantly. We are only three leagues from it and the other part of our regiment are not so far. We are with the Light division in front of the army so you may think we are pretty watchful. Their cavalry are encamped at the other side of the Aguida and we see them as plain as possible. We expect to have a difference with them in a short time concerning this country.

Maurice, as has been already said, visited the Peninsula this summer. Writing from Plymouth he explains to his mother—

Worcester is dying to make me buy a coat and cocked hat and feather, he says they are indispensably requisite for travelling in Portugal. If I can get one made cheap I will yield to his entreaties, if not let them take me for a merchant or what they please.

A little later he describes the costume he decided on:

Major Newton, the General's Major of Brigade, told me it was absolutely necessary for me to buy regimentals, so I have donned a uniform I believe peculiar to myself. I am a light Infantry Captain, that being the cheapest mode of dressing myself. I have a little jacket, a cap stuck most knowingly on one side with a little green feather: a second-hand sash and to finish all, a Turkish sabre, very very cheap and very elegant.' . . . ' Cintra is beyond everything magnificent I ever saw. It is a monstrous mountain of rocks on which are several smaller mountains of rock, on the top of the highest of which is built the Convent de Pena, or punishment for friars. In proportion to their fault, so long is their confinement, there is one old sinner who has been there fifty years and will remain the rest of his life: he must at least have put five families to death : the killing one man is so trivial a thing they would look over it. . . . We have a monstrous pleasant party of young men here who will go up the country in a body all well armed : We call ourselves the Junta Club, the members are as follows :—The Marquis of Worcester, Major, Lord George Granville do., M. F. Townshend, Captain, A. Boyle Townshend, Secretary to the Legation, G. P. Irwine, Corporal, H. S. Fox, ensign. The object of the Junta is, if we get into a row to stand by and put the Portuguese to death. We all figured away at the Minister's ball and flatter ourselves we won the hearts of several of the Portuguese nobility. Some of them are comparatively pretty, that is for a Portuguese, but positively frightful.

*John Townsend to his Mother.*

CAMP NEAR ALVERCA, *August* 19, 1810.

Almeida is now besieged, they began this morning to open their batteries from the town and at present there is very heavy firing there. Governor Cox is in high spirits, he expects to hold out ninety days. I hope we shall relieve it and give the Angel of Victory (Massena) a drubbing.

P.S. A cloak and promotion is all I want, 5 years and a half a subaltern is too long!

I hear there is a man in the 20 L. D., that will exchange to Infantry. Heavy Dragoons I won't go into, I had rather 'pad it' than wear Jack boots.

*John Townsend to his Mother.*

CAMP NEAR ALVERCA, *August* 30, 1810.

. . . You were only inclined to suppose I was in the unfortunate skirmish when our beloved commander fell, I was in it and had my left hand man killed and one covering me wounded, since that we have had two more brushes with the enemy. Almeida still remains in statu quo, the enemy have not as yet opened their batteries on it but the town continues to annoy them in their working. The infantry are close in our rear, so that I believe it is the intention of Lord Wellington to defend this position should the enemy advance. If they do advance we are confident they will get a most confounded drubbing as our army is in excellent health and spirits, but you must not publish anything I write, in the papers, as some gentlemen of the army have written home that the army were in full retreat and it was published, Lord Wellington was exceedingly displeased at it.

### *Maurice Townsend to his Mother.*

LISBON, *Sept.* 29, 1810.

... Two Mr. Napiers are wounded. Lord Wellington's position is so strong that he says it's impossible to force him. The French marched from Almeida to meet him with twelve days provisions on their backs, the weight was so great they were obliged to throw most of it away. The consequence is they are starving. The Portuguese have behaved inimitably. Lord Wellington does not know which to praise most them or the English.

In my humble opinion it would not be correct in Boyle to skip a term and if I stay here he will wish to stay also, so I think of leaving this place for England the first opportunity and keep my term at Oxford as usual. I give myself great credit for this resolution, Lisbon is so delightful a place I should like to stay here the rest of the winter. ... In talking of the engagement just now I forgot to mention the French have lost two Generals ... the account came in a letter from Lord Wellington, he says the engagement was pretty general, the whole of the French force being in action and most of ours. If this be true it is most glorious news and may perhaps sicken the French until after the winter. ... The ladies in Lisbon are delightfully pleasant and rather pretty, but the men are the most uncultivated stupid, dirty, ugly, lazy bears I ever met with, they are scarcely received into company by their own countrywomen.

### *A. Boyle Townsend to his Mother.*

LISBON, *Oct.* 27, 1810.

I hope that John will get his troop now and that Sir D. D. (David Dundas) won't send to the Highlands for one of his barelegged countrymen to fill the vacancy. If John does not get it, his Majesty does not deserve to have an officer in his service. . . . About a fortnight ago a navy officer landed his boats crew on one of the islands in the Tagus to pass the night, but the sailors instead of sleeping having found some mules did not cease riding them the whole night. . . . I have looked in almost every shop in Lisbon and have not seen above twenty garnets nor five saphires. . . . I am sure I don't know how I shall ever be thankful enough to you and my Father for your kindness in sending me abroad. I sincerely hope that I shall profit by it; I will endeavour to do so, and if I am too stupid I shall still have the satisfaction of being the dutiful and affectionate son of such generous parents.

*Maurice Townsend to his Mother.*

LISBON, *Nov.* 3, 1810.

In one of my letters I described our Tour up country, we went up as high as Celorico where we saw Jack in high health and spirits. Worcester delights in him and he in Worcester. I have written to Mr. Webber to thank him for his kindness in procuring us leave to skip this term. I have employed three or four people in looking for garnets for you, there is not such a thing in Lisbon, there are thousands of gold chains, not cheap but very thin. I have also seen sets of topazes not by any means dear. . . . Should there be anything like an engagement happen I shall know it, I have offers from two or three generals to take care of me in such a case, and Jack has promised me the use of a horse. Rely upon my not going to close to the French, if I got nine shillings a day for being shot at well and good, but as it is I may as well keep out of danger.

*John Townsend to his sister Eliza.*

PONTE DE ROLL, *Nov.* 10, 1810.

. . . I wrote to my father and told him all the news, this is a miserable place and completely uninhabited but still we contrive to eixst and are not quite brutes (from the want of society) tho' if we have another year in this country the same as the last we shall be perfect yahoos and not know how to behave ourselves in genteel company. When at Lisbon with the Boys (young gentlemen I should have said) I went to the

Ministers ball and lost my heart to an olive coloured young damsel whose mother said, that Maud (Maurice) Boyle and I were three madmen but I was the least mad of the three.

### *John Townsend to his Father.*

PONTE DE ROLL, *Nov.* 11, 1810.

Nothing particular has occurred between the two armies. The enemy from what we learn are daily decreasing by sickness deaths and desertion, the deaths are principally what occur in the foraging parties; the peasants whenever they meet with any of them mark them down and then surround them and murder them and fly to the mountains, which to a person unacquainted with them are impassable.

I wish you would call on Lord Bridgewater and ask him if I can get the troop or no; if not get me anything from the Lifeguards down to the Botany Bay corps. Having been recommended by Colonel Hervey and Lord Wellington I think I stand a very good chance.

### *John Townsend to his Mother.* *Nov.* 21.

I went out with a patrol from a place called Agembuja with a sergeant and four men of the 14th joined 5 of the 16th Light Dragoons and took fifty of them (the French) armed, they fired a volley at my party and then we charged them and they surrendered.

### *From Maurice Fitzgerald Townsend to his Mother.*

LISBON, *Saturday, Dec.* 15, 1810.

. . . I heard of Jack yesterday from Charles Syng, he is very well and has done one of the most gallant things that has as yet been done in Portugal—namely he with eight of his men surprised and brought home as prisoners fifty French Troopers, it has been the talk of the town for this last four or five days. . . . We are here the jolliest happy party under the sun, videlicit Worcester, Fox, Mellish who is become a dear Friend of mine, Irvine, Boyle, and myself. The Portugese ladies doat on us, I am desperately in love with two or three of them with whom as I am a great proficient in the language I talk nothing else but Portugese. I expect on my arrival at Cartago to find Jack three inches taller after that wonderful feat he was perpetrator of. Give my most kind and affectionate love to my father and tell him I wish Sir Wm. Manners was hanged drawn and quartered for his attempt at stopping the Leicestershire hunting. . . . You must have found out long ago that a Portugese has as much notion of a pen as a Highlander of a knee buckle.

In January, 1811, John Townsend sends word to his father,

We have races here every Tuesday, and Clifton and myself are the Buckle and Chifney of the Santarem Course.

And later on—

You must excuse bad writing as my pen is made out of the wing of a turkey we are going to have for dinner. Tell Maurice I beg he would send me a good pipe or else I shall have the ague, for the country here is very damp in the Spring, I have only one of my own manufacturing of a reed.

CAMPO ST. ANNA, NEAR CARTAGO, *Feb.* 22, 1811.

Since I wrote last I have dined twice at Lord Wellington's who always appears in the highest spirits, in fact he has been particularly civil to our regiment.

On June 13, 1811, John describes some of his services under Sir Stapleton Cotton, on the retreat from Gallejos and at the battle of Fuentes d'Onor, when he acted as one of the aides-de-camp.

On the 5th Sunday, they attacked our right flank with about 4000 cavalry 6 guns and some infantry, we had only about 1000 cavalry in all and stood them for some time, charged them, took three officers and about 200 men prisoners. They charged us in return and two of them rode at me and knocked me and my horse down (who was wounded in the hind leg just before), and took me prisoner for a few minutes but just at that moment Col. Ellez the A. A. G. brought up another squadron, charged the rascals and I and young Fitzclarence were taken again to my no small gratification. I have escaped unhurt but with an uncommon black eye.

Our loss was considerable . . . poor Knife shot thro' the breast with a grapeshot and I believe he cannot survive. I hope England will do something for Lord Wellington, he has beaten their best generals.

John Townsend succeeded Captain Knife in command of the long-desired troop—a letter from the Horseguards to his mother says he was strongly recommended by Lord Wellington, Sir Stapleton Cotton, and Col. Hawker.

He purposed sending his favourite horse Florist home as he was hurt in the leg, but he died of inflammation after twenty-four hours' illness, and his master wrote home that the other horses ought to wear crape for him. He also says—

'Tell Eliza I heard of her being at the review at Wimbledon common, *the prettiest girl in London.* . . . It may gratify you tho' it must go no further to know I was in the squadron of the 16th who were with the Royals the 6th of June under Dowson and was thanked by General Slade and Sir B. Spencer after the skirmish was over.

EL BODON, *Dec.* 10, 1811.

The guerillas are increasing in numbers and boldness throughout the Peninsula, and I think that the French interest greatly diminishes. Mina, one of the guerillas, took 1100 the other day in Aragon and has actually brought 700 of them thro' the Asturias to Corunna. Charles Synge is near here and very well. I am going to dine with him tomorrow and go fox hunting the next day with Lord Wellington's hounds on my old French horse. I shall make but a sorry hand of it I am afraid.

CAMP NEAR CUILLAR, *August* 2, 1812.

No doubt before this reaches you you will have heard of the glorious and decisive victory we gained over Marmont near Salamanca on the 22nd of July, since which time, and before we have had no halt until this day. You will see by the dispatches of Lord Wellington a much better account of the battle than I can give, but if he had had two hours more light we should certainly have annihilated the French army. . . . Wilks is going home and by him I will send Eliza a handsome watch that was taken by a man of my troop from an officer.

*The Honbl. A. J. Southwell to Maurice Townsend.*

PAU, *March* 9, 1814.

SIR,

I am extremely sorry to inform you that your brother John was made prisoner by the enemy the night of the 7th ultimo in a most unfortunate way, and at all events it will be a consolation to his family to know that no blame can be attached to him. The enemy came on at two o'clock in the morning and unfortunately surprised the advanced piquet of the squadron then on duty in support of the piquets, Townsend immediately mounted his horse and galloped to the front to ascertain what had attacked our advanced guard but which in fact at that time had been drove in by superior numbers. . . . Your brother must have found himself in the midst of the enemy. . . . I shall write to him and send him letters of recommendation to some French officers who were very kind to me while I was a prisoner in their hands, and from whom I am sure he will receive all possible attention. You may rest assured that Col. Hervey from his regard to your brother and his long and distinguished services will eagerly seize any opportunity of an exchange.

The next news of John is given in a letter from his brother Maurice, written when London was full of rejoicings at the peace.

MY DEAREST MOTHER,

The people in London are all mad, staring and gaping at emperors and princes, and many of us think you are all so for not being here at this joyful time. I am perfectly acquainted with all their faces. I met the Prince of Orange on Monday night at a Ball, he was most gracious to me and shook me most cordially several times by the hand. He inquired after all of you.

I have heard of Jack from several people, one account was that the last they saw of him was riding a steeplechase against a brother prisoner. I was last night at the illuminations at Carleton House, it is something superb, a great mob assembled there, who mistaking one of the noble visitors for his Royal Highness the fat P. R., set up a violent hissing, which they altered into as violent applause on ascertaining who it was in the carriage. They dragged old Blucher about the streets. There is a report about Town that the Duke of Wellington has been assassinated in Spain, but it is not given much credit to.

A letter from John, dated Toulouse, May 1, 1814, tells that he was at length released after having been remarkably well treated during his captivity: he also says in every town in France 'the people could not curb their joy at getting rid of the Tyrant.'

Maurice and some friends went to meet John in Paris. He writes home, July 1, 1814:—

Jack, Troy, Southwell, Walsh and myself are now assembled at the Hotel Versailles in high health, spirits and beauty. On Tuesday evening we leave this delightful scene of dissipation and frivolity for gloomy England. Jack would write but has sprained his thumb in an attempt to thrash me —which failed.—*That is false.* J. T.—Perfectly true. We dined all of us with Walsh's sister and had a most delightful grub. We hope soon to see you all, and believe me ever your most affectionate son,

MAURICE FITZGERALD TOWNSEND.

JOHN +<sup>his</sup> TOWNSEND
 <sub>mark</sub>

JOHN JAMES +<sup>his</sup> TROY
 <sub>mark</sub>

ARTHUR +<sup>his</sup> SOUTHWELL
 <sub>mark</sub>

Witness
 Paul the black valet de chambre.
 Troy has nearly purchased all Paris.

### John Townsend to his Father.

RADIPOLE, *Oct.* 6, 1814.

Colonel Baker and myself proceed tomorrow morning for Plymouth to embark with the squadron of the Regiment that accompanies the expedition to the southern part of the United States. My troop and Badcock's marched the day before yesterday, and I think without flattering the corps I never saw a squadron of finer men leave any barracks or in higher spirits, it would have done your heart good to hear them cheer. Are anxious to be employed again, for a Barrack life in England after having been actively employed for the last five years is one of the most sedentery and detestable that can be imagined and where there is neither honour nor glory to be gained. I am sure you will be gratified when I tell you that I was selected before 6 other captains to go with the squadron.

I remain my dearest Father
You ever affectionate son
J. TOWNSEND, Capt. 14 L. D. or
Royal American Heroes.

### John Townsend to his Sisters.

*Oct.* 6, 1814.

MY DARLING GIRLS,

Give the enclosed letter to my father and tell him that he must send to Bristol for the Fairy, a little favourite mare that I now give to you solely and wholly for your own riding; she was given me by our Col. for which reason I do not wish to part with her.

God bless you both, and if it is possible I will bring you at least two squaws home. I am really so happy at the thought of being actively employed that I don't know what I write.

### To his Mother (same date).

Tell the two darling girls that I have given their watches and chains which I meant to have given them in person to Schuyler, who has promised to have them conveyed safe to them. Tell Eliza I beg she will give you the little watch I gave her that I got at the battle of Salamanca in exchange for the one I send by Schuyler, which I know you will keep for my sake, as it is the only trophy of all our victories.

March 10, 1815, Boyle writes from Oxford to his mother that

In the late disastrous attacks on New Orleans, General Lambert says The conduct of the two squadrons of the 14th Light Dragoons has been the admiration of every one by the cheerfulness with which they have performed all description of service.

A letter from John was on its way at this time: it is dated Isle Dauphin, Feb. 20, 1815. He says:—

The whole of our little army is encamped on this island, not having a house or habitation of any description, but alligators and parrots on it. In short we have had no communication of any sort with the Americans, we are in want of everything nearly to make us comfortable, and tho' having plenty of dollars we cannot purchase a single thing, and being entirely on biscuit and salt pork we are worse here than I remember at any time to have been in the Peninsula. However we keep up our spirits, and have built a theatre which will open in a few days with 'Love à la mode.'

Colonel Townshend was very tender-hearted; when embarking for India in June, 1841, he could not bear to see the distress of the married men of his regiment whose wives had not been 'told off' for a free passage, and he paid himself for all the women and children who would otherwise have been left behind, expending, it is said, more than £800.

He died in 1845, aged fifty-six. A monument was erected to his memory in the church of Castle Townshend by the officers of his regiment.

In a military journal, under date May, 1845, is the

following record of Colonel Townshend's death and services :—

'On the 22nd of April, at his seat, Castle Townshend, County Cork, Colonel Townshend of the 14th (King's) Light Dragoons, in which regiment, without intermission, he served upwards of forty years in the four quarters of the globe, and to which corps he was most sincerely and devotedly attached. He was beloved in the extreme by every officer who served with or under him, and by the non-commissioned officers and men, their wives and offspring—not only beloved, but actually adored. His regiment is now serving on the burning plains of India, where he left them in November last for the recovery of his health, having had the Indian ague, which at last caused his death. He was born on the 11th of June, 1789[1]; therefore was in the fifty-seventh year of his age. He was appointed Cornet in the 14th Light Dragoons on the 24th of January, 1805: Lieutenant on the 8th of March, 1806, by purchase: Captain on the 6th June, without purchase (in place of Captain Knife who was mortally wounded in the battle of Fuentes d'Onor, and died a few days after): Brevet Major on the 21st of January, 1819, as a reward for active and zealous services during the Peninsular War: Major in the regiment, by purchase, on the 13th of September, 1821: Lieutenant-Colonel, by purchase, on the 16th of April, 1829: and Aide-de-camp to the Queen on the 23rd of November, 1841, consequently Colonel in the army. On the 16th of December, 1808, he sailed from Falmouth with his regiment for Portugal, and disembarked at Lisbon on the 24th of December, 1808. He was first engaged on the plains of Vogo, on the 10th of May, 1809, and in close pursuit of the enemy on the 11th, at the crossing of the Douro and capturing of Oporto on the 12th under Sir Arthur Wellesley (the enemy commanded by Marshal Soult). In the several skirmishes with the French rear-guard from Oporto to Gallicia in Spain, from the 13th to the 17th of May, 1809. In the engagements of the 27th and 28th of July, 1809, at Talavera. In an affair with the enemy's ad-

---

[1] Date corrected by Miss H. Somerville.

vanced posts on the 11th of July, 1810, in front of Ciudad Rodrigo, under the command of Lieut-Col. Talbot, who was killed with many others of the regiment. Engaged with the enemy on the 24th of July, 1810, at the passage of the Coa, near Almeida, under the command of Major-General Crawford. In the several skirmishes of the rear-guard from Almeida to Buzaco. Was present at Buzaco on the 27th of September, 1810 (cavalry not engaged). From Buzaco to Coimbra, and on to the great and ever-to-be-remembered lines of Torres Vedras, where the army arrived in the early part of October, 1810. From the 6th of March to the 4th of April, 1811, in the several affairs and skirmishes on the enemy's retreat from Santarem to the frontiers of Spain. (These are too numerous to particularise here, as the regiment was more or less engaged nearly every day). In the engagements of the 3rd and 5th of May, 1811, Fuentes d'Onor: employed as aide-de-camp to Sir Stapleton Cotton, on the 5th was slightly wounded and his horse shot. In the affair with the enemy's Lancers at Espega on the 25th September, 1811. Employed on duty at the siege of Ciudad Rodrigo in December, 1811, and January, 1812. Employed at the siege of Badajoz in March and April, 1812. In an affair with the enemy's cavalry on the 11th of April, 1812, at Usagre and Llarena, under the command of Sir Stapleton Cotton. In an affair on the 16th of June, 1812, in front of Salamanca. In an affair with the enemy's cavalry on the 18th of July, 1812, near Castrillos. At the battle of Salamanca on the 22nd of July, 1812. In an affair with the enemy's rear-guard near Penerando on the 23rd of July, 1812. In the several skirmishes with the enemy's rear-guard on their retreat from Salamanca to our taking of Madrid on the 13th of August, 1812. From the 24th of October to the 20th of November, 1812, in the several skirmishes from Madrid to Salamanca and from Salamanca to Ciudad Rodrigo. In the several affairs and skirmishes from the 26th of May (these are also too many to particularise, as they were nearly daily) to the battle of Vittoria on the 21st of June, when the whole of the enemy's baggage was taken or destroyed, together with nearly the whole of their artillery. On the 24th of June, 1813, at the taking of the enemy's last gun near Pampeluna, under the command of Major Brotherton of the same regiment. In the several engagements in the Pyrenees on the last three days of August, 1813. In the several engagements and skirmishes from the entrance of the British army into France, on the 1cth of November, 1813, to the battle of Orthes on the 27th of February, 1814, and to the 8th of March, 1814, when he was made prisoner of war in an affair with the enemy near the city of Pau. This took place about six weeks before the termination of the war by the abdication of Napoleon. (In consequence of the regiment being nearly daily engaged in France, it is impossible to particularise the affairs in that country, and bring them within the limits of a newspaper.) The whole of the above services were under the chief command of his Grace the Duke of Wellington. He was also present at New Orleans in America on the 8th of January, 1815, but not mounted. He was one of the Board of Officers appointed by the General commanding-in-chief in 1831 under Lord Edward Somerset for revising the formations and movements of the cavalry. He had been several times slightly wounded, but never quitted the field. He was Aide-de-camp to Her Majesty. He served in India with his regiment till November, 1844, when he embarked at Bombay. He arrived in his native country in January last, and expired, as before stated. A more humane, kind, tender-hearted and generous or a braver soldier did not exist, notwithstanding he was in every respect a strict disciplinarian.'

As Colonel Townshend lived with his regiment, his mother reigned at Castle Townshend in his stead. It was a literal reign, for the old feudal feeling of the tenants still survived, and they flew to obey a word from the 'Madam' as they called her, although she herself thoroughly disliked the title, which she considered only fit for the native Irish. She managed the entire estate, and was successful in several lawsuits. Her mind is said by one of her grandchildren to have been quite masculine in its power; but she had a feminine taste for collecting curiosities and old china.

Very proud and exclusive she was too; it has been said that 'Family pride was *le mot de l'enigme* of the existence of herself and belongings.' When old, she travelled post in her own pale yellow chariot, although when younger she had often ridden the sixty miles to Cork. She was devoted to her son, Colonel John Townshend, and after his death lost all interest in the management of affairs, and never even came downstairs, spending her time in a little business room called the Bull's Eye, writing letters in a most clear and beautiful hand, and arranging old papers. Unfortunately she had a great dislike to any one else looking at the family papers, so many of the most interesting records have not been copied. She died in 1848.

The other sons of Richard Boyle Townshend were the Rev. Maurice FitzGerald Stephens-Townshend, who succeeded his brother at Castle Townshend; the Rev. Abraham Boyle Townsend, Vicar of East Hampstead, Berks, Senior Student of Christ Church, Oxford; and Henry, a young naval officer, who served under his kinsman Lord James O'Brien, afterwards Marquis of Thomond, and died in the West Indies. The daughters were Henrietta Augusta, who married her cousin Thomas Somerville of Drishane, High Sheriff of Cork County in 1863; and Elizabeth Anne, who married the Rev. Robert St. Laurence, Rector of Moragh, and son of the Hon. and Right Rev. the Bishop of Cork.

Mrs. Somerville had a ready wit, and strong likes and dislikes. One day, a story goes, she drove to call on a lady for whom she had no love, and was told by the servant that his mistress was out. 'Indeed!' answered Mrs. Somerville. 'Will you tell your mistress that the next time she goes out I hope she will take her head with her, for now I see it sticking out of an upper window.'

Both the sisters were famed for their beauty. When they were presented at Court, Anthony St. Leger, the Queen's Chamberlain, standing by, said, 'Those are the *two* young ladies from Ireland I mean to marry.' (He was then a widower, and lived next door to them in Montague Square.) Queen Charlotte took snuff and answered, 'And you have very good taste, Mr. St. Leger.'

Eliza Townshend was witty as well as beautiful, and among her other admirers was Sir Robert Peel. She once made a pretty impromptu version of Malherbe's lines on the death of his friend Du Penrier's little daughter Rose :—

> 'Elle était du monde où les plus belles choses
> Ont le pire destin.
> Rose, elle a vécu ce que vivent les roses,
> L'espace d'un matin.'

Eliza tore her dress at a ball, and when Sir Robert Peel made some joke about it, she promptly answered,

> 'Robe, elle a vécu ce que vivent les robes,
> L'espace d'un festin.'

After her marriage she lived in Brussels, where her charming manners and conversation gathered a circle around her like that of a French salon of the old times. She died at Shanna Court, Castle Townshend, preserving her dignity and charm to the last.

The Rev. Maurice FitzGerald Townshend, who succeeded his brother at Castle Townshend, was educated at Westminster and Christ Church, Oxford. His brother John mentions in one of his letters from the Peninsula, 'I hear Maurice has taken his degree with great eclat.'

His letters from Lisbon and Paris have been already given. When a young man he lived much in the best London society, and danced at Almack's in the first quadrille ever performed in England.

In 1824 he was appointed Vicar of the Christ Church living of Thornbury, Gloucestershire, with its three dependencies, Rangeworthy, Oldbury and Falfield, which three places he caused to be erected into three separate livings, to his own loss.

He was at this time not a rich man, having only his younger son's portion of £5000, but finding the widow of his predecessor in poor circumstances, he remitted the sum due for dilapidations at the Vicarage. He repaired and added to it, and yet his daughter at his death in 1872 had to pay altogether £460 for dilapidations.

On the 16th of May, 1826, he married Alice Elizabeth, daughter of Richard Shute and his wife Harriet Willis, sister of Harry Willis Stephens, of Eastington and Chavenage, Gloucestershire, who died a monk at La Trappe. The Shute family is kin to Viscount Barrington. The Willis grandfather of Alice Elizabeth Shute was descended from Richard Stephens of Chavenage and his wife Anne, daughter of the heroic Cavalier Sir Hugh Cholmondeley. Richard Stephens was son of Nathaniel Stephens, M.P. for the county of Gloucester in the Long Parliament, but who abstained from voting at the time of King Charles's death, 1649. The Stephens and Cromwell families were connected by marriage, and Abigail, daughter of Nathaniel Stephens, married the well-known Sir Edward Harley of Brampton Bryan, and was mother of Queen Anne's Minister, the first Earl of Oxford.

Alice Elizabeth Shute was heiress by survival in her uncle Henry Stephens, and assumed his name. (Her husband bore three crests, Townshend, FitzGerald, and Stephens.) She was heiress of Chavenage and Lady of the Manors of Eastington, Horsley, Fretherne, and Alkerton. Mrs. Stephens-Townshend had three children, and died at Castle Townshend, aged only twenty-eight.

A fate seemed to hang over the mansion at Castle Townshend. One house was destroyed in the Jacobite wars, another fell down during alterations, and in November in 1852 the building raised by Richard Boyle Townshend was accidentally burnt to the ground. A quantity of plate, FitzGerald and Townshend heirlooms, was kept in a room at the top of the house, and so fierce was the blaze that the silver ran down in molten streams in large quantities, and Mr. Stephens-Townshend thought it worth while to send a Bristol silversmith to Ireland to search among the ruins and value the silver by the pound! His search was so well rewarded that he found it worth while to go off to America with his treasure, and he has never been heard of since!

Mr. Stephens-Townshend was a most benevolent landlord. On coming into the Castle Townshend and Dingle properties in 1845, the first thing he did was to draw his pen through £10,000 of arrears, hoping thus to enable his tenants to make a fresh start. He also remitted the toll fares at Skibbereen, a gift of £300 to the town.

In 1869, T. McCarthy Downing, M.P. for Co. Cork, presented to him in the name of his tenantry a testimonial in acknowledgment of his unbounded generosity during the years of famine and the unusually long leases with which he had almost gifted them with his estates— said to be let between £1500 and £2000 below their actual annual value [1]. A ripe classical scholar, of original wit and retentive memory, he was a delightful companion.

He died in 1872 at Thornbury, and at his own wish was buried in a simple grave among the poor of his parish.

His only son, Henry John, died in 1869. He was educated at Eton, and for ten years held a commission in the Second Lifeguards. He married in 1864 his cousin Jane Adeliza Hussey de Burgh, eldest daughter of John Hamilton Hussey de Burgh of Kilfinnan Castle, Glandore, and Louise Jane Townshend of Shepperton. Her great-great-grandfather was the well-known orator Walter Hussey Burgh, famous for his oration in 1779. Henry John Townshend left two sons, Maurice Fitz-Gerald Stephens, born in 1865, and Hubert de Burgh Fitz-Gerald, born 1867.

Mr. Stephens-Townshend left a 'life interest successively' in the Castle Townshend property, and the whole of his Dingle and Kerry estates, to be divided between his two daughters. The elder of these, Geraldine Henrietta, married Major-General Pierrepont Mundy, late Royal Horse Artillery, the following sketch of whose life appeared in *The Bristol Times and Mirror*:—

'He was the sixth son of General Godfrey Basil Mundy, who was the second son of Mr. E. Miller Mundy of Shipley, Derbyshire, M.P., by his first wife Frances Meynell, daughter and co-heir of Mr. Godfrey Meynell, "father of the Meynell Hunt." General G. B. Mundy, who served in the Cavalry and was for many years A.D.C. to his brother-in-law

---

[1] Father Davis of Baltimore also signed this testimonial.

General Lord Charles FitzRoy (who married Miss Mundy of Shipley), married the Hon. Sarah Rodney, youngest daughter of the great Admiral Lord Rodney, by whom he had several sons and one daughter, the mother of the present Godfrey, Lord Tredegar. Born in Derbyshire, August 4th, 1815, and educated at Dr. Everard's school at Brighton, known as the "House of Lords," General Pierrepont Mundy's schoolfellows included the present Dukes of Beaufort and of Rutland. He entered the Royal Military Academy of Woolwich at the age of 14 (in 1829-30), and was head of his batch on leaving, with the choice of entering Engineers or Artillery. Choosing the latter for its "smartness," he continued in the regiment until he was a full Colonel, when his lameness from a dislocated hip becoming more trying, he retired on full pay, with the honorary rank of Major-General. He applied to go to the Crimea in 1854-5: but the head of the War Office, his first-cousin, Lord Lincoln, afterwards Duke of Newcastle (whose mother was Miss Mundy of Shipley), procured for him the more pacific office of buying horses for remounts, and the war was over before the opportunity for Captain Mundy's distinction in other fields but those of cricket and hunting and every "manly exercise" occurred. Later he was sent out in command of the Artillery troops to New Brunswick (1862), but the Mason and Slidell business had ended peacefully before he landed. In 1859 he married Mrs. Richards, widow of E. P. Richards, Esq., of Plâs Newydd, near Cardiff. Mrs. Pierrepont Mundy died in 1865, and subsequently General Mundy married Miss (Geraldine Henrietta) Townsend. After his second marriage, General Mundy resided in Gloucestershire at his hunting box, Thornbury House, where he became well known to all who frequented cricket matches or the hunting field. We believe that the General was an original member of Pratt's Club, and the "I Zingari" Cricket Club. He was known as one of the best racquet-players in England. In fact there were few games in which he did not excel. In cricket he on one occasion played with the Gentlemen of England v. the Players, on the winning side. He was a thorough gentleman and an ardent sportsman, a smart officer, with a host of friends and never a foe. In the "Badminton Library" an article on Tandem Driving contains a sketch of him as "Mentor," by his friend Sir C. Teesdale, who writes of himself as "Telemachus."

' Subjoined is an anecdote showing the humorous straightforwardness of General "Pip" Mundy in very early life. His parents lived at Brighton (owning Norfolk House, now the hotel of that name), for the education of their children. The King loved children, and often gave balls to amuse them and himself. At one of these dances little Pierrepont Mundy was sitting on his Majesty's knee—who remarked on his small and beautiful feet and hands and then said, "What pretty shoes"! "They are not *my* shoes, George the Fourth," replied the child, "they are my sister's!" (probably a long-discarded pair used for the occasion). In treating of the General's subsequent prowess in every "field of exercise," it should be added that his many-sided character included the charm of wit and pleasantry—the life and soul of his domestic circle. He was a clever draughtsman and devoted to music, with a wonderful ear for it. He read a good deal, and *"never was bored in his life"*!'

The second daughter of Mr. Stephens-Townshend, Alice Gertrude, married in 1856 the Honourable and Rev. Courtenay Vernon, brother and heir to Lord Lyveden and great-nephew of Sydney Smith.

The pleasure shown by the tenants on Mrs. Mundy's arrival at Castle Townshend had its comic side. As her carriage was passing through the crowded streets of Skibbereen on a market day, an old woman was accidentally knocked down. Of course the carriage was stopped, and inquiries were made after the woman's injuries. But the poor thing was found, half-fainting, held up between two men who were shaking her and scolding her soundly for getting in the way and frightening 'the Madam' when she was coming home at last!

When they reached Castle Townshend there was a great welcome, and in the evening a man asked to see Mrs. Mundy. He greeted her with, 'Oh, it's the fine day that sees your ladyship in the old place,' and sinking his voice, 'and if there's any one you'd like rowlled in the river—why,' pointing to himself, 'I'm your man.' 'What!' cried Mrs. Mundy; 'why should I want any one rolled in the river?' 'Och, bedad! and it isn't out of it he'd come in a hurry, and if you *should* want any one put in, I'd just like your ladyship to know I'm your man!' An old woman, too, came to beg that a neighbour she disliked might be put out of a cottage near, and when Mrs. Mundy tried to explain that she did not turn out tenants without some good reason, the old woman sidled up to her, and slipping a sovereign into her hand whispered, 'Ah, now, ye'll just turn her out and not say a word about it, and that's for yourself!'

A good deal of Irish history seems to be explained by these anecdotes.

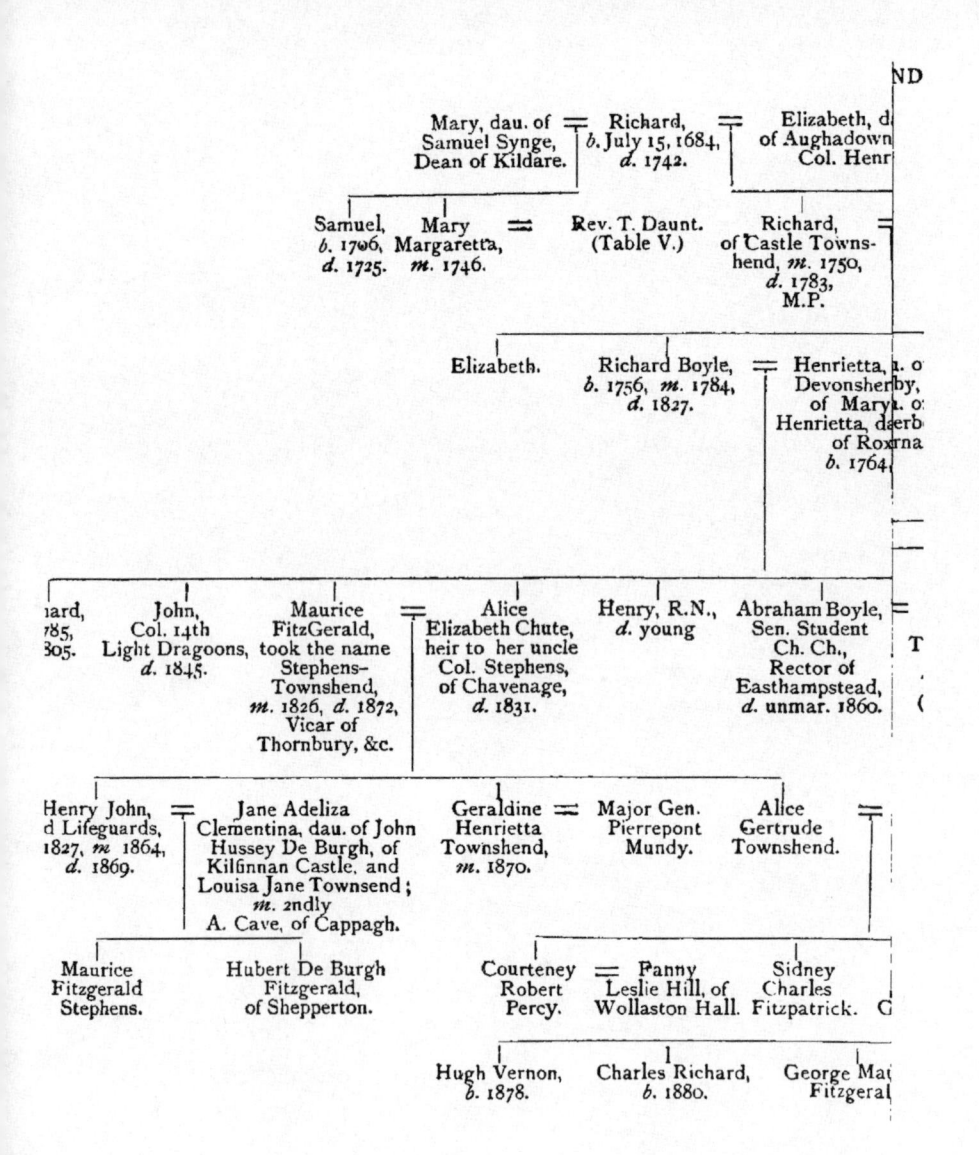

| | | | |
|---|---|---|---|
| Mary, dau. of Samuel Synge, Dean of Kildare. | = | Richard, b. July 15, 1684, d. 1742. | = Elizabeth, d. of Aughadown Col. Henr... |

Samuel, b. 1706, d. 1725. — Mary Margaretta, m. 1746. = Rev. T. Daunt. (Table V.) — Richard, of Castle Townshend, m. 1750, d. 1783, M.P.

Elizabeth. — Richard Boyle, b. 1756, m. 1784, d. 1827. = Henrietta, ... of Devonsher...by, of Mary... o... Henrietta, daerb... of Rox...rna b. 1764.

...ard, ...785, ...805, — John, Col. 14th Light Dragoons, d. 1845. — Maurice FitzGerald, took the name Stephens-Townshend, m. 1826, d. 1872, Vicar of Thornbury, &c. = Alice Elizabeth Chute, heir to her uncle Col. Stephens, of Chavenage, d. 1831. — Henry, R.N., d. young — Abraham Boyle, Sen. Student Ch. Ch., Rector of Easthampstead, d. unmar. 1860.

Henry John, d Lifeguards, 1827, m. 1864, d. 1869. = Jane Adeliza Clementina, dau. of John Hussey De Burgh, of Kilfinnan Castle, and Louisa Jane Townsend; m. 2ndly A. Cave, of Cappagh. — Geraldine Henrietta Townshend, m. 1870. = Major Gen. Pierrepont Mundy. — Alice Gertrude Townshend.

Maurice Fitzgerald Stephens. — Hubert De Burgh Fitzgerald, of Shepperton. — Courteney Robert Percy. = Fanny Leslie Hill, of Wollaston Hall. — Sidney Charles Fitzpatrick.

Hugh Vernon, b. 1878. — Charles Richard, b. 1880. — George Ma... Fitzgeral...

# APPENDIX A.

*A Memorandum given by Judge Townsend to Mrs. Pierrepont Mundy.*

RICHARD TOWNSEND of Castle Townshend, eldest son of Colonel Bryan Townsend, was owner of the Castle Townshend estates, which comprised at that time not only the lands granted by patent to his grandfather Colonel Richard Townesend, but also certain lands which had been annexed by the augmentation act to the Archiepiscopal See of Dublin, although the lands lie in the county of Cork. These latter were—
1. North and South Aghills (since called Shepperton).
2. Drishane and Farrendagh.
3. East and West Myross.
4. Kilcoe.
5. Glannafoyne (near Loch Ine).

Richard Townshend, who died in 1742, held these See lands as tenant to the Archbishop of Dublin.

By his will he directed that the leases should be changed into leases for lives, which was done after his death. Richard Townshend devised all his estates to his wife Elizabeth, daughter of Henry Becher, and a question arose whether she was entitled to them absolutely, or only for life, with a power of disposing of them among his sons Richard, John, and Henry.

Richard died in 1742. After his death his widow made her will, appointing the estates among her three sons just mentioned. To Richard she appointed what are still called the Castle Townshend estates. To John[1] she appointed the See lands; and to Henry, the youngest son, she appointed the lands of Dunbeacon, Ardra, and Ballintona, all in the County of Cork.

[1] Commissioner of Excise, and M.P. for Clonakilty.

This Henry died unmarried, and left his property to Richard, the eldest son of his brother John. (This Richard was usually known in the family as Dick of the Point.) Therefore there was no necessity for John to make any provision for his eldest son, and he was enabled to divide the See lands between his other sons, Jonas Morris, Henry, and Abraham. John built a residence on Aghills which he called 'Shepperton,' so that his branch of the family were usually called the Shepperton family. Shepperton he left to his second son Jonas Morris, who married Jane Digby; Kilcoe he left to Henry, and Drishane and Glannafoyne to Abraham.

But John had previously made a lease of Drishane and Farrendagh to his son-in-law Thomas Somerville, with a covenant to renew to his heirs as often as he (John) should renew with the Archbishop of Dublin. He made a similar lease with a similar covenant to a person named Atkins of the land of Glannafoyne.

After Jonas Morris's death his son John Morris became entitled to Shepperton and to another estate called Cahira which Commissioner John had purchased. John Morris died leaving all his estates to his mother (Jane Digby).

After Henry's death, John FitzHenry, the writer of this note, became entitled to Kilcoe, and also under the will of his uncle Abraham to Drishane and Glannafoyne, subject to the leases and covenants.

Mrs. Morris Townshend and John FitzHenry joined in purchasing the fee simple of the Church-lands, so Shepperton became the estate in fee simple of Mrs. Morris Townshend. John FitzHenry (being bound by the Church Temporalities Act) conveyed the fee simple in Drishane to Thomas Somerville. John FitzHenry is now owner of Kilcoe and Myros, and a rent charge out of Glannafoyne. Dunbeacon belonged to the late Richard Mellifont Townshend, who died at Nice.

Ballintona and Ardra were sold in the Landed Estates Court, and are no longer the property of any of the Townshend family.

# APPENDIX B.

## *The Somerville Family.*

THE Rev. William Somerville fled to Ireland in an open boat in 1692 to escape the persecution that was then being inflicted on the Episcopal Clergy in Scotland.

He was accompanied by his two sons and his daughter with her husband, afterwards Archdeacon Cameron.

One of the sons, Thomas, was educated in Dublin and became a clergyman. His first curacy was Christchurch, Cork. He was reader of St. Barry's, and planted the lime-trees round the churchyard. He married Anne, eldest daughter of John Neville, of Newcastle, near Dublin, widow of John Perry of Woodruffe, and granddaughter of Edward and Anne Riggs of Riggsdale. The Nevilles trace their descent from John of Gaunt through Edward fifth Lord Abergavenny. John Neville, by his second wife, Miss Allen, left a daughter Alice, who married Thomas Corker, father of Archdeacon Corker[1]. (See notes, Table XII.)

It is supposed that William, the elder brother of the Rev. Thomas Somerville, returned to Scotland, as a letter from him is preserved in which he says, 'I received your last through Lord Somerville. I suppose it was he who sealed it, as when writing to the head of the family it is not usual to use the arms.' Lord Somerville was at this time quartered at Cork. On taking the livings of Myros and Castlehaven Thomas Somerville took a lease of Castlehaven castle, where the family resided till Thomas Townsend Somerville built a house on the present site of Drishane. During the long minority of his son the castle was let to an Englishman, who pulled down portions of it whenever he wanted stone, so that it was reduced to a ruin[2].

After the sons of Henry Townshend of Castle Townshend and the children of Mrs. Courtenay Vernon his sister, the

---

[1] Mrs. Judith Cameron.    [2] Miss H. Somerville.

# CHAPTER VIII.

THE OTHER CHILDREN OF COLONEL RICHARD TOWNES-END, VIZ. JOHN, FRANCIS, HORATIO, PHILIP, CORNELIUS, CATHERINE, DOROTHEA, AND MRS. OWEN, WITH NOTES ON THE EARLS OF BARRYMORE AND THE COPINGER AND BECHER FAMILIES.

(Tables III–VIII.)

## NOTES ON TABLE III.

[1] JOHN TOWNESEND was probably born before Colonel Townesend came to Ireland in 1647, but the place and date of his birth are not at present known. He married in 1666 Lady Catherine Barry, then aged about sixteen. She was the daughter of Richard, second Earl of Barrymore.

The great family of Barry was descended from William de Barri and Angareth, daughter of Princess Nesta of Wales and sister of FitzGerald, ancestor of the Geraldines. In the end of the sixteenth century the Great Barry, Barrymore, was also Lord of Ibawne and Viscount Buttevant, and in the time of Charles I the young Lord David was created Earl of Barrymore. He was a person 'of great generosity, humanity, and Christian charity [2],' and required his family to accompany him to hear sermons twice a day on Sundays, Wednesdays, and Fridays.

[1] The greater part of this notice is extracted from Judge FitzHenry Townshend's article on the Earls of Barrymore, printed in the *Abbeystrewry Magazine*.    [2] Lodge.

## TABLE III.

### ELDEST SON OF COLONEL TOWNESEND.

John Townsend = Lady Catherine Barry.

- Richard Fitzjohn, *d. young.*
- Catherine, *d. young.*
- Susannah = Colonel James Barry, of Lisnagar and Rathcormac. The McAdam Barry.
  - David, *d. unmarried.*
  - Patrick, *d. unmarried.*
- Elizabeth = Niblett Dunscumbe, M.P., of Mount Desert, High Sheriff 1730, *d.* 1735.
  *d. s. p.*
- Catherine = John Townshend. (Table IX.)

His wife was Alicia, daughter of the great Earl of Cork, and sister of Lord Broghill and the learned Robert Boyle. Her father[1] devised to her the monastery of Castlelyons (granted to him at the dissolution of the religious houses) 'to buy her gloves and pins.' When Earl David closed his creditable career and was buried in the Boyle vault at Youghal, the old Earl of Cork[2] showed his concern for his daughter's early widowhood by leaving bequests to her three children, and especially recommending a good education for the boy.

She consoled herself by marrying Colonel James Barry of Liscarrol, having it seems taken a fancy to the family. He was generally known as Colonel Jack Barry, and was a Roman Catholic. He served under Ormonde, and kept up a correspondence with his brother-in-law Broghill, and so prudently kept in favour with both sides. By the wish of the talented Countess Ranelagh, his aunt, the young Earl of Barrymore was placed under the care of John Milton in his house at the Barbican[3], but Milton soon after gave up taking pupils, and does not seem to have had so much influence over young Barrymore as over Lord Ranelagh's son, with whom he kept up a long correspondence.

When Cork declared for the Parliament in 1649 Lord Inchiquin was staying with Colonel Jack Barry, but the young Earl was away in France getting married to one of the maids of honour—Susan, daughter of Sir William Killigrew. The Dowager Countess does not seem to have liked her new daughter-in-law, and a letter of condolence to her on the marriage is printed in Robert Boyle's works. However, the young Countess

---

[1] Archdale, *Monas. Hib.*    [2] Masson's *Milton*, iii. 660.
[3] Wood's *Fasti*, i. 483.

allowed her second daughter to be named Catherine, after Lady Ranelagh, so it is to be hoped that the family made friends after all. The Earl was a soldier, and his commission as Colonel of Infantry is still in the possession of Judge Townshend, who also has the Earl's handsome snuff-box.

As it has been said, Lord Barrymore's second daughter, Catherine, married John Townsend, and it is believed that Colonel Townesend built the large mansion at Castle Townshend for the young pair, who meanwhile lived at Timoleague. But their married life did not last long. John Townsend died before his father, and his son Richard FitzJohn followed him while still young. Lady Catherine married as her second husband Captain Charles Barclay, of London [1], and had one daughter, Elizabeth, who married Captain Richard Wills. Lady Catherine gave her as a marriage portion three hundred pounds then owing by Bryan Townsend, and a hundred pounds more of her own, and an annuity of ten pounds for fifty years provided her own jointure lasted so long. No money seemed to come to Elizabeth from her father, and there is no mention of property belonging to her husband, nor of where he came from [2].

Bishop Dives Downes (who married Horatio Townsend's widow) mentions in his tour that he stayed with Lady Catherine 'Berkeley' at Skibbereen.

The Earls of Barrymore did not all imitate the virtues of Earl David, and it is hardly surprising that their race dwindled and the title died out. Sir Egerton Bridges says of the seventh Earl:—

[1] The marriage settlement of Lady Catherine and Captain Barclay is among the Castle Townshend deeds.

[2] Letter from Miss E. Townshend (afterwards Mrs. St. Laurence), Feb. 1845.

'With talents to shine in the course of honourable ambition, with wit, good-nature and engaging manners, he shone a meteor of ten-fold wonder and regret by freaks which would have disgraced a Buckingham or a Rochester, till the accidental explosion of a musket put an end to his troubles and follies on 9th March, 1793.'

He was popularly called 'Hellgate,' and his brother, the eighth and last Earl, who succeeded him, was clubfooted, and so known as 'Cripplegate'; the third brother was styled 'Newgate,' because he passed much of his time in prison as a debtor, and their only sister was honoured by the title of 'Billingsgate'! It is said that the Barry race were placed under a 'Mailloch,' an Irish curse of great vigour, by some old woman whose husband and sons the Lord Barrymore had hung in the rebellion of 1641. Judge Townshend heard the legend and curse (in the Irish tongue) from Mr. James Redmond Barry of Glandore, who claimed to be Viscount Buttevant, but somehow the House of Lords did not think his proofs satisfactory. Among the documents in his possession was the settlement executed on the marriage of John Townesend and Lady Catherine Barry.

The Barry estates are now in the possession of the Smith-Barrys, but if Mr. Redmond Barry is not heir-male, the heir-general of the Barrymore family must be sought in the descendants of Catherine Townesend, for the rest of her father's line is extinct. If we could find him, he would it seems be entitled to style himself Lord Barry, because the Barony was *in fee*, and would descend to the heir-general of Earl Richard, Lady Catherine's father. The Earldom is clearly extinct, but both Viscounty and Barony rest 'in gremio legis' or 'in nubibus.'

Richard Mellifont Townshend[1] inherited John Townesend's seal. It was a curious one, and seems to have had three stones[2], one plain, one engraved with a stag, and the third was missing.

Susanna, the only surviving child of John and Catherine, married her cousin, Colonel James Barry of Lisnagar, the McAdam Barry. He descended from Sir Robert de Barri, an elder brother of the ancestors of the Earls of Barrymore.

A Chancery suit[3] shows that Colonel James Barry was a widower when he married Susanna Townsend, but the children of his first wife, Mary Anselme, died unmarried. By Susanna he left two daughters, one of whom left no descendants; the other married John Townsend of Skirtagh (Table IX), whose descendants now represent the families of Barrymore and McAdam Barry. In the male line the children of Colonel James Barry's step-brother carry on the family of Lisnagar.

Mrs. Townsend of Skirtagh and her sister were left bequests by their step-brother Redmond, as 'My sisters Townshend and Dunscombe.'

### Notes on Table IV.

The date of Francis Townsend's birth is not known. The settlement on his marriage with Catherine Honnor is dated Nov. 10th, 1679, and was lately in the possession of Richard Mellifont Townshend[4]. It is sealed with the arms of the Honnor family, Or, on a bend az. between two hawks' heads erased sa. three cinquefoils of the second. William Honnor lived at Madame, near Clonakilty[5]. It had originally belonged to

---

[1] Table I.  [2] Described by John Sealy Townshend.
[3] Feb. 23rd, 1750; quoted by John Sealy Townshend.
[4] Of Nice, France; Table I.  [5] J. Sealy Townshend.

# TABLE IV.

## Third Son of Colonel Townesend.

Francis, = Katherine, daughter of W. Honnor,
a captain in   of Madame, near Clonakilty.
the army.

- Dorothy.
- Jane.
- Richard = Miss Minchin.
  - Francis, = Miss Roche,
    of Clogheen.  of West Carbery.
    - Butler,
      died at 21
      of a fever.
    - Elizabeth = Rev. W. Stewart,
      of Wellfield or
      Kilgariff.
      - H. W. Stewart, = Grace
        D.D., Rector of Townshend.
        Templemanus.  (Table XIII.)
  - Butler, = Frances, dau. of John Roche,
    in holy orders,  of West Carbery.
    ob. s. p.
  - Mary = Francis Beamish,
    of Kilmaluda.
    - Townsend = Mary, dau. of W. Atkins.
      - A son who died young
        and was succeeded by Sampson Beamish.

Dermond McFinnin McCartie, who mortgaged it to Sir Robert Travers.

Francis Townsend was a captain in the army. He was proscribed as a traitor by James II's Irish Parliament, and took his wife and five children to England for safety. At that time the Trinity College (Dublin) MS. list of fugitives says his estates were worth £340 yearly. Francis signed a bond for the debts of his brother-in-law, Dominic Copinger, and his brother Philip laid claim to some of Dominic's land in 1684 on behalf of Francis's eldest son Richard. In the year 1705 Dorothy and Jane Townsend were living. Judge Townshend believes they were daughters of Francis, but the only descendant given in most pedigrees is Richard, who lived near Bandon and married Miss Minchin. Richard's eldest son, Francis of Clogeen, was sworn freeman of Clonakilty, 1728. The second son, Butler [1], entered Trinity College, Dublin, 1727, aged 17. Ordained priest at Cork 1743. Licensed August 26th, 1747, to the curacy of Kilgariffe, Ross. He died in the same week as his nephew Butler, leaving no children. Francis and Richard both married ladies of the name of Roche, who bore the arms of Roche, Lord Fermoy. Francis left two daughters, one of whom, Elizabeth, married William Stewart of Wellfield, whose arms were those of Scotland 'in a border gobonated arg. and az.' Wellfield is described as—

'The seat of Rev. W. Stewart, a gentleman honourably distinguished for spirited and judicious improvements. It stands upon a part of Lord Shannon's estate, taken on a lease of three lives. It was then in a rude and impoverished state, with a good deal of wet and waste ground, destitute of trees or proper enclosures. By draining, dressing and enclosing

[1] Brady's *Records*.

it is now a very handsome as well as productive farm, with the addition of an excellent house, garden, and plantations[1].'

His son, the Rev. H. W. Stewart, was head of the classical school at Clonakilty. The *Statistical Survey* speaks of his 'combination of talent and diligence,' and says that in a very short time the number of boarders had increased from twelve to fifty.

### NOTES ON TABLE V.

Horatio Townsend was captain of the Lynn sloop of war. His gallant exploits have been already described in treating of his father's life, but the most romantic part of the story has yet to be told. He landed one day on Shirkin Island, and visited the castle, when he unexpectedly came on Mrs. Becher, combing the long hair of her lovely daughter Elizabeth, who was sitting at her mother's feet. The impressionable sailor was struck motionless with admiration. But the course of true love did not run smooth; perhaps Mrs. Becher hoped for a better match, for at the time of the landing of James II in Ireland Horatio was only worth a hundred a year. Mrs. Becher took care that the lovers had few chances of meeting, but they kept up a constant correspondence, and at last their constancy was rewarded, and they were married. They only had one daughter, Penelope, and then Horatio died of a fever on board his ship, leaving all his small property to his 'affectionate wife,' who was sole executrix. His short will is dated 1697, and was proved in 1705; but, alas for the romance, by that time Elizabeth Townsend was the wife of Bishop Dives Downes! Sir Thomas Becher[2]

---

[1] *Statist. Surv.*, Townsend, i. 331.   [2] Caulfield, *Kinsale*.

## TABLE V.

### FOURTH SON OF COLONEL TOWNESEND.

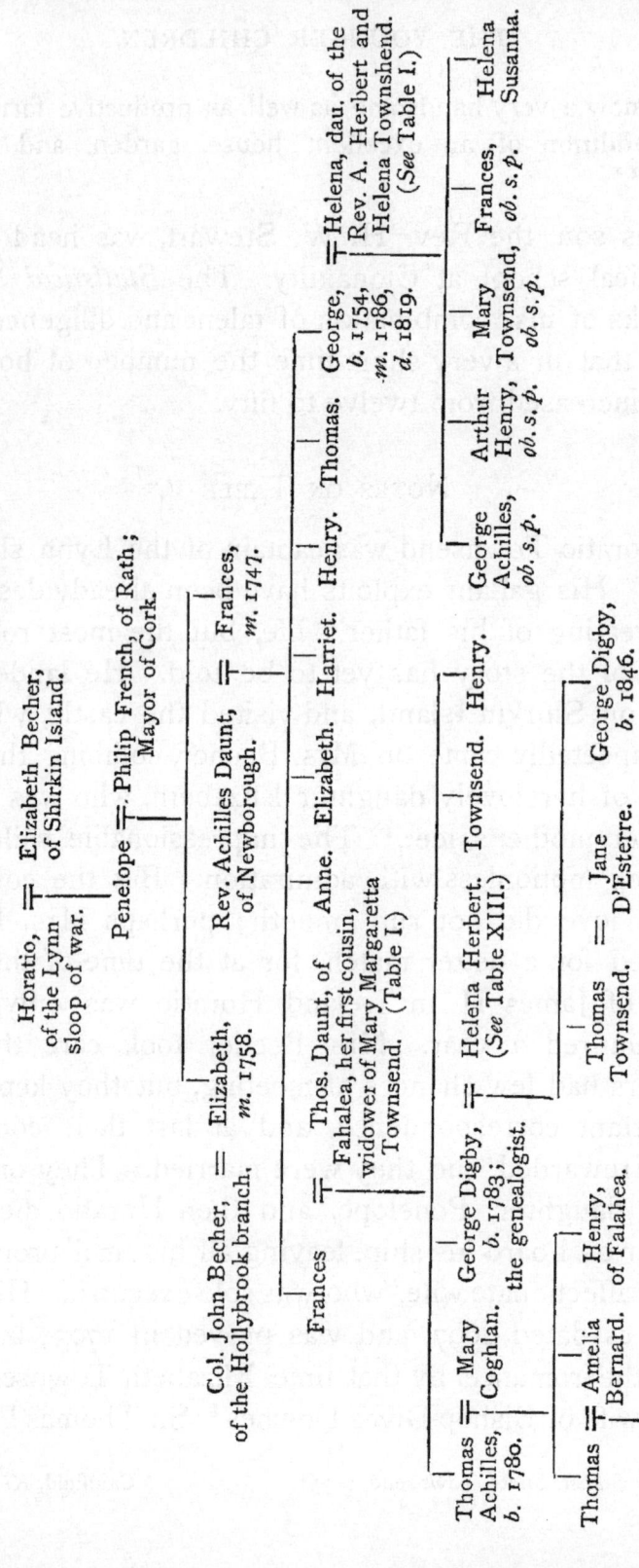

Horatio, of the Lynn sloop of war. = Elizabeth Becher, of Shirkin Island.

├── Penelope = Philip French, of Rath; Mayor of Cork.
│   └── Rev. Achilles Daunt, of Newborough. = Frances, m. 1747.
│       ├── Thos. Daunt, of Fahalea, her first cousin, widower of Mary Margaretta Townsend. (Table I.) = Frances
│       ├── Anne.
│       ├── Elizabeth.
│       ├── Harriet.
│       ├── Henry.
│       ├── Thomas.
│       └── George, b. 1754, m. 1786, d. 1819. = Helena, dau. of the Rev. A. Herbert and Helena Townshend. (See Table I.)
│           ├── George Achilles, ob. s. p.
│           ├── Henry.
│           ├── Townsend. = Jane D'Esterre.
│           │   └── Thomas Townsend. — George Digby, b. 1846.
│           ├── Helena Herbert. (See Table XIII.)
│           ├── Arthur Henry, ob. s. p.
│           ├── Mary Townsend, ob. s. p.
│           ├── Frances, ob. s. p.
│           └── Helena Susanna.
└── Col. John Becher, of the Hollybrook branch. = Elizabeth, m. 1758.
    ├── Thomas Achilles, b. 1780. = Mary Coghlan.
    │   ├── George Digby, b. 1783; the genealogist.
    │   └── Henry, Bernard. of Falahea.
    └── Thomas = Amelia
        └── Four sons and four daughters.

wrote from Shirkin Island on July 30th, 1701, 'I have married my daughter Townsend to the Bishop of Cork.' He must have been a great contrast to her sailor husband, for he was 'remarkable for his prudence and gravity, as well as for his learning.' She bore him one daughter, Elizabeth, and died young, her will being proved August, 1707.

## NOTES ON BECHER.

The Becher family claim descent from Sir Eustace Bridgecourt, who came from Hainault as a follower of Queen Philippa in 1328, and they settled in Cork in the time of Elizabeth.

Colonel Thomas Becher of Baltimore lived in the castle on Shirkin Island. He was an active, powerful man in those stirring times, and his name is constantly met with in County Cork records. When James II landed in Cork and most of the English settlers placed their families in safety, Thomas Becher, his wife and seven children, were among those who left the country. He was one of the richest of the gentry, his estates being valued at £898 a year. He acted as aide-de-camp to King William at the battle of the Boyne, and was presented by the King with his own watch; it has a beautiful chased silver case, and only one hand, which points to the hours; the minutes are marked on a small dial, which revolves in the centre of the large face [1].

Colonel Becher married Elizabeth, daughter of Major Henry Turner and Dorothy daughter of the Right Reverend Richard Boyle, Archbishop of Tuam. His daughter Elizabeth was the heroine of Horatio Townsend's romantic story [2], and the next daughter Susanna [3]

---

[1] Now in the possession of J. R. Becher of Loch Ine.
[2] Table V. and notes.  [3] Chap. xi.

married Thomas Hungerford of the Island. The eldest son, Henry, married Catherine, daughter and heir of Colonel Henry Owen, a cousin of Colonel Arnop, who is described in Orrery's letter [1] as 'somewhat crazed.' Her brother John had married a daughter of Colonel Richard Townesend, but died without children. The Owens were an Oxfordshire family who had fought on the King's side in the civil wars, and settled at Baltimore about 1650. Colonel Owen's wife was Margaret, daughter of Sir William Piers, of Finsternagh, County Westmeath, and granddaughter of Archbishop Jones, the ancestor of Lord Ranelagh [2].

Aughadown House, the principal residence of the Becher family, was pulled down some years ago. It was a strong castellated mansion, entered by a drawbridge, surrounded by beautiful grounds, and having a gazebo on one of the heights behind the house. No vestige of the old house at Creagh remains.

## NOTES ON TABLE VII.

Philip Townsend was born 1664 at Kilbrittan Castle, near Timoleague, one of the castles forfeited by McCarthy Reagh in 1642. Colonel Townesend resided there while Castle Townsend was building. It was a stately building, environed with a large bawn, and fortified with turrets on the top [3].

Philip entered Trinity College, Dublin, 1684 [4]. He was a captain of horse in King William's army, and afterwards took holy orders. He was Prebendary of Liscleary (Cork), Rector and Vicar of Aghingh (Cloyne), and Vicar of Christchurch (Cork). This latter preferment he held from 1707 till his death. He was

[1] Chap. v.      [2] See Barrymore history, Table II.
[3] Smith's *Hist. Co. Cork.*      [4] Brady's *Records*, i, 112.

executor to his father's will, 1692, and claimed land from Domenic Copinger, on behalf of his nephew Richard, in 1684. He married, about 1708, Helena, daughter of John Galway, who died of consumption in 1711. Philip died in 1735, and was buried in Christchurch, Cork, May 26.

## TABLE VII.

### SIXTH SON OF COLONEL TOWNESEND.

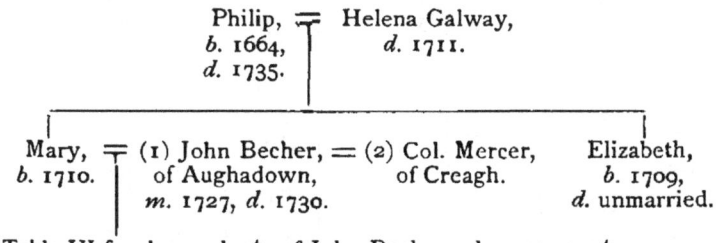

Philip, = Helena Galway,
b. 1664, d. 1711.
d. 1735.

| Mary, = (1) John Becher, = (2) Col. Mercer, | Elizabeth, |
| b. 1710. of Aughadown, of Creagh. | b. 1709, |
| m. 1727, d. 1730. | d. unmarried. |

(*See* Table VI for descendants of John Becher who represent Philip Townesend.)

His daughter Mary married, as her first husband[1], John Becher of Aughadown, who died in 1738, when Samuel Townsend of Whitehall was made guardian of young Thomas Becher, Elizabeth, widow of Richard Townsend of Castle Townsend, being guardian of the other children. The descendants of Mary Becher now represent Philip Townsend's line.

### NOTES ON TABLE VIII.

Tradition says that Cornelius Townsend was born in 1666 in the mansion of an Irish chieftain who had sheltered Mrs. Townesend during the disturbances of that year, and after whom the infant was named Cornelius.

This story is firmly believed in the family, having

[1] Both Philip Townsend and John Becher settled considerable estates on this marriage. Reg. Deed, August 19, 1727.

## TABLE VIII.

### EIGHTH SON OF COLONEL TOWNESEND.

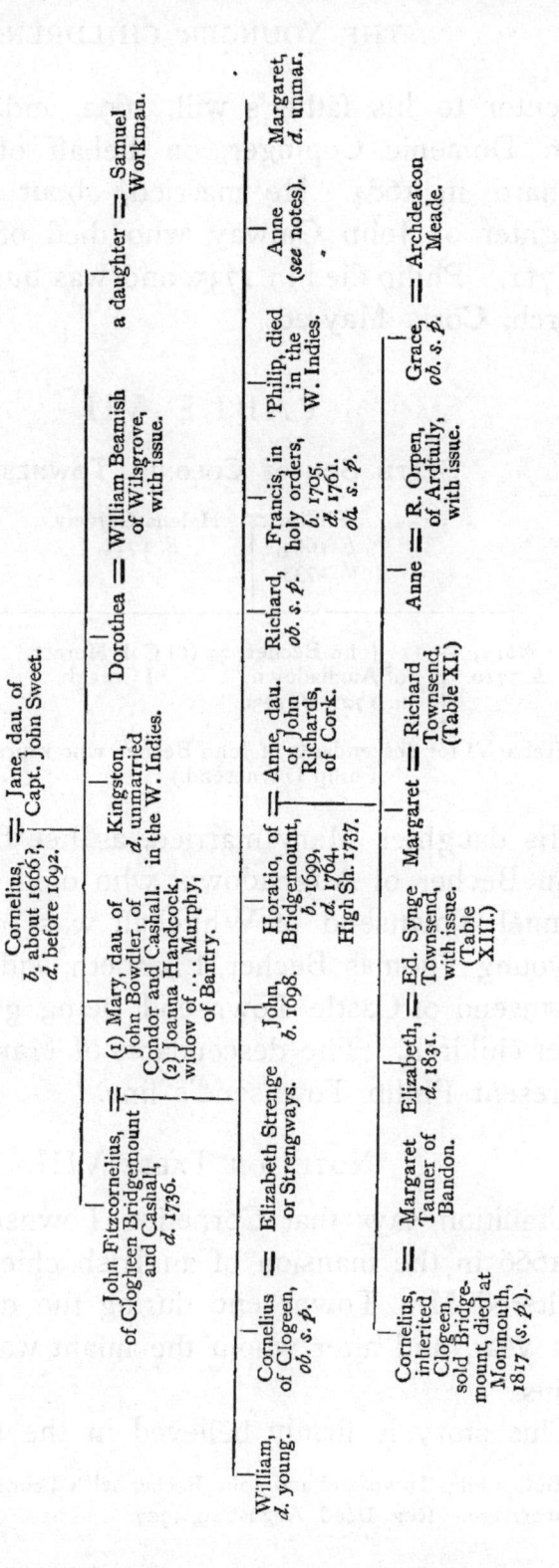

Cornelius, b. about 1666?, d. before 1692. = Jane, dau. of Capt. John Sweet.

Children:

- **John Fitzcornelius,** of Clogheen Bridgemount and Cashall, d. 1736. = (1) Mary, dau. of John Bowdler, of Condor and Cashall. (2) Joanna Handcock, widow of ... Murphy, of Bantry.
- **Kingston,** d. unmarried in the W. Indies.
- **Dorothea** = William Beamish of Wilsgrove, with issue.
- **a daughter** = Samuel Workman.

Children of John Fitzcornelius:

- **William,** d. young.
- **Cornelius,** of Clogeen, ob. s. p. = Elizabeth Strenge or Strengways.
- **John,** b. 1698.
- **Horatio,** of Bridgemount, b. 1699, d. 1764. High Sh. 1737. = Anne, dau. of John Richards, of Cork.
- **Richard,** ob. s. p.
- **Francis,** in holy orders, b. 1705, d. 1761. ob. s. p.
- **Philip,** died in the W. Indies.
- **Anne** (see notes).
- **Margaret,** d. unmar.

Children of Horatio:

- **Cornelius,** inherited Clogeen, sold Bridgemount, died at Monmouth, 1817 (s. p.). = Margaret Tanner of Bandon.
- **Elizabeth,** d. 1831.
- **Margaret** = Richard Townsend. (Table XI.)
- **Anne** = R. Orpen, of Ardtully, with issue.
- **Grace,** ob. s. p.
- = Ed. Synge Townsend, with issue (Table XIII.)
- = Archdeacon Meade.

been handed down by John Sealy Townsend, Master in Chancery, whose father, Dr. Richard Townsend of Derry, was born only forty years after the death of Cornelius; and Judge Fitz-Henry Townshend heard it in 1828 from his aunt, Catherine Helena Townshend. But there must be some confusion about the dates, unless there was an earlier Cornelius Townsend belonging to some other family, for on the Council-book of Clonakilty 'Cornelius Tounsend' is entered as present at a meeting in 1675, and as elected sovereign in 1676, when the subject of this memoir should only have been ten years old. He married Jane, daughter of Captain John Sweet[1], one of the officers who served the king before 1649, or ''49 officers' as they were called. It is curious to see how quickly the memories of the civil wars faded, and how Colonel Townesend's children married into the opposite party.

When Cornelius married, his father settled on him the land of Kilcrane, mortgaged to him by the Earl of Barrymore. Cornelius died young, and during the minority of his son there was a lawsuit instituted concerning this land against the O'Heas and Daniel McCarthie Reagh.

One of the sons of Cornelius Townshend died unmarried in the West Indies; the elder, John Fitz-Cornelius, married twice.

First, Margaret, daughter of Captain William Bowdler of Condor, Salop, who bore as his arms three Cornish choughs on a silver shield. He was a captain in Cromwell's Irish army, and acquired lands in County Cork in the neighbourhood of Rosscarbery. In his

[1] Colonel R. Townesend was overseer of the will of John Sweet of Mohanah, Barony Ibaune, 1676.

will[1], dated 1706, he leaves the estate of Cashall, Dunscullige, Dromullihy and Kilbogg to the eldest surviving son of his late daughter Margaret. Failing her descendants, the lands were to go to his nephew, W. Bowdler of Longnor, in the parish of Condor. To each of his granddaughters he leaves the sum of fourscore pounds on her attaining the age of eighteen. His will makes no mention of his other daughter, Joyce, who was married to the Quaker Captain Morris, but Captain Morris is one of the executors, and the burial is ordered to take place in Castle Salem burying-ground.

John Fitz-Cornelius bought the estate of Bridgemount, situated in a wild and rugged country between Macroom and Milstreet[2], and he also resided much at his wife's estate of Cashall.

His second wife was Joanna, daughter of Mr. Hancock and widow of Thomas Murphy of Bantry. A Chancery suit, December 7th, 1724, shows that she had a fortune of about £2000.

John Fitz-Cornelius died in 1736 and was buried in Ross Cathedral. He left no children by his second wife. His fourth son, Horatio, eventually became head of this branch of the family, and married Anne Richards. An amusing letter which he wrote to his wife from London is still in existence:—

*To Mrs. Anne Townsend to be left at Mr. John Baily's in Queen Street, Dublin.*

MY DEAREST LIFE,   *May 24, 1733.*

I am heartily sorry to hear by Frank Price's of the 15th inst. to me, you are indisposed with that confounded dis-

---
[1] Now in the possession of the Rev. Ed. Mansell Townshend.
[2] *Statist. Surv.*, II. 158.

temper, and whether by sympathy or other I am just in the same state. . . . My life, it would be endless for me to undertake giving you a history of my voyage and journey, this much may suffice that I was seven days and nights I did not put off one screed, and all that owing to the number of passengers of whom there were about a hundred. . . .

I am my dearest Life and Soule
Yours for ever and ever,
HORATIO TOWNSHEND.

It is said that many of the Romanist gentry, thrown back to an idle and obscure life by the penal laws, fell into lawless habits, and the English Protestants who lived among them became too often assimilated to their neighbours[1]. One of the most terribly common crimes was the abduction of Protestant ladies: and such was the sad fate of Horatio Townshend's sister Anne. Her step-mother's son, Thomas Murphy, was determined to obtain possession of her, and carrying her off, he kept her imprisoned in a cave in a lonely part of the country, till she consented to become his wife. Her family searched for her in vain. At last her youngest brother, Philip, came on some of the Murphy family, and drawing his pistol, threatened to fire if they did not disclose Anne's place of concealment. One of the women seized his arm, the pistol went off, Murphy's brother fell, and Philip, believing that he was a murderer, fled. This new misfortune seems to have ended the pursuit. Thomas married the luckless Anne, the wounded man recovered, and in a thoroughly Irish fashion the innocent Philip was the most afraid of the consequences. Nothing could be heard of him, and at last his friends wrote to enquire of their uncle Kingston in Barbadoes, to ask

[1] *Hist. Kingdom of Ireland*, Walpole, 372.

if he knew anything of the fugitive. After awhile the letter was answered by Philip himself from that island, and saying he was in such distress as to be tempted to return and take his chance of a trial. He however remained in Barbadoes, and died there unmarried. In 1739 he signed a paper appointing his loving brothers Cornelius and Horatio his 'Atturnies' to manage any money he might receive at his father's death. It is witnessed by his great-uncle Kingston. Poor Anne had one daughter, Catherine, who seems to have inherited her father's disposition, for she eloped with her uncle's butler, Thomas Bennett of Bridgmount, and selected for the performance the year that her uncle was High Sheriff!

Cornelius, the only surviving son of Horatio Townshend, sold the estates of Bridgemount, having lost much money in attempted agricultural improvements. He died in England, leaving no children. Arthur Young in his *Tour in Ireland*, 1776–1779, mentions that about 1768 Cornelius Townsend, Esq., at Brokham (probably a mistake for Bridgemount) 'fixed two Sussex farmers to improve a stony mountain. These men, Messrs. Crampe and Johnson, bought very fine horses and brought over all their implements at great expense. Mr. Townsend built the most handsome houses, barns, &c., for them. The land was so stony that £100 was spent in clearing one field of eight acres. The men were ruined, and Mr. Townsend suffered considerably. To persist in improving such a spot was inexcusable in point of prudence, and the sure way to bring ridicule on English husbandry. Planting is the only proper improvement for such land.'

It is said that some of Cornelius Townshend's land is now included in the estate of Lisselan; and the

## THE YOUNGER CHILDREN.

remains of some farm buildings are still known as Townshend's Folly.

With Cornelius ended in the male line the descendants of Colonel Richard Townesend's eighth son.

His four sisters married, and two of them left children: Anne, who married, 1766, Richard Orpen of Ardtully, Co. Kerry (see Burke's *Landed Gentry*), and Elizabeth, who married, also in 1766, the Rev. Edward Synge Townsend, Rector of Clondrohid near Macroom; she died at Kinsale, April 12, 1831, aged 89. For her descendants, see Table XIII.

### DAUGHTERS OF COLONEL RICHARD TOWNESEND.

An account has already been given[1] of one of Colonel Townesend's daughters, Catherine Gun. One, whose name has not been preserved, married John, son of Colonel Henry Owen and Margaret daughter of Sir William Piers of West Meath. Colonel Owen settled in Baltimore about 1650, and was cousin to the Lieutenant-Colonel Arnop mentioned by Orrery when raising the Militia in 1660. John Owen leaving no children, the estates passed to his sister Margaret, who married Henry Becher of Aughadown, of a family which intermarried so frequently with the Townshends that a sketch of it is inserted after Table VI. Another daughter, Mary, is believed to have married an Irish chieftain; and a third, Dorothea, married Domenic Copinger. The Coppinger or Copinger family came from Denmark as early as the tenth century. Sir Walter Copinger was settled at Baltimore shortly before its destruction by the Algerian pirates, but having quarrelled with the famous Fineen O'Driscoll left, and determined to build

[1] Chapter v.

a finer town for himself on the little Rowry River near Glandore, which he proposed to convert into a canal. He raised the walls of a splendid mansion there, but the rebellion of 1641 put an end to his projects, and only the ruins of Copinger's Court remain. He is said to have been a cruel and tyrannical lord to the peasantry, who still tell many legends about him, and show a beam projecting from the wall of the mansion which is said to have been used for a gallows. His grandson was also named Walter, and had a son Domenic, who married Dorothea Townesend. Domenic was a Romanist, seated at Rincolisky; he died before the Protestant ascendency was re-established; his will is dated May 8, 1688. In it he leaves his father sole guardian of his son James, and in consideration of a debt of sixty pounds, also leaves him his 'peanted brass beds, bedstead, linen and other household stuff, his sorle horse, watch and pistols.' The only mention of his wife is that she is to see the doctor paid, and give him the grey mare. Letters of administration are dated October 6, 1693. Old Walter and his second son were outlawed by William III for high treason in 1691, and so was young James. He petitioned the Chichester House Commissioners, in whom were vested all estates forfeited for high treason in 1700, but in vain; the lands of Copinger's Court, Clogan Castle, Rincolisky and Lissapole were lost for ever. This was the only branch of the Copingers that did not ultimately get back a great proportion of their estates. Domenic and Dorothea had three children, Mary, Walter, and James of Lissapole. The latter married Ann Youd of Cork, 1718, and had a son John, who settled in Brittany and then in Cornwall. This branch is now represented by W. A. Copinger, Esq., of the Priory, Manchester, and Tynycoed Tower, Merioneth, author of the History of the Copinger family, whom I have to thank for the above information. Domenic Copinger leased land to Francis Townesend, and in 1684 Philip made a claim on it for his nephew Richard. Francis also signed a bond for Domenic's debts. Domenic leased land to 'one Brian Townsend' for £80 per annum for a term of thirty-one years, and Bryan's son Samuel eventually became owner of estates at Rincolisky, where he built Whitehall.

# CHAPTER IX.

SKIRTAGH HOUSE, AND NOTES ON MORRIS.

(Table IX.)

### NOTES ON TABLE IX.

*By the Hon. Judge John Fitz-Henry Townshend, LL.D., D.L.C.*

JOHN TOWNSHEND of Skirtagh was born May 26, 1696. He was called to the Irish Bar, but did not, I think, practise long at it. He married Katherine, daughter of Colonel James Barry of Rathcormac, as already mentioned (Table III), and died before February, 1750. I never heard anything of the personal appearance or character of John Townshend of Skirtagh. His wife died December 20, 1754. They left three sons and four daughters; one other son died young.

Their eldest son, the Rev. Richard Townshend, became Rector and Vicar of Schull, diocese of Cork, November 1, 1780[1]. He had been ordained April 29, 1753, and held different clerical offices in the United Diocese of Cork and Ross. He married Susan, daughter of Colonel Alexander Gay; she was widow of Thomas Wheatley, of Bristol. Her father Colonel Gay had married Elizabeth, only daughter of James Fitzgerald, Esq., and Elizabeth, daughter of Redmond Barry of Rathcormac and Mary Boyle (see notes, Table III). The

[1] Brady, *Records*, I. 246.

| John Towneser
  b. May 26, |

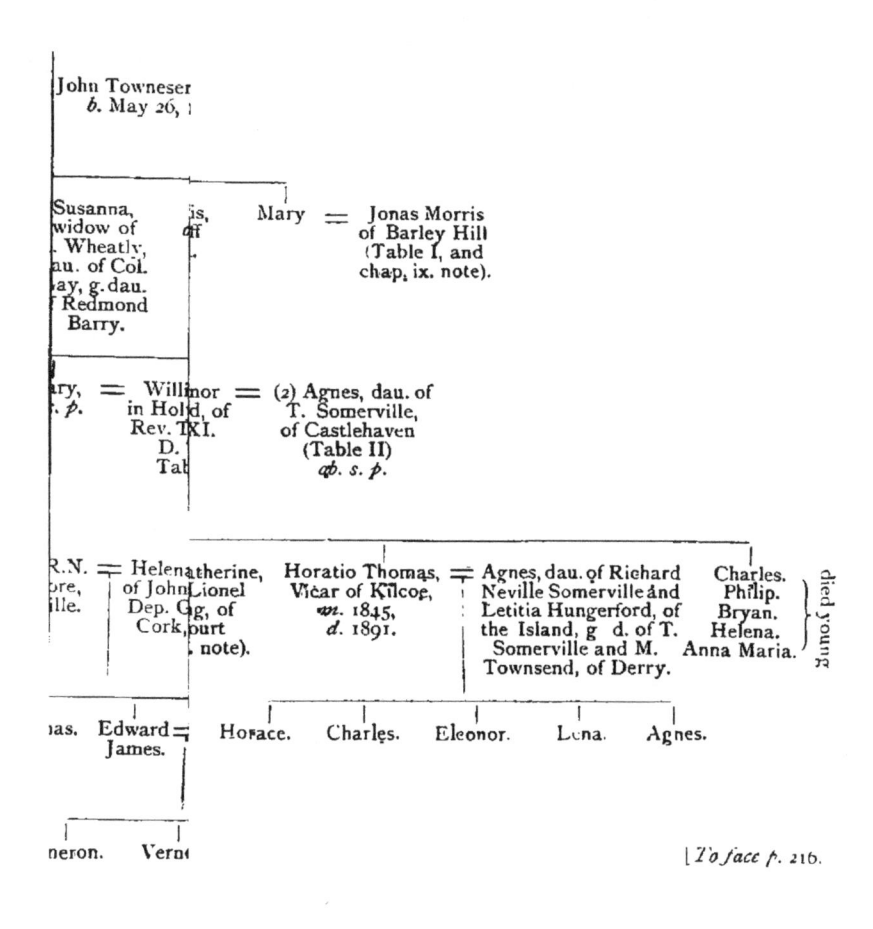

| Susanna, | is, | Mary | = | Jonas Morris |
| widow of | of | | | of Barley Hill |
| . Wheatly, | | | | (Table I, and |
| au. of Col. | | | | chap. ix. note). |
| ay, g. dau. |
| f Redmond |
| Barry. |

ry, = Willinor = (2) Agnes, dau. of
. p.   in Hold, of    T. Somerville,
       Rev. T. I.     of Castlehaven
       D.             (Table II)
       Tab            *ob. s. p.*

R.N. = Helen atherine, Horatio Thomas, = Agnes, dau. of Richard   Charles.  } died young
ore,   of John Lionel  Vicar of Kilcoe,   Neville Somerville and   Philip.   }
lle.   Dep. Gg, of     m. 1845,           Letitia Hungerford, of   Bryan.    }
       Cork, ourt      d. 1891.           the Island, g d. of T.   Helena.   }
       . note).                           Somerville and M.        Anna Maria.}
                                          Townsend, of Derry.

ias.  Edward = Horace.  Charles.  Eleonor.  Luna.  Agnes.
      James.

neron.  Verne                                      [*To face p.* 216.

Rev. Richard Townshend died May 17, 1793, leaving no children [1].

Their second son, John Townshend, of Court Macsherry, Co. Cork, married Elizabeth, daughter of Colonel Reddish, of London; they had issue (besides a son James Townshend, who was called to the Bar, but died unmarried) two sons, John and Richard, and three daughters, Barbara, Dorothea, and Mary. The elder son John took orders April 23, 1775 [1], and next year became Curate of the Island, and from 1788 to 1791 was Curate of Marmullane. He married Martha, daughter of Carré Williams, of Ashgrove, Cork, Esq., by whom he had a daughter Martha, who married Carré-Columbine Williams, of the City of Cork, Esq. His arms, as given by Major Edward Townshend, were Sable, a lion rampant argent.

The second son of John Townshend and Elizabeth Reddish married Dorothea, daughter of the Rev. Thomas Robinson of Coronea, a nice house near Skibbereen. These Robinsons claimed to be of the Rokeby family, and used the same arms. One of the Rokeby family was Primate of Ireland, which circumstance may have brought over some of his Robinson relatives to eat of the crumbs which fell from his Grace's table. The Robinsons intermarried several times with the Whitehall branch of the Townshend family.

The eldest son of Richard Townshend and Dorothea Robinson was John; he was ordained in 1807, married Alicia, daughter of Sir Robert Warren of Crokestown, and had issue a son Richard, who married Miss Wilkinson and went to America with the family after the famine of 1846. I heard that he and they all perished

[1] Brady, *Records*, I. 246.

of fever, but Dr. Edward Townshend informs me that a son of this Richard has called on him in Cork.

On the death of the last Earl of Barrymore, the heir-general of that family was to be sought in the female descendants of Richard second Earl of Barrymore. It seems to me that Richard Townshend who married Miss Wilkinson was representative of one of the co-heirs of that nobleman, and was entitled to quarter the arms of Barry.

I now go to Thomas, younger brother of the Rev. John Townshend. He was in the navy, and had the rank of Commander at his death. A worthy honest gentleman, he had seen a good deal of service in the Baltic. He married Helena, daughter of John Freke of Baltimore, Esq., and died April 28, 1848, much regretted. He had lived for many years at Smithville, near Castle Townshend, and was buried at the old burial-place south of Skibbereen. Mr. John Freke was a trusted friend of the late Lord Carbery, agent to Lord Carbery's estate in North Carbery, and Deputy Governor of the County Cork during the rebellion of 1798[1]. Richard, the eldest son of Captain Thomas Townshend, obtained a fellowship in Trinity College, Dublin, and was ordained in 1860. He married Miss Barrett, a first cousin of his mother, and had no issue. He is described as a 'splendid-looking man, one of the first mathematicians of his day, one of the kindest and most agreeable of men, and a model of what a Tutor and Professor should be.' A mathematical exhibition has been founded in his memory at Trinity College, Dublin[2].

The second son of Captain T. Townshend was James, of Baltimore, who married Mary, daughter of Samuel

---

[1] Mrs. Pierrepont Mundy.
[2] The Very Rev. the Dean of Cloyne.

Townshend of Derreny, second son of Samuel Townshend of Whitehall.

One of the remaining brothers went to Australia, and another to America, and became a County Court Judge in California.

I return to the third son of John Townshend of Skirtagh—Philip, who married Mary Delap of Londonderry. Their eldest son, Richard of Cononagh, was a Doctor of Medicine. His first wife was Helena, daughter of Richard Hungerford of Cahirmore; she died without issue. His second wife was a daughter of Francis Jennison, of Union Hall, a member of a respectable family. These Jennisons were connected with the family of Morris of Benduff, but have since decayed. Mr. Francis Jennison of Castle Townshend married a daughter of William Morris of Benduff. He had a daughter married to Mr. Potter, proprietor of the *West Cork Eagle*, and a son and two daughters unmarried.

Richard Townshend of Cononagh had two sons, both of whom died unmarried. The elder was the only descendant of Bryan Townshend[1] I ever heard of who was named after him. This unfortunate gentleman led a life of poverty and obscurity, and in his latter days was mainly supported by the humanity of my brother-in-law, the late Charles Armstrong, M.D. He died at Crookhaven, 1868. His sister Elizabeth married Edward Morris, son of William Morris of Benduff Castle, whose mother was Barbara Jennison. A further record of the Morris family will be found in the note to this chapter.

[1] A son of Commissioner John Townshend was also named Bryan, and died of consumption, see page 222 and chapter vi. on the disuse of the name Bryan.

[1] The second son of Philip Townshend and Mary Delap was John, born in 1764. He entered the navy about 1778, and saw much active service during the stirring times of the great French War. He was in the fleet which, under Admiral Rodney, pursued the French to the West Indies, and was under Elliot at the defence of Gibraltar, and at the taking of a rich prize returning home from South America. Promotion was quick in those days for young men of spirit, and at twenty years of age John Townshend was commanding the Bush revenue cutter. His little vessel was anchored at Kingstown, and he was entertaining a party of friends at dinner in the cabin, when a signal was sent up from the Bailie Lighthouse at Howth that a French privateer was in sight. Orders were instantly given to man the boats and put the guests ashore; but before this could be done a second signal shot up. Townshend refused to delay a minute longer: in vain did the guests beg him to wait; they were hurried to sea by their impetuous host with the prospect of a livelier form of entertainment than that to which they had been invited.

One of the visitors was his brother-in-law Thomas, who told the story afterwards to John Sealy Townshend. 'My God, John!' he said, 'as the danger grew greater he only grew the bolder.' The Bush overhauled the French vessel, and grappling to her, boarded and took her, after a hard fight. Commander Townshend received the French captain's sword, and conveyed his prize and his visitors in safety to Kingstown. For this service he received a substantial reward in prize-money.

[1] This portion of the chapter is from notes by Mrs. Edward Townshend, grand-daughter of John Townshend.

When the French fleet anchored in Bantry Bay in 1798, and the news was brought in haste to Cork, not a ship of all those lying there would put to sea to carry the tidings to England; no one dared face the gale which wrecked and scattered the French fleet, till John Townshend volunteered. Those who saw him set sail in the teeth of that north-easter never expected to see him again; but he beat across to Bristol in safety, and received a letter of thanks from the Admiralty for the delivery of such important despatches. His gallant little vessel met her end in Galway Bay; she struck on some rocks in a fearful snowstorm at nine o'clock in the evening. She partially sank, and then remained jammed with the masts above water, and the sailors took refuge in the rigging. In the hurry and darkness a little cabin boy was left behind, but the Commander went back for him and found him, and wrapping him in his own coat carried him up the mast and held him in his arms through the terrible night. But when the day dawned he found he was only holding the little body, the terrible cold had killed the boy. John Townshend often spoke of the sorrow of that day-break.

Among other things that were thrown over to lighten the vessel was a box of books, which were afterwards recovered, among others a great Bible, in which John Townshend entered the names of all his children on the water-stained fly-leaf.

He next commanded the Minerva of seventy men. There are many stories preserved of his hand-to-hand fights when boarding ships, and of the sinking of the Ville de Paris, for John Townshend was a man of iron nerve and splendid physique. On account of his fine sight he was frequently chosen for night duty, but the strain of constantly using a night-glass injured his eyes, and he was obliged to retire comparatively early from the service. He then settled in Clonakilty, Co. Cork, and became Recorder of the town. When he was over eighty the authorities assumed that he must be dead, and as he did not receive his pension as usual, he applied for its continuance. He received a letter of apology from Sir Robert Peel himself, couched in the most complimentary terms, thanking him for his services during his naval career, and assuring him such a mistake should not occur again; and the veteran did live to receive it for several years after.

When a young man John Townshend had adopted the infidel opinions that were common at the time, becoming a total unbeliever in the existence of any spiritual world, or of any survival of the soul after death. This was his state of mind when his wife died of typhus fever in 1817. His grand-daughter tells the following occurrence, which has never been questioned by his descendants:—

'A year after his wife's death, on a bright summer evening, Commander Townshend was standing at his open hall door when he perceived a lady dressed in white coming across the grass towards the house. Remembering that there was to be a ball in the town that evening he paid no attention to the circumstance until she had advanced to within a couple of yards of him, when looking in her face he recognised his lost wife. As she continued to advance he walked backwards with his eyes fixed on her, until in this way they had reached the foot of the staircase. John Townshend walked past it, but when she reached it, she ascended it to the drawing room. In that room were sitting her eldest surviving son Richard Boyle Townshend, who was studying for his examinations in Trinity College, Dublin, and a younger brother Brian, who was also reading: he was in bad health, and died of consumption not long after. Richard afterwards said he heard on the stairs outside the drawing-room door, which was slightly ajar, a noise like the rustling of wings. Thinking some of the fowl had escaped from the yard and had got into the house he raised his eyes from his book and looked towards the door, when he saw a lady in white entering. His first thought was how could she manage to pass through such a small opening. He then looked at her face and recognised his mother. He was about to exclaim and touch his brother's arm, but remembering his bad health, he was afraid of the shock to him, and remained perfectly quiet, gazing at the visitor. She advanced into the room, where she remained a few minutes, he thought, and then returned to the door and passed out, as she had entered, through the narrow opening. It is said that a number of workmen who were waiting in a room of the hall, to be paid their wages, as it was Saturday evening, saw and recognised her, both when going upstairs and when she returned and went out at the hall door.'

From that time Commander Townshend's religious opinions underwent a complete change, so that his relations and friends believed that it was for this object that she was permitted to return and appear to him.

John and Eleanor Townshend had been married on the 9th of February, 1788. He died the 5th of March, 1849.

The eldest of their sons who lived to grow up was Richard Boyle, born January 27, 1795. He entered the Church, and became Rector of Abbeystrewry. He was a most saintly man, devoted to the care of his poor. During the potato famine of 1847 he was examined before Parliament on the causes of the distress, and went through England collecting subscriptions for the sufferers. Lord Dufferin[1] described visiting Skibbereen at that time and finding Mrs. Townshend sewing shrouds, with two maidservants lying dead of typhus in

[1] *From Oxford to Skibbereen.* By Lord Dufferin and the Hon. G. T. Boyle.

the house. Richard Boyle Townshend established a temporary hospital in Skibbereen, and worked night and day among his people, till he caught the famine fever and literally died for those he was helping. All classes and creeds loved him, and mourned for him, and he was followed forty miles to his grave by several Roman Catholic priests at the head of their flocks.

His second brother was John Sealy, who became a barrister in Dublin. He was born June 25, 1805, and died April 27, 1883. He, like his brother, was deeply religious; he was also a man of most studious tastes and habits, employing his leisure hours in accumulating stores of information on all imaginable subjects, religious, scientific, or historical.

The greater part of our information about Colonel Richard Townesend is due to the industry of John Sealy Townshend, who left elaborate manuscript notes on his life. His legal knowledge and accuracy and experience in weighing evidence of course made him a most valuable authority on the subject.

He took a great interest in the study of the evidences of Christianity. A story goes, that he once by chance entered an infidel lecture-hall in London, and after listening to the speaker for a short time, was unable to stand the nonsense he heard, and hissed. The audience got excited, and carried him bodily up on the platform to argue the matter out. Nothing could have pleased John Sealy better, though he said he was never so astounded as at the position he found himself in, but the poor lecturer had not suspected that he would have to do with a student at the Bar; he soon found himself no match for John Sealy, either in learning or in logical power, and was fairly argued down, so he covered his retreat by promising to meet him again the following week and entirely confute him. The audience had been so well entertained that they chaired the victor round the room, and all assembled to hear the end of the debate the next week. John Sealy had spent the intervening time in making notes for his discussion at the British Museum, but the lecturer had had enough of it and never came back to meet his Irish opponent.

These very notes formed the basis of a pamphlet which John Sealy afterwards published against Bishop Colenso's views on the Pentateuch, which the *Saturday Review*, among others, said was one of the best answers written. He married Judith, daughter of Becher Fleming of New Court[1] and his wife Judith Somerville. He left one daughter, Judith, married in 1864 to Edward Townshend, now (1891) Professor of Engineering and Register of Queen's College, Galway[2]. Their eldest son Edwin entered Trinity College, Dublin, in 1885, B.A. in 1889. The second, John, obtained an entrance exhibition to Dublin University and a mathematical scholarship, and also at his degree examination he gained the first moderatorship in mathematics and second in experimental physics, thus gaining a studentship. He also gained two gold medals.

There is a story told of a clergyman belonging to this branch of the Townshend family—although which particular member he was is not said. It was in the last century, when clergymen wore gowns as their ordinary dress, and Mr. Townshend was riding home one evening when a man insulted him. Mr. Townshend sprang from his horse, and throwing down his gown, he cried, 'Lie thou there, Divinity, till I make thine

---
[1] See Note A, on Fleming family, Chap. xi.
[2] See Table XIII, Chapter xii.

enemies thy footstool,' and then knocked the man down.

## NOTE A, ON MORRIS OF BENDUFF.

This family have intermarried so frequently with that of Townshend, that some account of their mansion and pedigree will not be out of place.

Benduff or Castle Salem was a Norman fortress situated in a secluded valley about a mile from Rosscarbery. Some say it was built by the O'Donovan family, others that Katherine, daughter of the eighth Earl of Desmond, founded the castle of the 'Black Peak,' and still haunts it as the 'Black Lady.' The building was one of great strength, with walls eleven feet thick, and was surrounded by a beautiful oak wood and a large deer-park, whose ruined walls are still visible. The pleasure-grounds were laid out in the old Dutch style, with ponds and little islands and clipped yew-trees, and so sheltered was the situation that fig-trees flourished in the open air.

Dr. Donovan[1] says the first of the Morris family who owned Benduff was Major Apollo Morris, an officer in Cromwell's army. He obtained a grant of the estate, and on the Restoration was fortunate enough to have the grant confirmed through the interest of a relative who was private secretary to the king.

A portrait of Cromwell was preserved at Benduff,— a stern figure in complete armour, but bareheaded.

The genealogist, Mr. D. O'C. Fisher, gave a pedigree to Judge Townshend, which calls Cromwell's officer

[1] *Sketches in Carbery*, D. Donovan, M.D., p. 213.

Captain William Morris. He married Joyce, daughter and co-heir of his fellow-soldier, Captain John Bowdler of Condor. Her sister Mary was wife of John Fitz-Cornelius Townshend. Captain Morris became a quaker in 1675, and died 1680, leaving a son, Fortunatus, who married, 1682, Elizabeth Morris. The names of her parents are not given, but her arms are the same as those of Morris of Benduff. William Morris, the son of Fortunatus, was an intimate friend and correspondent of William Penn. He married Dorothy Leckey of Ballyhealy, whose family still exists in County Carlow. He became a member of the Church of England, and his descendants continued to belong to it. But the ancient quaker burying-ground is still shown at Benduff, and the simple graves, with plain head and foot-stones, facing north and south, which the 'Friends' used to make, no monuments being allowed by that sect. Around the graveyard is a grove of laurel-trees, so large that an old established colony of rooks live in them. It was such a favourite place of burial that even from Cork the Quakers brought their dead to lie under the shade of the old castle. But when William Morris died, and a very simple rude tomb was erected to his memory, the Quakers were so shocked at this breach of their customs that they never buried in that ground again.

The sons of William Morris, William and Jonas, married daughters of John Townshend of Skirtagh[1]. Jonas Morris had a son Abraham, whose fine house and grounds at Dunkettle are described in the Statistical Survey of Co. Cork. He married Thomasine, daughter of W. Connor of Connorsville, and had a daughter, Catherine, who married Horatio Townshend

---

[1] Table IX, Chapter ix, see also p. 219.

(Table XIII). All the family papers were preserved at Benduff till the late William Morris placed them in the hands of a bookseller in Cork with a view to publication. The bookseller failed, and the papers were lost[1]

[1] *Carbery Sketches*, Donovan.

SAMUEL TOWNSHEND, OF WHITEHALL
*Born 1689 or 1692*

# CHAPTER X.

### WHITEHALL HOUSE.

### (Table X.)

SAMUEL, fifth son of Bryan Townsend, settled at Rincolisky on Roaring Water Bay. The remains of the fortified wall that surrounded his house, Whitehall, still stand there, looking over the lonely bay towards Cape Clear. Above on the heights are the remains of a castle built by the O'Driscolls[1] when they were lords of the country, and that passed from their hands into those of the Copingers, for Rincolisky was one of the estates forfeited in 1690 by the unlucky young James Copinger, Colonel Townesend's Roman Catholic grandson.

As in many other old houses there is a story of an underground passage, which is said to connect Whitehall with the ruined castle. There is also a legend that when one of the family tried to explore it, his two negro servant boys ran eagerly on in front and were lost in the darkness. The rest of the party found the passage grow more and more stifling, and shouted to the boys to come back, but in vain. They were not answered and, overpowered by the foul air, they hurried back to the entrance and the boys were never seen again. So after that the passage was closed up.

[1] Smith's *Hist. Co. Cork.*

Samuel Townshend was born Sept. 23, 1689 or 1692[1]. He became a freeman of Clonakilty, 1717, High Sheriff, 1742, and died 1759. He married Dorothea, daughter of Sir Edward Mansell of Iscoed, Carmarthen, Bart. The Mansell family came to England at the Conquest, and from them descended Sir Rhys Mansell, who died 1589. He was father to Sir Edward who married Anne, daughter of Henry Earl of Dorchester, and by her had Sir Frances Mansel, created Baronet in 1621, who married Catherine, daughter and co-heir of Henry Morgan of Muddlescombe. Their son, Sir Anthony, fell at Newbury fighting on the Royalist side, and was father to the Sir Edward Mansell first mentioned.

What strange memories must have haunted that lonely house of Whitehall, among its wind-swept trees, when its master, the grandson of a Parliamentarian officer, married to the grand-daughter of a man who died for King Charles, was living on the property forfeited by their kinsman for his fidelity to King James!

Samuel Townshend travelled in Italy, and his miniature painted there makes him look a very Sir Charles Grandison, with large blue eyes and short proud upper lip, very splendid in blue velvet coat and powdered wig. He was a man of taste and culture, and altered his house in the Italian style, adding a handsome double staircase and pilasters painted to imitate marble.

When his third son Samuel was entering the army, Samuel Townshend wrote him the following farewell letter[2], which, it is pleasant to see, the young man preserved with affectionate care.

[1] From a list of Bryan Townshend's children on the blank leaf of *The Christian Pattern*, 1707.
[2] The original still is in the possession of Mrs. John Townshend, widow of Samuel Townshend's great grandson. Table XIII.

My dear Sam,

We are now parting for a time, but I hope we shall have a happy meeting againe and as much satisfaction in it as this world can afford. My anxiety will be great for you, and you will seldom or ever be absent from my thoughts. I know you soe well that I am persuaded your conduct will be as happy and as well as possible, and that your usual sobriety and goodness will ever subsist with you, however as 'tis an ease to my mind at parting to repeat something to you that I have often observed to you before, tho' I am obliged to doe it in a hurry I would not omit it. First then lett your strictest Duty to God be your constant care we can hope for noe Blessing or happyness but through the Almighty. This world is transient and triffling filled with troubles and uncertainty, we must however doe the best we can in it, in the most prudent and virtuous man$^r$. A Blessed Eternity is what we must have the greatest Regard to, and indeed is the only thing worth our anxiety and care.

Next to your Duty to God, that of your Duty to your King and Country you are not to forgett.

Be courteous and obliging to Every Body and never on any passion or hurry in your thoughts or expressions.

Consider seriously in everything you Doe and every steppe you take that you may by that means always act with prudence and Discretion, and not hurry your selfe into anything that may not afterwards answer to your satisfaction.

Be carefull to read dilligently and to gett the best instruction you can in your intended profession. When you think you can read in ye Country I think Captain Gwynne[1] at Upham in Hampshire will be a convenient place where you may be assured of a sincere welcome. Trimsaran[2] I think in ye same way of, but you will have more Company there than at Upham however I would have you use both places as your discretion will Direct you.

Be punctual in your Expenses, but dont want whatever is

---

[1] Captain Gwyn was married to Eliz. daughter of Richard Townshend of Castle Townshend. Table I.

[2] Trimsaran, Sir Edward Mansel's seat, S. Wales.

necessary for a gentleman. You pritty well know my situation and circumstances and that I shall answer your calls while I am able for I begrudge you nothing. You are centred in my heart and from your Conduct and behaviour with virtue Honour and discretion will be placed the greatest Happyness I can have in life. I am Hurryd soe I am forced to conclude. May the Great God always bless and preserve you, and have you in his keeping. Write often, never omitt a month at a time at most.

Be carefull in your Choice of company, keep none that are wicked or wild or of loose bad characters for such bring discredit and lead a man into misfortunes.

Samuel Townshend proved himself worthy of his father's tender anxiety. He entered the army in 1759 in Drogheda's Light Horse, since named the 18th Hussars, then being raised by Charles Earl of Drogheda. He was Aide-de-camp to his Majesty George III during the memorable riots of 1780, and was afterwards Commandant at Chatham and Inspector-General. He married Elizabeth, daughter of a Mr. Aikenhead of Lanark, and widow of Gilbert Ford, Attorney-General of Jamaica, and died at 23 Wimpole Street, in May, 1794. His body was lying in the house when the illuminations took place in honour of Lord Howe's victory of the 1st of June. He was buried in St. Martin's Church. His portrait in full uniform is at Whitehall.

His only daughter, Elizabeth Trelawney[1], was a beautiful and accomplished girl, and being an excellent musician, was often asked to play to King George. General Townshend's elder brother, Edward Mansell, inherited the estates of Whitehall. He was known in the family as 'Splendid Ned.' His portrait is at Whitehall in a brown coat and red waistcoat.

[1] She married Horatio Townshend, Table XIII.

His eldest son, Samuel, is fully described in the following account given by his grandson, Samuel Nugent Townshend. He is also remembered by Judge Townshend as 'an agreeable and accomplished gentleman'; and his kinsman, Horace of Derry, says[1], 'When hounds became a subject of heavy taxation, Samuel Townsend, Esq., of Whitehall, wisely exchanged the pleasures of the chase for those of the garden. This he superintends himself with care as well as *con amore*, and for, I believe, a smaller expense than that of dogs, hunters and their appendages, finds a constant source of very substantial gratification. His grapes in particular exceed any I have seen both in size and flavour.' And in another place is mentioned a sort of seaweed which is an excellent manure for potatoes and found near 'The estate of Samuel Townshend, one of the few gentlemen in that quarter who have paid much attention to agricultural improvement[2].'

## TOWNSENDS, TOWNSHENDS, OR TOWNESENDES OF WHITEHALL.

### *By Samuel Nugent Townshend.*

The Whitehall property having gone in the female line its family monuments and archives, save as recorded in the last edition but one of *Burke's Landed Gentry*[3], appear to have absolutely vanished, and though now the lineal head of the family, I can only afford such information as was verbally given me by my father, who was born in 1800, and was a man of most accurate and

---

[1] *Satist. Surv.*, Co. Cork, ii. 113.  [2] *Statist. Surv.*, Co. Cork, i. 301.
[3] In consequence of the Whitehall Estate having gone in the female line, Burke has now merged that house ancestry in Townshend of Castletownshend. Formerly it was given under its own heading.

detailed memory. Edward, 'Splendid Ned,' his grandfather, was a great horse breeder and agriculturist in his later years. Earlier, viz. from October 15, 1756, as 'Adjutant of Militia Dragoons in the County of Corke,' commanded by Richard Townsend, Esq., he had plenty of work of a non-agricultural nature to attend to, as anyone reading the Irish history of that day can easily enough see. On his eldest son's marriage he assigned Whitehall and all his property to him, reserving a life annuity. This son—my grandfather—Samuel, was early in life sent to Oxford, and thence on the *Grand Tour* regardless of expense, and with the most aristocratic youth of the day. He was naturally gifted, and an accomplished musician. The reverse of his father, he did nothing to improve the estate, and spent much time in England, often in Dublin, always a grand Juror in Cork, and in 1798 High Sheriff of the County. This was the year of the Rebellion, and large quantities of troops and Militia Dragoons were placed at his disposal. These wherever employed were quartered on the inhabitants and ate them into subjection. In his own parish of Aughadown, to avoid the ruin of the tenantry, who were very prosperous, and largely consisted of Cromwellian soldiers' descendants, he, together with the Parish Priest and Protestant Rector, a combination previously unheard of, decided to guarantee the peace of the parish, and at the Priest's request he, the High Sheriff, addressed in the Chapel Yard the Catholic Congregation, and told them of the guarantee.

No troops therefore were quartered in Aughadown, and there was no disturbance there. After the year of my grandfather's Shrievalty expired, Lord Shannon intimated to him that the Lord Lieutenant was willing to knight him. My grandfather, as most country gentlemen then, having a profound contempt for a title almost exclusively given to the Castle tradesmen and City Aldermen, replied with a hidden sarcasm aping humility 'that he was unaware of his having done anything to deserve such an offer from the Irish government.' Passing years did not conquer his taste for London life, and after the Peninsular War he repaired to the metropolis for a long visit, leaving his wife and large family at Whitehall.

Up to this time none of the female heads of the house appear to have been in any way conspicuous, but this Mrs. Townsend, a Miss Baldwin of Curavody, on the first and only occasion she got, certainly was so.

Whitehall was then an old three-storied house, square and utterly unimposing. The rooms were not large, the windows were small, and her ten children probably uncomfortably filled them.

The lady rose to the first occasion on which she probably ever had a chance to assert herself independently of her brilliant and versatile husband. He was well across the seas, and she lost no time in sending for an architect, and with almost magic swiftness there rose to her order a series of noble rooms, forming a new front to the old house, and rendering it quite unrecognisable. Samuel Townsend duly returned home, and his astonishment is said to have been more than paralleled by his disgust at the magnitude of the builder's bills. That bill, £1700, was never paid, and descended as a charge with the unentailed property to the younger branch.

However, Whitehall was now too much of a mansion not to be put to higher social uses than of old, and thither came often the neighbouring Earls of Bantry and Kingston, and Lord Audley, and sometimes the

Earls of Shannon and Bandon, and from time to time potentates from afar off, so that the cost of the mansion as it then stood was as nought to the keeping of it up as it then was. After his wife's death my grandfather decided to retrench somewhat by letting Whitehall to Lord Audley, and go abroad for a season, but this retrenchment was rather a disappointment, for the trip abroad cost more than was anticipated on the one hand, and Lord Audley never paid a penny of rent. Indeed I think his Lordship went into liquidation just as my grandfather returned.

The Whiteboy disturbance was the last thing that brought my grandfather to the front before—after many quiet years of retirement at Whitehall, retirement only broken by the semi-annual grand juries in Cork— he passed away in that city. These Whiteboy outbreaks in his vicinity he however coped with and suppressed with all his old skilful ability. The old parish priest had passed away, and his successor probably could not, if he would, join in any guarantee with the squire and the parson that would effectively protect life and property. The priest, an old St. Omer one, cursed the Whiteboys, and the only effect was that the Whiteboys cursed the priest, so my grandfather, though determined not to have his neighbours' substance eaten up by soldiers, saw that something even stronger than ecclesiastical anathema must be put in force.

He applied to Dublin Castle for permission to raise a troop of Yeomanry Cavalry, and for arms for the troop. The permission promptly came, and with it a Commission appointing my grandfather its Captain-Commandant, and another appointing his second son, my father, Adjutant. The arms, however, were a very long time indeed in arriving. Perpetual patrols at all hours for nearly two years perfectly restored quiet, and the government of the day, like the governments of many a day since and before, thinking that Ireland was at last permanently quiet *disbanded the yeomanry*. A more mischievous and uncalled-for action towards a loyal force in Ireland, that then cost them actually nothing and would have saved the regulars much worry and the exchequer much expense, was never done. My grandfather was thunderstruck and disgusted, but he declined to make any protest, and ordered his tried and trusty men to turn in their arms to him at Whitehall.

Scarcely was it known that the yeomanry were disbanded than the whole condition of the West Riding became so unsettled, that in response to repeated applications to the officer commanding in Cork to send an escort to receive these arms, the only replies were that an escort sufficiently large to be quite safe could not be spared from Bandon. Application was then made to the Admiralty to the same effect, but with no better result. Then it was that my grandfather's eldest son Edward had completed his first racing yacht, the Blonde of 30 tons, and the two elder sons being in a very great state of anxiety in consequence of the ever-recurring rumours of incendiarism and forcible robbery of this large stand of arms from Whitehall, and well knowing their father would risk and lose his life in defence of his trust, petitioned the Admiralty or War Office to permit the shipment to the arsenal at Cove of the arms in the Blonde. Promptly the reply came back that the law prohibited arms being shipped in any vessels other than Her Majesty's ships, and that the Blonde would be confiscated if she attempted to ship any of the arms.

Irritated to the quick by such extraordinary treatment, for these applications extended over years, and stung by new apprehensions of a cruel raid on his father's home, my father as adjutant, in whose legal custody these arms were, called a few of his men together at midnight, and placing the arms in carts, without any undue solemnity, drove them to the Castle cliff and shot them bodily into the Atlantic.

Strangely enough, the War Office never asked a question as to these arms, though my father was quite certain he would be severely punished instead of praised for having adopted the only practicable course to prevent the yeomanry armament from falling into mischievous and disloyal hands. Never probably has a yeomanry cavalry equipment come to such an untimely end. My grandfather was told nothing of the matter then, if ever. His name was one of those on the first list of Deputy Lieutenants appointed in Ireland, but he only survived this appointment [1] three years.

During the latter years of his life his eldest son Edward, although chiefly a bookworm and student, and also a B. N. C. Oxford man, had been designing and building, and my father been racing for him, yacht after yacht, commencing with the Blonde 30 tons, and ending with the Medina 48 tons. These yachts carried my uncle's flag, usually a winning one, all round the British coast, and amongst other valuable prizes a very unique salver, won in the Isle of Man regatta, is now at Whitehall. My uncle however after he had succeeded to the estate again buried himself in his books up to his last days at Whitehall.

Speaking of my Uncle Edward, it might be interesting to note that while the Royal Cork Yacht Club, the oldest in existence, was very badly supported and could

[1] This D. L. Commission is signed by the Earl of Shannon, Feb. 18, 1832.

# CHAPTER XI.

DERRY HOUSE, WITH NOTES ON FLEMING, CORKER,
AND OLIVER.

(Tables XI and XII.)

PHILIP TOWNSEND was born August 5, 1700, and on April 28, 1733, he married Elizabeth, daughter of Thomas Hungerford, of the Island, and Susanna Becher[1]. Mr. Hungerford died early, and his widow was re-married to Sampson Jarvis of Braad, so Philip's wedding took place at Braad Church, whose ruins are still seen above the trees of Myros Wood. The service was read by Philip's favourite brother Horace, who married another of the daughters of Thomas Hungerford, making a double link of affection.

Thomas Hungerford of Inchydony, the Island that lies at the mouth of Clonakilty Bay, was the son of Richard Hungerford, and Mary More, daughter of the Sir Emmanuel More who so narrowly escaped the pains of high treason for being too good a Protestant in 1686[2]. Richard Hungerford's brother Thomas had married Barbara Townshend of Castle Townshend, his first cousin through the Synges. Richard Hungerford was called 'cousin' in the will of John Hungerford of Hungerford in 1729. The family was seated for many generations at Farley Castle in Somerset, and Richard's father had come to Ireland in 1647[3].

[1] See Chapter viii, Table VI.   [2] See Chapter v.   [3] See p. 36.

Susanna Becher, the mother of Captain Philip Townsend's wife, had four gold pieces of Philip and Mary that were dug up on Shirkin Island, near the residence of her father, Colonel Thomas Becher. The coins were handed down in the female line; she left them first to her daughters who married Philip and Horatio Townsend. Elizabeth Townsend left hers to her daughters Susanna French and Mary Somerville. Mary Townsend left hers to her daughters Susan Meade and Mary Newman. Susan Meade having no children bequeathed her piece to her niece Mary Synge Townsend, and from her it passed to her nephew, Major Edward Townsend.

Philip Townsend inherited Derry, Rosscarbery, from his father Bryan (who had bought it in 1686); his youngest son Samuel, who died in infancy, was born there in 1745.

Philip Townsend was captain in General O'Farrel's regiment, the 22nd, during the struggle between England and France for the supremacy in North America.

His regiment embarked at Cork. Captain Townsend took his youngest son, Tom, with him as a volunteer, the eldest, Dick, was studying medicine, and Mrs. Townsend and the younger children were left in the care of Horace Townsend, rector of Coolmona, who had married Mary Hungerford, sister of Philip's wife Elizabeth.

The beautifully written letters from Captain Philip to his brother Horace and his 'dearest dear Bess' have been carefully preserved, but space will only allow of extracts being given; he constantly sends messages to Jack Townsend at Castletown, 'my brother Sam,' Jack Townsend at Mardyke, and Barbara, who seems to have been one of his most regular correspondents.

*To Mrs. Elizabeth Townsend.*

My dearest dear Life,  NEW YORK, *Feb.* 11, 1757.

After a long tedious passage of almost fourteen weeks and a great deal of bad weather we (God be praised) arrived safe Wednesday last, we were separated from our Fleet and indeed ye whole Fleet separated from ye commadore in about a week after we sailed so that no two ships came in together or were at all in company on the passage. There are still five of our ships not arrived, two of which are at Philadelphia and one att Virginia, one of them on board which was German officers and draughts was taken by a french man of war, two of ye German officers volunteering went to France and carried with them 60 of ye draughts. The ship and the Rest were Ransomed for five hundred pounds. The ship was in great distress before she met with ye French man having lost two of her masts and was very laky with four foot of water in her hold. ... One of the ships in which Col. Rollo was, had ye good fortune to take a French ship and retake an English one that had been a long time in the hands of ye French. Those of our regiment that arrived before us are quartered about this place in little vilages as I shall be next week. This town is very large with spacious streets and buildings, but yett it does not seem populous as might be expected from ye space it stands on. Some here tell me it is as large as Cork, but in my apprehension it is not two thirds of Cork. Everything here is very dear but provisions them I think very cheap.

Colonel Rollo has been extremely kind in respect of Tom, before I came here he recommended him to Lord Loudon our Commander in Chief for a pair of colours in our regiment and the better to recommend him told his lordship he carried arms in our regiment, and when he landed to show he did, made him march with a soldier's coat on from the ships to his quarters. So Tom is now a soldier with daily pay and an allowance of provisions daily. He is in very good health and seems now very well pleased tho' he was not so at first. ...

You now will perhaps expect I should tell you some thing of your poor old Pett, at first I was very sick for three or four days, after that I grew better but still sick but I could eat and crawl on deck in a fine day, in this way I continued about a month still growing sicker as the ship altered her manner of sailing, but in five or six weeks I conquered all and have since been in as good health as ever I was in my life, and God be praised I want nothing but returning to my heart's delight again, and I shall never have true comfort or satisfaction until I do. Could I but hear from you I should think myself as happy as I can be at this distance from you, and I trust God as He has delivered me from this very dangerous passage at this season of the year He will also protect and send me safe back to the arms of my dearest dear life, till which I can have no real comfort or satisfaction.'

He adds in a postscript—

Our fresh provisions held out bravely (during the voyage) and better butter I never tasted than that sent me by Horace.

EAST CHESTER, *March* 2, 1757.

... The winter has been severely bad, the inhabitants say they have not for years past had so severe a winter and indeed in ye great frost ye weather was not half so cold as some days I have met with here.... The country here about is as rough almost as ours in respect of stones and hills much like that land about Drimoleague Church. The cattle much such as ye Carbury cattle, ye horses ye same as ye punch nags we formerly had in Ireland but large, and all of them swift pacers. There are variety of animals of ye wild kind but no hares. Rabbitts, Patriges and Quail in good plenty each kind as big again as those of ours. The people in this place are all estated men, Descendants of English and tho' the country is pritty thick inhabited they have not hands for labour, for they are above working for any one but themselves which is a great detriment to them, and if any will stoop as some doe who are reduced they expect ye same treatment as any of ye family and to sitt at ye table. This is the mischief of these small estates as no one here, I mean in this neighbourhood, haveing above 500 acres and some not more than 30 and each wooded tho' not near so well as some other parts of the country. They have no notion of any other manure than dung, no limestone near them. What lime they use for their houses which are mostly wood, is oyster shells which they have in great abundance but very insipid, and not at all like ours in taste. Further inland I am told there is charming fine country as any in ye world, whence they supply New York with cattle and very fine bullocks of about 5 to 7 hundred. The inhabitants about New York are mostly Descendants of Dutch this being originally a Dutch settlement and given in exchange for Surinam. . . . The people seem to me to be in a disponding way from ye many ill successes they have met with which they think owing to corruption, and instead of a bold enterprising people as we always thought them they seem rather indolent and slothful, and though they, every government gives a small number of men each campaigne, yett they goe with unwillingness to defend their own properties. Great complaints are made of Shirley here, of his not marching up to Braddock with his and Pepperil's regiments though Braddock waited a fortnight for him. Dunbarr too is condemned for delaying 10 days with his regiment. These delays they say caused Braddock's misfortune. . . . These are all different governments, and ye currency quite different in every one of them. The money is all Spanish very like English and the piece that passes here only for eight shillings (a dollar) goes for pounds in the next government which I imagine a great detriment to trade besides so many different governments, different laws and customs breeds discontent and great confusion and I think this country will never be happy till it is under one and ye same government or legislature and such a one as we have in Ireland would in my apprehension soon make them a flourishing people who by having a good man for a viceroy would always make them firm to the constitution which I fear many of them are nott at this time. They are so situated that they might with industry (which I think they want greatly) have every necessary of life. They have fruits in abundance in a manner wild, as fine apples as you would wish there are planted, peaches grapes and cherries wild and I am told ye grapes are very luscious but no attempt has ever been to make wine of them, their only drink is cyder and punch which last they drink in ye morning as freely as in Europe in ye afternoon but small. New York is a large town. I believe half or near it of Cork. The houses for the most part timber which makes them subject to fire. . . . There are now ships going with flower to Cork, Dublin, Derry and many parts of Great Britain and it is said there is great scarcity there but I hope its not so bad as is said here, it is too soon to feel such wants. . . . . Direct your letters to be forwarded by Mr. Hugh Wallace merchant in New York, there are four paquet boats going constantly from London to New York.—God bless you all and send me safe to you for I can have no comfort till that happens.

Yr owne<br>P. T.

*To his brother Horatio.*

FORT HEREKHEIMER, *March* 1, 1758.

. . . The highlanders are all arrived. I have not yett seen one of them. I must here tell you a remark ye Indians made when they saw ye first highland regiment which was that they had long lost one of their tribes and were sure this was it for ye Indian dress is something like theirs, they wear stockings and shoes of deerskin, a shirt and a Blankett, no Breeches. . . . I was very uneasy at not hearing from you, and tho' I gave no great credit to dreams, yet I had some of both you and my dear Bess that made me in my retired quarters very melancholy.

I suppose my brother Sam has given you a full account as I desired him of ye melancholy affair here the day or two after I wrote to my Bess lest he has not I will. I am quartered here in a small Frontier Fort on ye Mohock River, this place is called ye German Flats from ye very fine flat land by ye River inhabited by ye descendants of high germans settled here about 55 years ago, about five or six days after I came here a body of French or Indians to ye number of 350 (but till all was over I was informed 800) fell upon the inhabitants of a flat on ye Other side of the River from me, and above a mile and a half above me, burned their houses and Barns, killed twelve of them and carryed away about 100 prisoners and destroyed their stock. It is supposed ye loss amounted to £40,000. All this in my sight without my being able to give the least assistance. . . . On Sunday last was sevenights another small party sett a House and Barn on fire just opposite to me and miserably butchered four young ladds and a girle, ye snow was so deep that we could not get over to them for want of snow shoes, a contrivance to walk without sinking in ye snow. These little rapines and crueltys are ye chief advantage they take, which are considered among ye Indians as very extraordinary exploits.

*To Mrs. Elizabeth Townsend.*

FROM ABOARD THE THORNTON TRANSPORT, NEW YORK, *April* 19, 1758.

. . . I told him of the mischief done by the Indians and more cruel French. I cannot help calling them so, as by all accounts the Indians never used such cruelty untill instructed by them.

. . . I fear (the Indians) are secretly in our enemy's interest as they leave no stone unturned to gain them over. This they doe by large presents but most of all by their missionaries to whom they pay a sort of adoration whilst we almost totally neglect them, they are a people of strong natural parts and make very shrewd remarks upon us and our neglect of religion, and by all I can gather if proper care were taken by sending persons among them to instruct them in ye principals of ye Christian religion which they all profess it would greatly redound to ye English interest. . . .

Poor Tom studies to lessen my expense and avoid every thing that might run him into it so much that I am sometimes obliged to force him among ye young gentlemen of the regiment, all of whom court his company and I think have very good regard for him. He has att last gott a commission and Col. Rollo who is very good to him and to whom I think I am alone obliged for his preferment has appointed him to my company, but while he is youngest Ensign he'll have no pay but this cannot hold long if common justice is done to the regiment.

FROM ABOARD THE THORNTON TRANSPORT, HALIFAX, *May* 2, 1758.

We hear we are to sail at two or three days at furthest for Louisburg, with a fine fleet consisting of 20 sail of the line besides frigates, fire ships, and Bomb ketches, all in high spirits and full of Resentment for ye many cruelties committed by ye French and ye Indians for which this campaigne will I doubt not make them severely suffer. . . . In a former letter I mentioned Lord Loudon being recalled [1] and now can assure you his being recalled is a very great concern to the soldiery here who have ye highest opinion of him, I wish his successors might deserve as well. General Abercromby is a very good man and well liked. He succeeds Lord Loudon here in all his appointments on this side ye water and goes with ye army into ye Heart of ye country, and Brigadere General Forbes with another to ye Ohio. . . . My dearest dear Bess's owne for ever and ever

P. S.

I now write from Hallifax a country abounding in nothing but trees and Indians. As to the bringing my hearts delight here I could never think of it if it was the finest place in the world while we are in this unsettled way. My heart hangs too much after my friends att home to think of it on any account tho' there's no earthly pleasure to me so great as being with my Bess.

Your last paragraph gives me pleasure and uneasiness for why should my dear Bess's dear dear heart so ake. I am I bless God in good health and have been so since I come here except a cough I got last winter in that excessive cold. I find no other disorder than my eyes being so weak that I am at last forced to use spectacles when I read and if the day be dark when I write. This I look upon as caused as much by the sharp smoak of ye wood fires (for ye chimnies are all very smoaky) as from any thing else. · · ·

I long nay I pine after you all and daily pray for a joyful meeting never after to part this side the grave.

[1] By Pitt.

*To his brother Horatio.*

LOUISBURG, *Sept.* 18, 1758.

I wrote from hence to my dearest Bess in which I gave her an account of my illness and the cause of it, and promised to write you a long letter with a full account of the siege. I told you I had applyed for leave to go to New York this winter for the benefit of my health as it is a much warmer climate than this but was indifferent whether I obtained it or not as I recovered very fast, but since I wrote I have obtained leave and expect this day to be called on to go aboard a large schooner bound to New London which is part of ye government of New England . . . from thence I intend rideing to New York about one hundred English miles thro' a well settled thick inhabited and plentifull country, from thence I will write to you or my Bess (I mean York) but perhaps not immediately when I gett there for I intend applying to General Abercrombie for leave to sell. I have my Colonel's leave to do so. If I succeed you may expect next Summer to see another *schuler*[1] stalking into Coolmona. Commissions here went for about Twelve hundred pounds, but the expenses of going home &c. might perhaps reduce it to Eleven. This will near clear my debts and if a good farm is to be had I might be able then to live, but as I have them two boys[2] to educate, I don't know but a town life would be the best, but if it pleases God that I succeed in my schemes and can have ye unspeakable happiness of once more seing my dearest Bess, you &c. again, we can at leisure talk these matters over. As to our successes here you have to be sure many particular accounts, which you should have had early from me but that I was taken ill the day before the surrender of the place, and my disorder was so lingering that until within this fortnight or three weeks I had such a tremour that I could scarce write, but God be praised all that is now over and only that I have not yett quite recovered my strength I should think myself as well as ever. Providence seemed greatly of our side ye day of landing, which was ye eighth of June, when we

---

[1] Tramp.   [2] Horace, aged 9; William, aged 7.

landed in ye face (as it were) of a Noble Breastwork well lined with men some pieces of cannon and several large swivels ye sea very rough which made a great surge on ye Rocks and large Breakers on a strand ye chief landing place. A frigate ye Sleningboug fired almost incessantly on the Breastwork from whence ye enemy kept a very hot fire on our boats full of men until a Number of Light Infantry landed on the right of the division who gott on ye flank of their Breastwork and fired upon them. This and seing our grenadiers land struck such a terror in them that they immediately quitted ye Breastwork and took to ye woods which saved their Bacons or our light Infantry would have slaughtered them. However many of them were killed and about 150 (I am not exact in the number) taken prisoners and had we well known ye country we might easily have cutt off 500 from ye town who as we have been informed since did not gett in intill ye second day after. The whole army lay on their arms that night, the next day we encamped about three miles from ye town, we gott ashore our canon and amunition as soon as possible and laid regular siege which took up a great deal of time as we were obliged to make roads for our canon &c. through a very stony rough country and large deep swamps in ye face of their canon which they fired upon us in great, I may say I think profusion, in the end we battered their walls and the whole town so and Burned two fine publick buildings, one built when we had possession of it last war for a barrack, ye other a stately chappel and Barrack, and burned three of their ships, that they scarcely had a battery to fire from. However they still stood it out and Never made a sally ye whole siege but one unlucky one in which by surprising Lord Dundonald and part of his grenadier company they killed him and seven of his men and took one of his lieutenants prisoner the rest of them made their escape to the camp but Capt. Schaach of our regiment gott ample revenge, he marched into ye Breastwork with his grenadiers, Drove the enemy from it killed near twenty of them, took a Capt. prisoner who was wounded and after died of his wounds and killed their commanding officer. Thus about a hundred grenadiers drove from a breastwork they had possessed themselves off eight hundred men, retook a working party of ours who they had taken prisoner without ye loss of one man. This will appear fabulous but ye fact is truth and the numbers of the enemy reported to be so great by ye french captain who after died of his wounds. Schaach received ye thanks of ye general officers and ye grenadiers ye applause of ye whole army. Two ships still remained in ye Harbour, ye admiral ordered a number of boats from ye fleet to be manned and sent in att Night boarded the two ships without any resistance ye largest of which was aground, her they Burned and took away ye other, this is ye only thing was done ye whole siege by ye admiral in ye ffleet besides ye letting a very fine frigate out of ye Harbour one night with all ye Rich effects of ye town and yett perhaps ye honour will be all given to Admiral Boscawen. Now the town thought propper to surrender on 26 of July and would have made terms but no terms were allowed them but ye garrison prisoners of warr, the Inhabitants to be sent to France and all this was done with ye loss of 2 captains 10 sub. and 150 killed, 4 cap.'s 19 sub. 323 wounded, 1 Lt. and 22 of which were drowned ye Day of landing. I now shall only add that this town is well situated a very fine harbour but not so fine a one as Hallifax but Never can be made very strong one reason is ye frosts are so great that ye lime will not sement and ye sods molder away. Another and ye greatest that several hills command it, and from them are a Number of little Hillocks which make ye approaches easier, it takes up time to make the Roads over these Hills chiefly composed of a number of stones and swamps from Hillock to Hillock and these so exposed to ye enemy that they are only to be passed in ye night. This side of ye Island is all a rough peice of land or rather stones and Rocks some small pasture ground is cleared where there is tollerable herbage but it all abounds with strawberries Hurts rassberries and cranberries and abundance of currant shrubs these bring great quantities of grey plover and small curlew which grow most immoderately fatt, but I am told other parts of ye island are very fertile, have plenty of cattle and vegetables and Spanish river plenty of fish of all kinds particularly salmon.

... I have now made ye most of my time I had to write and perhaps tired your patience so shall only beg you'll give my affect. Service to all Friends not forgetting dear Mary and all ye rest at Coolmona

I am My dear Horace<br>
truly affect.<br>
P. T.

Tell my Bess I love her a wee bit.

*To Mrs. Elizabeth Townsend.*

NEW YORK, *Nov.* 26, 1758.

... I am still in some expectation this summer to see my dear dear Petts sweet face again which is my greatest happyness in this life. ... The miserable situation of many officers wives and now widdows makes me pleased when I reflect that my dearest Pett is not here with me, for at best if you was here your life would be a very uneasy one, I don't mean from the country for it is in general a very fine one but this, that we could be together only the winter, then the parting every spring when we are in doubts of ever seing each other and att that time reflecting on ye wretched situation you would be in in a country distant from Friends and perhaps relief If I should fall, would make us both miserable every time of parting though at times I would give any thing to have you with me.

Sure Dick if he has not been idle has by this time taken his degree. What you say of making a present to Susan is very true yett I would be glad to make her some small present that she might see I do not forget her. Poor Moll has not had any thing this long while and by what you tell me I judge you don't afford yourself ye propper necessaries.

*May* 5, 1759.

I now write from Boston a very clever town (on a Peninsula) by much the largest on this continent and had much ye greatest trade but New York.

New York has so much the advantage (paper is torn here) in a very little time it will flourish more than this place and indeed will in all probability by ye mistress of America though it has a powerful rival in Philadelphia but then ships are froze up there in ye winter, at York there's free passage in or out lett ye season be never so rigorous.

'Here the government is the Presbyterian, it is so too in Connecticut and their severity differs very little from Popish persecutions as far as imprisoning, fining and whipping. I cannot help telling you one instance of this which was at Newhaven in Connecticut government. The Master of one of their ships had been through misfortune from home three or four years. His friends all thought him dead, his wife was in mourning for him, when he came home unexpectedly on a Sunday. He went toward the church to meet her and as they were a remarkably fond couple, he ran to her, took her in his arms and kissed her in the street, and for doing this on the Sabbath, he was prosecuted, fined and whipped: how should you like to have your Philly served so when he goes home, for I fancy he would take you in his arms even at the church door. In this town, the justices put the captain of a man of war in the stocks for almost the like, but the captain dissembled his resentment, invited the justices on board, then ordered them to be tied one by one, and gave them two dozen lashes each. They complained at home, and all the satisfaction was, that they ought to have received two dozen more and indeed I think so.'

.

*To his brother Horatio.*

My brother Sam . . . I hear with great concern poor man is dead. It was told me by a Bandon man who says he saw his corps carried out of Town. I much doubted it, because my Bess in her letter says he had the gout at Bandon.

. . . My Bess takes no sort of notice of ye Death of Molly Morris[1] or Nelly Herbert[2]. Molly I hear from Barbara died of the smallpox, and Nelly, Arthur's Brother says, died in child bed. A few more losses which I hope I shall never see would make me determine never to go back again and

[1] Mary daughter of John Townsend of Skirtagh.
[2] Helena daughter of Rich. Townsend of Castle Townsend, married Rev. Arthur Herbert.

indeed was it not for the desire of being with my friends I could I think live happily here the rest of my Days. It's a Noble country and was it inhabited well enough to manufacture for themselves they need not care a farthing for Europe, but this cannot be for centuries to come. . . .

In my last I told you I had a squirrel for my Moll and Susan, the prettiest pet of the kind even here where they are plentiful. But Tom's kindness for him was his loss, for he fell overboard playing about the ship and was drowned which vexed me heartily.

*To Mrs. Eliz. Townsend.*

LOUISBURG, *June* 3, 1759.

I cannot miss this hasty opportunity of acquainting my Hearts darling of my safe arrival here and God be praised pritty hearty and well. In my last I mentioned to you of an expectation I had of purchasing a Lieutcy. for Thom, but am I find disappointed in it. He is very high in ye Rank of Ensign is grown a lusty fellow and what is better is well liked by everyone. . . .

Its said 7 or eight ships saild from old France and that some of them are fallen into ye Hands of some of ye New York Privateers which I heartily wish might be truth. The People of that town deserve good success as no people on this continent have their spirit for Privateering for all ye continent besides have not so many as this one place.

In my letter to Horace I gave him an account of our success at Quebec contrary to our most sanguine expectations. Mr. Wolff by several feints for five or six days up the river as if he intended landing there, drew a great part of the enemy up that way. He slipped them in the night which was very dark and the current being strong he was luckily obliged to land nearer to the town than he had intended, where if he had landed he would have met with great difficulty, the enemy being aware of his landing there.

Captain Townsend's memorial to General Amherst asking for permission to dispose of his commission, says his health has given way owing to the fatigues he suffered at Louisburg. He seems to have succeeded in selling his commission and returning home, for the next letter is in Tom's round schoolboy hand, dated 1763. 'I find by my dear father's letter from Dublin in which he mentions Dick being very near marriage, &c.' This was Captain Townsend's eldest son Richard, born at Braad, February 1737. His god-parents were Samuel Jervois of Braad and Lieutenant Thomas Bate. His father complained in some of his letters that Dick could not apply himself to his books; but he improved, for he qualified for a doctor of medicine and practised in Dublin. There he married three times, first Eleanor Sealy of Bandon, second, Margaret, daughter of Horatio Townsend of Bridgemount [1], and third, Elizabeth Morris. He sold the estate of Derry to his youngest brother Horatio.

It is believed in the family that Tom was near General Wolff when he fell at Quebec, and that he sat for his portrait to be introduced in the painting of the death of Wolff. He continued in the 22nd Regiment, and was in the siege of Ravenna. When he returned to Ireland, Lord Townshend, the viceroy, gave him a post in the Battleaxe Guards, and always treated him as a cousin. Tom was said to have been the handsomest man in the Battleaxe Guards; but he never married, and lived with his brother Will, who had also been in the army, at Derry when they were both old men.

Captain Philip Townsend died in 1786, leaving four sons and two daughters. Susanna, his eldest child, was married to Michael French of Rath; and Mary, born at Castletown, August 1789, married Thomas Somerville [2] of Castlehaven and Drishane.

A quaint account of Derry and the two old soldiers

[1] See Table VIII.   [2] See Table II.

is presented in notes by Somerville Reeves, grandson of Mary and Thomas Somerville. His mother died when he was very young, and as he was sickly the Somerville aunts fetched the little fellow from Cork to try the effects of country air. 'Aunt Hungerford' (she had been Kitty Somerville) and Bessie Townsend (daughter of Richard Townsend the eldest of the Derry Branch), left Cork with the boy in a post-chaise on Easter Sunday, 1747. They started at five in the morning, and ended their forty miles drive at Derry at six that evening. There they found Uncles Tom and Will, and Tom Townsend (Mrs. Harrison's father). The party had finished dinner, but a side table was laid for the new comers. Aunt Hungerford was explaining to the old gentleman how delicate little Somerville was, and how he must eat no vegetables nor fat meat, when dinner was carried in, and to her horror it consisted of fat boiled pork and greens. Uncle Will paid no attention to her protests, and said it didn't matter for once, they could attend to her rules another time. But next day he proposed to keep the child at Derry, so that he might have the advantage of being near the grammar school, and the rules for the diet were all forgotten. The family used to kill a pig and live on it, and then a calf was consumed in the same way; and, strange to say, the delicate boy flourished and grew strong. This was partly owing to the kindness of the housekeeper, who took care of him like a mother, care which he was able to repay by pensioning her in her old age. He used to walk into school at Ross every day, and soon made light of the long mile, and though his master was anxious to prevent his working too hard, he speedily got to the head of his class above much older boys.

Not long after Somerville came to Derry, Uncle

Tom died of a paralytic stroke, and Uncle Will was sole master of the quaint little castellated house which stood on the site of the present dairy, near 'Frank Townsend's field.' A chief part of Uncle Will's land was a very stony hill; they were always hauling sand to improve it, but the sand seemed to sink in and the land grew no better. Uncle Will wore a red waistcoat, trimmed with silver buttons, with a fox engraved on each; but there was no hunting, the horses were too busy with the land for that, but there was plenty of coursing, and Somerville learned to shoot and fish and fence. The evenings Uncle Will and the boy spent in the panelled parlour with its rush-strewn floor, where the old officer used to busy himself in cutting out wooden soles for his own shoes, to which the leather was afterwards nailed. The shelves round the room were filled with tools and finished shoe-soles. While he worked he used to tell endless stories of his adventures by flood and field, how he swam the Rhine with dispatches in his mouth, and had to disguise himself as a peasant to bring them safely across France. He used to talk of sport too, and tell the best way to trap otters and catch fish, for he was the most successful fisherman in the neighbourhood. All his life long Somerville Reeves used to quote Uncle Will's wise sayings; for although the veteran had no great literary attainments he was a man of shrewd sense and much natural talent. He was very courteous in his manner, though when he chose he could override everyone about him. He kept plantations of useful herbs in the garden, and used to doctor the poor, to whom he was very kind; he grew great quantities of flax and employed many women in spinning and weaving.

He was Captain of Yeomanry, and his old military

experience was useful in the troubled times of 1798. Sir John Moore commanded the soldiers then quartered in Clonakilty, and used to ask Uncle Will to guide him about the country. Somerville remembered the bonfires on the hills at that time, and running along the roads with other boys after the rebels. He was as happy as a king at Derry, and only wished to spend his whole life there with his uncle, whom he always called 'Billy.'

Derry was the only house in that neighbourhood that was not attacked by the rebels. The windows were barricaded, and lights kept burning, and once Uncle Will paced up and down all night before the door, keeping guard, but no enemy appeared. After the rising was suppressed and people were afraid of their houses being searched for arms, numbers of pikes were found piled at the hall door every morning, the house at one time being almost filled with them.

Once Uncle Will and Somerville walked over to the village of Castle Townshend for a christening. On their way home the old man said, 'Somerville, my boy, I thought they would have made me godfather, and I brought my present in my pocket, but as they did not ask me, I shall give it to you;' and he pulled out a handful of gold pieces, old Spanish doubloons, and handed them to the boy. No doubt they were the relics of some prize-money gained in the wars. Somerville bought a watch with the gold, which he wore for the rest of his life.

After a time his happy life at Derry had to come to an end. When he next visited it, he wrote in his diary, 'I found my uncle had removed to a house he built in Ross, and my Uncle Horace was building and living at Derry. Uncle Tom Hungerford was also living at Ross and the Frenchs at Clonakilty.' Somerville was as welcome at Derry as ever, and his Uncle Horace used to help him with his Latin lessons.

William Townshend died at Ross in 1816.

His younger brother, Horatio, was born in 1750. His god-parents were Richard Townshend of Castle Townshend, Thomas Becher, Mrs. Penelope French and Mrs. D. Robinson.

His father mentioned in the letters from America, 'I always suspect my Horace of tending a little to idleness, but I know fair means and a little coaxing will make him do anything.' If Horace was idle at seven years old, he showed little signs of it afterwards, for he was a singularly active man both in mind and body. He entered Trinity College, Dublin, and when he left home to go up there as a freshman, his foster-brother ran after him to press his little savings of a guinea on him as a farewell present. He rode all the way up to Dublin, a journey which took about a week. He took an 'ad eundem' in order to accompany his kinsman, Richard Boyle Townshend, of Castle Townshend, to Magdalen College, Oxford. Afterwards he went on the continent with him, Mr. St. Leger (afterwards Lord Doneraile), and the Hon. W. Spencer. He wrote an account of these travels in *Blackwood's Magazine*, under the title of 'A Trip to Spa[1].' He was a most amusing companion. Long afterwards Bishop Spencer of Madras, meeting Harriet Townshend in India, asked if she could be any relation to a delightful Horace Townshend with whom his father had travelled as a young man, and whose conversation he had never forgotten. When he returned home Horace took holy orders. He was ordained Priest

[1] See Chapter iv.

THE REV. HORATIO TOWNSHEND, OF DERRY

in 1770, and was first Curate of Abbey-Strewrey, and afterwards removed to Saint Michael's, Cork, and Carrigaline. In 1785-6 he was Rector of Dungourney, and afterwards he was Prebendary of the Island, Vicar of Kilgariffe and Desert, Vicar of Kilkerranmore and Castle Ventry, and Rector of Carrigaline.

With all these functions he combined those first of tutor and then of agent to Lord Shannon, besides which he was sovereign of Clonakilty and Justice of the Peace.

These varied offices gave him much influence in the neighbourhood, and being a talented, practical and kind-hearted man, he was able to do so much for his poorer neighbours, that he was named among them the 'Friend of the poor.' He was a tall, strong man, with red hair and blue eyes, a good horseman, and a most interesting and witty companion. At an election when a roar of laughter went up from a knot of gentlemen, it used to be said, 'That must be a Horatian jest.'

He wrote quantities of 'vers de société,' both political and complimentary, and also *The Statistical Survey of the County of Cork*, a book which contains a quantity of varied information about the county. In this book he tells with simple delight how, in 1786, when he obtained the living of Clonakilty, as there was no residence for the clergyman, Lord Shannon 'was pleased to accommodate me with his villa at Courtmacsherry; consisting of a house and upwards of a hundred acres, including the woods, a most acceptable acquisition to me, wholly unprovided with house or land. I there had the first opportunity of practising on a small scale an art which, even in theory, had always been productive of entertainment.' That is to say, he added farming to his other pursuits, and endeavoured to show the people that important improvements in their methods of agriculture need not be very costly nor difficult. The *Statistical Survey* is full of useful hints on the subject.

Horace Townshend married in 1795 Helena, only daughter and heiress of the Rev. Richard Meade of Ballintober. He had written charming verses describing her beauty of mind and person, and when she died, after only one year of married life, he was so overwhelmed with grief that his friends feared some tragic result.

As the simplest way of consoling him they persuaded him to marry again, and he was accepted by Catherine, daughter of Archdeacon Corker, grand-daughter of Bishop Jemmett Brown. She was a gentle, religious woman; her portrait is that of a pretty blue-eyed girl.

Somerville Reeves in his notes gives a glowing account of holidays spent at Courtmacsherry, and of learning to swim. Mrs. Townsend's brother, Chambré Corker, was there, and Joanna, the only daughter of Horatio's first marriage, and the whole party used to go out fishing at night. About 1810 or 1820 Horatio and his brother Thomas joined in buying Derry from their elder brother Richard.

As a Magistrate and Clergyman, Horatio had busy times during the troubles of 1798. His cousin, Samuel Townsend, the High Sheriff, was able to keep the peace in the extreme west, but Horatio was the most important man in the neighbourhood of Clonakilty. He rode through the town to the large Roman Catholic Church, which was crowded with peasantry. There he went up into the pulpit, and told the congregation they knew well he was their friend and might believe his words, that the insurgents had no chance of success, and that the punishment of those who were found in possession of arms would be very dreadful. He said he would not ask the hearers to bring any concealed arms to him, but there was a certain field where, if he found arms piled, he should know they were left there for him, and he should ask no questions. Quantities of pikes were found in the appointed place, and were taken out by boat-loads and sunk in Courtmacsherry Bay, with the result that the country was quite peaceful, and when the military did come they found no excuse for the atrocities that had been practised elsewhere.

Once, it is said, they made a beginning, and Horace Townsend riding by, saw a party of soldiers preparing to hang two men up by the feet over their own doors. He promptly had the men cut down, and he was too important a person to be disobeyed. Long afterwards his daughter, Susan, when driving, heard a woman say to her children, 'See, there's the daughter of the man who saved your father's life.'

The house which Horatio built at Derry was soon filled with children; three sons and eight daughters lived to grow up. He was a most tender father, and prepared his sons for college himself, and wrote nursery rhymes for his little ones. One of these was printed in a newspaper[1], but may be preserved here.

> 'When winter came and days were short,
> And chilling winds began to blow,
> The children thought it pretty sport,
> To watch the gently falling snow.
>
> "Oh dear," cried Car, in great surprise,
> "'Tis sure the strangest of all weathers,
> For if I may believe my eyes,
> I vow 'tis raining white goose feathers!"

[1] *Cork Constitution*, Christmas, 1878.

"I'll gather some for Dolly's bed!"
"Indeed, Miss Car, you're quite mistaken,
"'Tis raining salt," smart Harry said,
"Enough to salt Papa's fat bacon."

Dick, thinking none were in the right,
With hopes to gain a better prize,
Said "powdered sugar, nice and white,
Was kindly falling from the skies."

They begged for leave abroad to go,
And promised not to stay too long;
In order finally to know
Whose guess was right and whose was wrong.

Car's feathers melted at the touch,
Experience Harry's error taught her,
And Dick, whose hopes were raised too much,
Found nothing in his mouth but water!'

It must be remembered that snow is very seldom seen in the mild and sheltered south-west of Ireland.

Horace Townsend was much injured by an accidental explosion of gunpowder—his sight never quite recovered, and he had to give up his long rides. He went to Harrogate for his health in 1820. He died in the year 1837[1]. It is said that on the day of his death the petty sessions were being held, and the first case was just being dealt with, when a loud voice was heard crying out from the body of the court, 'Gintlemen, is this a time for ye to be sitting here, while the Poor Man's Friend is lying dead upon his bed?' There was a great silence, and the speaker went on, 'God knows our hearts are broken; and is this a time for ye to be sitting here?' This was the first tidings the magistrates had received, and they at once rose and adjourned the Court. He was buried in Ross Cathedral.

His sister Mary spent her married life in the tapestried rooms of the old Castle of Castlehaven. After

[1] Rev. John Hume Townsend.

her husband's death she lived in a nice house on the Mall at Castle Townshend, and was described by her son[1] Harry as 'a dear little prim old lady. She used to give little feasts off the most beautiful old china, and when all was over she and her daughter washed it up themselves in a snow-white wooden bowl.'

Horatio Townsend lost his wife early from fever in 1811, soon after the birth of Richard, and his eldest daughter, Kate, had the responsibility of a large household thrown on her young shoulders.

The tone of society then was far lower than at the present day, and drinking and gambling were paving the road to ruin of many of the best families in the county. Kate and Eliza, the two eldest sisters of the Derry family, were sent to school in Clifton with Miss Mills, the favourite pupil of Hannah More, and the aunt of the historian Macaulay. The piety that the girls learned from Miss Mills became the centre of a quickened religious life in their neighbourhood, and the influence of their brothers widened the circle of good. The two eldest, Chambré and Horace, entered the Church, and were well known as preachers. There is a touching story told at length in the *British Messenger* of a little servant girl at Clonakilty whose mistress reproved her for never going to church: 'you must leave my service,' she said, 'I won't have a heathen in my house.' The girl's curiosity was at last aroused, and she thought she would go to church for once and see what it was like. When she came home, 'Ma'am,' she said, 'it wasn't a man in the pulpit, but an angel, with a red glory round his head, and he read about the dry bones, and I'm just dead and dry bones myself.' The good mistress was delighted at the effect of the red-haired rector's

[1] To Miss H. Somerville.

```
                                                                              Cather
                                                                              with is
                                  (1) Frances Vere, ═ Chambré Cor ohn, so
                                      dau. of           of Derry Flemi
                                  Robert Vere Stewart, b. 1797, d. 18 court,
                                                                      Somer
                                                                      and n
┌──────────┬──────────┬──────────┬──────────┬──────────┬──────────┐
Horatio,  ═ Mary    Nathaniel ═ Maria    Chambré ═ Emily,    Richa  orace,
of Derry,   Susanna, Wilmot     Strawson. Corker    dau. of J. Baxt
took the    dau. of  Oliver,                        Gibson.
name of     Lt.-Col. of
Payne       Kirby.   Derry.
Townshend.
┌──────────┬──────────────────┬──────────┬──────────┬──────────┐
Charlotte,  Mary     ═ Hugh Cholmondely, Wilmot.  Horatio. William.  Dudley      El
of Derry.   Stewart.   with issue.                                   Ryder.
                       Cicily.
```

posed and used daily while Master in Chancery, is extant, asking for 'health, knowledge, and integrity.'

His grandson, General Townshend, is author of several books of travel, *Wild Life in Florida,* and others.

## Notes on Table XII.

NOTE A.—Eliza, eldest daughter of the second family of Horace of Derry, married Lionel John Fleming. His family was of Scotch origin; there are many Fleming monuments in Glasgow Cathedral, and in the east window are the crest and motto borne by the present Flemings of New Court. The first of this family acted as agent to the Becher's, and settled in the neighbourhood of the estates he managed. There were others of the name already in the county, possibly they invited this young man over. Sir Henry Sidney, Elizabeth's viceroy, speaks of Flemings among the ancient English settlers in Cork, and others are mentioned in Charles the Second's Courts of Claims.

Lionel Fleming, of Thornfield, married Martha, daughter of Major Ancram, and sister of Mrs. Richard Townsend 'of the Point[1].' They had two children, Becher, who married Judith Somerville[2], and was the father of the Lionel John above mentioned, and Eliz. Martha, who married Redmond Uniacke, of Carrig, Cork, who died 1802.

NOTE B.—The Cor Cors or Cœur Cœurs were an ancient family believed to have come to England in the time of William the Conqueror, and afterwards granted Nostall Abbey by Queen Elizabeth. An account of Abbot Maurus Corker will be found in the Dictionary of National Biography.

[1] Table I, Chapter vii.     [2] Table II.

Some relatives of Catherine Corker seem to have come from St. Buryan's, Cornwall. Others were officers in the army of 1648. Eliza, sister to Catherine Corker, married the Rev. Philip French.

NOTE C.—The Oliver family descend from Captain Robert Oliver, M.P. for County Limerick, and Valentine, daughter of Sir Claud Hamilton.

Colonel Robert Oliver, of Castle Oliver, had a son John, Archdeacon of Ardagh, who married Elizabeth, daughter of the Most Rev. R. Ryder, Archbishop of Tuam, and was the father of General Nathaniel Wilmot Oliver, R.A., whose only daughter married the Rev. C. C. Townsend of Derry. General Oliver's sister Alicia married James Hewitt, Lord Lifford, Dean of Armagh, and his sister Eliza married R. Aldworth of Newmarket.

Colonel Robert Oliver above mentioned had also a son Philip, M.P. for Kilmallock, whose daughter Elizabeth married Charles Coote of Mount Coote, and had a son Chidley, who married Anne, daughter and heir of the Honourable William Hewitt, and their son Charles Eyre Coote married the daughter of Major Crofton Croker, and had a daughter Mary Anne Harriott, who married William Uniacke Townsend of the elder Derry branch.

NOTE D.—Susanna Townsend, who married Michael French, of Rath, had among other children Michael, who married Mary Hungerford, of Caermore, and had a son John whose daughter Ellen married James Edward Somerville, M.D., of Park Cottage.

# CHAPTER XII.

### Donoughmore House.
(Table XIII.)

### Notes on Table XIII.

*Most of this branch write their name without H.*

HORATIO TOWNSEND was born at Castletownsend, September 1, 1706. He entered Trinity College, Dublin, when sixteen, and became a Scholar in 1724. Ordained Deacon, June 23, 1728. Married, 1739[1], Mary Hungerford.

Having purchased Knockane in the parish of Donoughmore, he resided there while building the glebe house of Coolmona. He also purchased 224 acres at Ardinpinane from Lord Kingston, in April, 1754. This land is in the deed described as 'the ploughland of Coosheen in the parish of Scull.' He also bought several hundred acres from Sir Charles Moore.

A warm affection seems to have united him with his brother Philip, who began many of his letters from America 'My dear, dear Horace.'

Philip's wife was sister to Horace's wife, and lived in their family while her husband was on foreign service.

His son, Samuel Philip, of Firmount, is described by his first cousin, Horace of Derry, in the *Statistical Survey*, as 'a gentleman of the soundest judgment, the

[1] Brady's *Records*.

sweetest disposition, and the most undeviating rectitude. He enjoyed the singular felicity of passing through life certainly without giving, and as I have reason to believe, without receiving offence. To the common people of his neighbourhood his loss is irreparable. He was their friend in distress, their adviser in difficulty, and by a sort of general acquiescence in his justice, their umpire in every dispute. Agriculture was among his favourite pursuits, and few understood it better [1].'

The same author says [2] that Richard Townsend, of Palace Town, was also distinguished among other good qualities for his agricultural skill. Palace Town is near Kinsale, and has the advantage of a small estuary washing its eastern border.

The next member of this branch of whom I have been able to collect any anecdotes is Mrs. Richard Townsend of Magourney, daughter of Dean Hume. When set free from other ties, she set out at the age of sixty to join her only son, Edward Hume Townsend, in India. She rode across the isthmus of Suez on a donkey, being the first European lady who crossed the desert; her pluck was commemorated in a paragraph in the *Times*. But this first adventure nearly proved her last, for riding briskly ahead of her party, they missed her, and she was for some time completely lost in the desert.

The Rev. Edward Synge Townsend was known in the family as 'the apostle': his portrait is that of a most benevolent looking old man with flowing white locks.

The Rev. Aubrey Townshend, his grandson, son of Horatio Townshend and Elizabeth Trelawney Townshend [3], was born in 1812. He graduated with honours at Trinity College, Dublin, in 1836, and was ordained by

---

[1] *Statis. Surv.*, ii. 157.   [2] Id. ii. 39.   [3] Table X.

Bishop Sumner to the curacy of Godalming, but he soon accepted the curacy of Hatfield, where the present Marquis of Salisbury was his holiday pupil. When Curate of St. Michael's, Bath, he found time to edit the works of the Martyr Bradford for the Parker Society, and formed a remarkable collection of black-letter books. He was presented by the Bishop of Bath and Wells to the living of Puxton in 1874. Here, beloved by all, he ministered in spite of failing health down to the very last Sunday of his life, retaining in his old age all his keen interest in historical and theological study, and his wonderful memory for genealogical data. 'His figure, aged beyond his years, was well known at all gatherings of the clergy throughout the diocese, and his well-weighed words at Ruridecanal Chapters often struck a deeper note than usual, and his hearers felt they were the words of one who was indeed living very closely with his God. He died August, 1891 [1].'

Commander John Townshend, his brother, entered the navy as 'volunteer of the first class' in 1829 on board the 'Britannia,' at Plymouth, and was midshipman in the 'Druid' during the insurrections of Monte Video and Rio Janeiro. He was present at the bombardment of St. John D'Acre, when his ship was the first to engage the enemy, and among other spoils he brought home a large six-and-half foot Syrian rifle, and a pair of bronze candlesticks from a mosque. He and a party of friends rode to Damascus, but the plague was so deadly in the city that the only relic they dared bring away was a horseshoe nail. They rode past the ruins of Baalbec and over the Anti-Lebanon, and one night he and his companions unconsciously encamped on the flat roof of a house, which was built against a hill side,

[1] *Bristol Times and Mirror.*

and tied their horses to a chimney which in the dark they mistook for a post. He was a senior lieutenant of the 'Plover,' under Captain Collison, surveying the coast of China, in which service she went on shore repeatedly and was once nearly wrecked. At Hong-kong he horrified the ship's surgeon during the prevalence of fever in the rainy season, by starting across country with a party of young men in flannels, playing follow-my-leader. However the exercise agreed with them, while the careful surgeon caught the fever and died.

He was exceedingly fond of athletic sports, and always organized a cricket club when possible. He was said to be one of the strongest men in the Mediterranean fleet, carrying weights on his little finger which not every one could lift. When a midshipman he climbed to the cross above the ball on St. Paul's, and his favourite reading place used to be the truck on the mast-head. His last service, during the Russian War, 1855, was as senior lieutenant of the 'Himalaya' conveying troops to the Crimea, and he preserved among his relics a piece of grape-shot, picked up when riding through a storm of shot and shell in 'the Valley of Death' at Sebastopol.

After serving under three sovereigns for thirty-seven years, and winning four war-medals, Commander Townsend retired from the service and settled at Weston-super-Mare, and took a prominent part in improving and beautifying that watering-place. It is said at one time he sat on twenty-seven committees, and was Town Commissioner and Chairman of the Local Government Board.

Edward Hume Townsend was the son of the Rev. Richard Townsend, Rector of Magourney, who married the daughter of the Rev. John Hume, Dean of Derry.

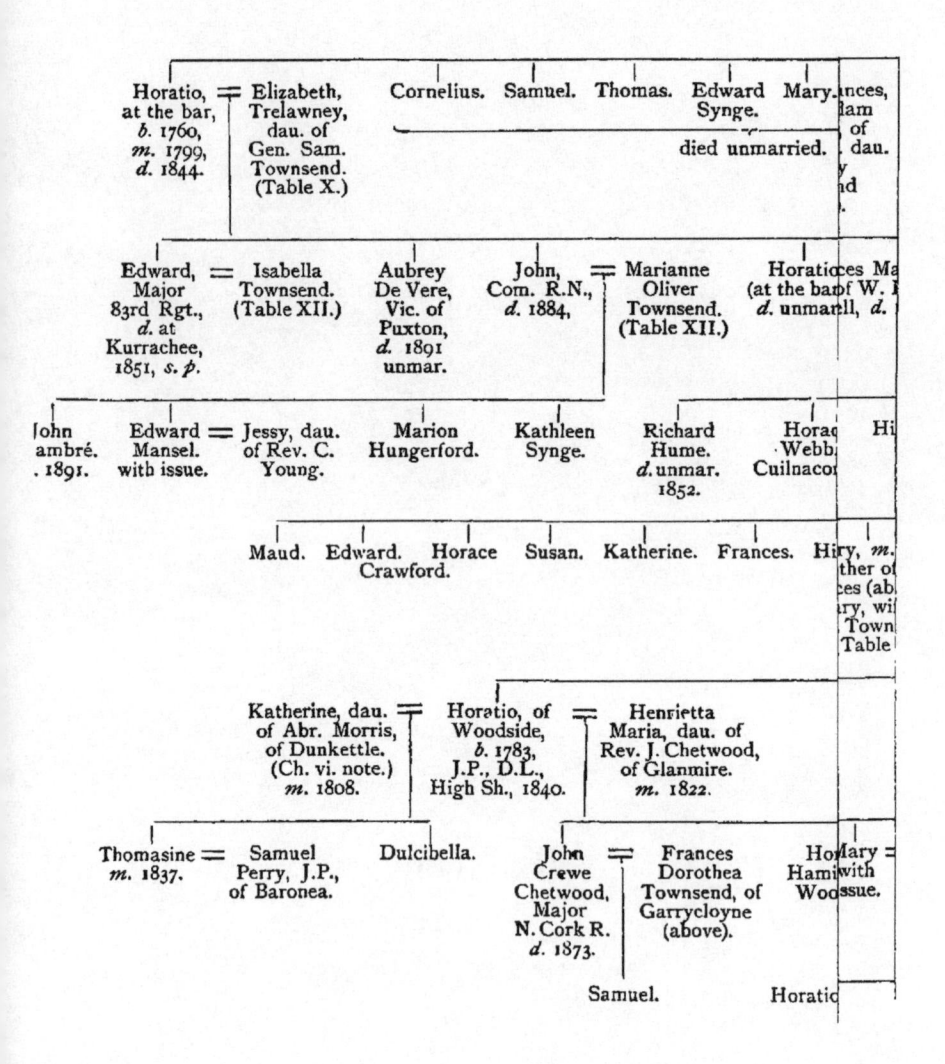

| Horatio, = Elizabeth, | Cornelius. | Samuel. | Thomas. | Edward | Mary. | ...nces, |
| at the bar, | Trelawney, | | | | Synge. | | ...lam |
| b. 1760, | dau. of | | | | | | of |
| m. 1799, | Gen. Sam. | | | | died unmarried. | | . dau. |
| d. 1844. | Townsend. | | | | | | ...y |
| | (Table X.) | | | | | | ...d |

| Edward, = Isabella | Aubrey | John, = Marianne | Horatio ...ces Ma |
| Major | Townsend. | De Vere, | Com. R.N., | Oliver | (at the ba... of W. |
| 83rd Rgt., | (Table XII.) | Vic. of | d. 1884, | Townsend. | d. unmar... ll, d. |
| d. at | | Puxton, | | (Table XII.) | |
| Kurrachee, | | d. 1891 | | | |
| 1851, s. p. | | unmar. | | | |

| John | Edward = Jessy, dau. | Marion | Kathleen | Richard | Hora... | Hi... |
| ambré. | Mansel. | of Rev. C. | Hungerford. | Synge. | Hume. | Webb... | |
| . 1891. | with issue. | Young. | | | d. unmar. | Cuilnaco... |
| | | | | | 1852. | |

| Maud. | Edward. | Horace | Susan. | Katherine. | Frances. | Hi...ry, m. |
| | | Crawford. | | | | ther of |
| | | | | | | ...es (ab... |
| | | | | | | ...ry, wi... |
| | | | | | | Town... |
| | | | | | | Table... |

| Katherine, dau. = Horatio, of = Henrietta |
| of Abr. Morris, | Woodside, | Maria, dau. of |
| of Dunkettle. | b. 1783, | Rev. J. Chetwood, |
| (Ch. vi. note.) | J.P., D.L., | of Glanmire. |
| m. 1808. | High Sh., 1840. | m. 1822. |

| Thomasine = Samuel | Dulcibella. | John = Frances | Ho...ary = |
| m. 1837. | Perry, J.P., | | Crewe | Dorothea | Hami... with |
| | of Baronea. | | Chetwood, | Townsend, of | Woo... ssue. |
| | | | Major | Garrycloyne | |
| | | | N. Cork R. | (above). | |
| | | | d. 1873. | | |
| | | | Samuel. | | Horatio |

...rd,
R.N.

His education was begun at Clonakilty school, and carried on at Westminster and Foyle College, Londonderry, where the Lawrences and Herbert Edwards, so famous afterwards in the terrible days of the Indian Mutiny, were among his schoolfellows. Having been nominated to a writership in the Honourable East India Company's Service, he was removed to Haileybury College; here he obtained various distinctions, and finally gained the Sanscrit gold medal of his year. He sailed for India in 1822, when nineteen years of age, and in a short time his abilities brought him special notice and promotion from Lord Clive, the Governor of Bombay. The thirty years that followed were spent in India, and he became in time Secretary to Government, and finally Revenue Commissioner to the Presidency. Here his talent for languages showed itself; in his court he was accustomed to speak in four of the native tongues: one of these, Marathi, he spoke like a native. He was a devoted Christian and a warm supporter of missionaries of all Protestant denominations. A native scholarship in the Robert Money school was founded to perpetuate his memory. One incident in his life deserves especial notice. A friend having called his attention to the fact that numbers of rescued slaves were brought by H.M. ships to Bombay and there absorbed in the population, he, as secretary, laid before Government a plan for educating in the Christian faith the children thus rescued, in the full belief that they would become pioneers for missionary work in their own lands. The proposal was adopted, and steps taken for carrying it into effect. It is well known to all how the C. M. S. has prospered in this work; how Jacob Wainwright, one of the children thus rescued and taught, was the means of helping Dr. Livingstone, and finally of bringing his body back to England; but it may not be known who were the originators of the plan which has worked so well. Mr. Townsend was also a prominent supporter of total abstinence. Upon his return from India he lived with his family for a short time in Bath, for some years near Dublin, and for the last eighteen years of his life on a property which he purchased at Clonakilty. While in India he did not amass a fortune, but spent the greater part of his large income in philanthropic and religious works in that country, holding it as a principle that money should be spent for the benefit of the country whence it was obtained. During the years of famine in Ireland he collected some thousands of pounds annually to send to his native country, and out of his private means contributed large sums every year for the same object. His liberality was very great, but as he generally preferred to give anonymously, the amount of his beneficence can never be known. He was a good landlord and magistrate, a devoted husband, and a wise and loving father.

*Communicated by the Very Rev. Dean of Tuam.*

The Rev. William Robinson Townsend, for thirty years Rector of Aghada, County Cork, was born in 1785. He was a man of a most benevolent and unselfish disposition, and it was truly said of him that he had a passion for doing good. He began his clerical duties in 1810 as Curate of the parish of Innis-tarra. His stipend was only £75 Irish, and he paid £22 a year for his house and farm, while the Rector had £2000 a year, and two glebes. W. Townsend established a farming society, and the first dispensary known in the country, and previously had acted himself as the physician of the poor under the direction of the Doctor. He also established an excellent free school in his parish, and a Sunday school for those obliged to work on week-days. In 1822 there was a famine in the country, and a Central Committee of landed proprietors was formed. Without Mr. Townsend's knowledge he was chosen Secretary, and entered zealously on the duties of his office. He was afterwards appointed to the Curacy of Coens; the Rector was seldom resident, and the stipend £100 a year. While there, a visitation of cholera prevailed, along with great scarcity of food; Mr. Townsend was appointed Secretary of both Relief Committees. The Bishop of Cork presented him with the living of Nohonal, and in 1837 he was removed to the living of Aghada, where, in addition to his parish duties, he had the care of a large family of his own, three sons and five daughters. He took up the question of agriculture with enthusiasm, wrote several pamphlets on farming, and at one time conducted a farming journal, which sold well. He wrote under the name of 'Agricola,' and was considered a second Martin Doyle. At the age of eighty he obtained first prize of £30 for an essay on the best way of managing a farm of forty acres.

During the cholera and famine years of 1846–7 his energies were severely taxed. He wrote letters in the English and Irish papers, and contributions of money and clothes poured in. Seeing the evil of giving alms, he planned various means of supplying work to the people. He organised drainage operations (acting as his own engineer), and by this means 137 acres, which had been only fit for shooting snipe, were turned into profitable pastures. He also set the people to make clogs, rough shoes such as are worn in Cumberland,

and sent to Liverpool for soles, and to Cork for hides; waterproof cloaks and coats were also manufactured under his direction. The culture of flax was also carried on with great success. Mr. Townsend encouraged the establishment of the Queen's College, Cork, when most of the Clergy stood aloof. He aided and took a lively interest in the meeting of the British Association in Cork, and was a supporter of the National School system, believing it to be the best to be had under the circumstances. During his long and useful life he was ever to the front in any scheme for benefiting the moral and spiritual condition of the people. Free Libraries were always one of the first things he established in any parish that he was connected with, and this at a time when books were dearer and scarcer than at present. He married Isabella, daughter of Major-General Brook Young, R.A. His eldest son, Samuel Philip, the ideal of a brave Christian soldier, was killed at Inkerman, November 5, 1854, just as he had been gazetted to a Colonelcy in the Royal Artillery. His second son, Brook Young Townsend, Staff Assistant-Surgeon, was thrown from his horse at Hobart Town, Tasmania, and killed, while on his way to see a patient. His third son, William Chambers, is now Dean of Tuam. He married first, Emma Mary Fitzgerald, and second, Emma Mary Fetherstonhaugh.

Dr. Edward Townsend, of Cork, was on the 'Kent' East-India-man, at the time of the well-known fire. His son, Rear-Admiral Townsend, entered the navy in 1844 as a midshipman on board the 'Dragon' in the Mediterranean. He was afterwards mate in the 'Retribution,' and promoted to Lieutenant 1852. He was then appointed to H.M.S. 'Sans Pareil.' He assisted in landing our troops at Varna, and was present in the attack of the 17th October upon the sea-forts of Sebastopol, when the 'Sans Pareil' sustained a loss of eleven killed and fifty-nine wounded, receiving thirty-two shells in her hull alone. Lieutenant Townsend then was attached with the Naval Brigade to Sir Colin Campbell's Division. He received command of the 'Boxer,' was three times mentioned in despatches, and received the Turkish and Crimean medals with the clasps, and fifth Order of the Medjide. In September, 1859, he was appointed First Lieutenant of the Royal Yacht 'Victoria and Albert,' and was Commander 1861. Employed in coastguard service at Skibbereen, and on the China station. As captain he commanded the 'Crocodile' troopship, the 'Nymph,' the 'Hercules,' and the 'Warrior.' Awarded good service pension 1883. Rear-Admiral 1885.

## Why every Maiden in the Family of W. Hume Townsend learns to Milk a Cow.

*Told by the Rev. J. Hume Townsend.*

I have often heard my father tell the story of an ancestress of his who lived with her husband and children on their estate in the north of Ireland, somewhere near Letterkenny I imagine. It was, I believe, during the Rebellion of 1668(?); her husband was away on military service; her children had been sent somewhere to be in safe keeping; and she, with her servants, remained in the family mansion, which was on high ground surrounded with sloping woods. One night she got an intimation suddenly that the Rebels were close at hand, so hiding a few valuables about her person she hastily made her escape in the darkness, and before long heard loud yells which told her that the attack had begun: soon the sky was lit up with the glare of the flames rising from the burning house. In terror she fled all the night through, but in what direction she knew not; at last, when the winter's morning dawned, she saw a farmhouse not far off, and terrified at the thought of discovery, bethought herself of some plan to escape detection. She had no idea where she was, but summoning all her courage, went to the farmhouse and asked the farmer's wife if she wanted a servant. 'Yes,' was the reply, 'take this pail and stool, and go and milk the cows.' She took it, and went into the byre and tried to milk a cow, thinking it would be easy work, but the cow only kicked her and the pail, and her efforts were all in vain; at last, overcome by fear and sorrow and loneliness she sat down, and burying her face in her hands, gave way to a burst of uncontrolled sobs; the farmer's wife meanwhile, thinking that she would see how her new maid was getting on, looked in, and found her sitting at the *wrong side of the cow* weeping bitterly. The good woman took in the situation at a glance, and going up to her said, 'Ah! I see how it is, you are one of the poor things trying to hide; come along with me, I'll keep you safe as long as there is any danger, and no one shall know where you are;' and so she did, and the poor wanderer found a safe hiding-place in the kind woman's farmhouse until the troubles had passed away, and her husband returned from the war. The practical issue of the whole thing was that my ancestress left in her will a strict command on all her female issue that they should learn how to milk a cow, which command has been faithfully obeyed in our branch of the family.

Many years ago, when I was taking a long drive in that neighbourhood with my cousin, Dr. Thomas Barnard Hart, of Glanalla, he pointed out some trees in the distance, and said, 'There stood in former days the house of the lady who left in her will the injunction that all her female descendants should learn to milk a cow.'

# ADDENDA.

The editors will be exceedingly grateful for any further information that may be sent.

Page 128. Richard Townesend matriculated at Hart Hall, 1634, aged nineteen, and as he therefore must have been born in 1615 he evidently cannot be Colonel Richard Townesend.

P. 133. Catherine Gunn is ancestress of Lord Ventry and of the family of Gunn of Rattoo.

P. 141. Capt. Joseph Cuff is ancestor of the Earls of Dysart.

P. 144. In October, 1695, Col. Townsend received leave of absence from his parliamentary duties to go into England for a month, and in August, 1697, leave to go into the country on urgent occasions.—*Commons Journals of Ireland.*

P. 150. In June, 1723, Dean Swift spent the summer at Myross, for his health, having, he said, when he went there, no acquaintances in West Carbery. It is believed that he wrote *Carberiæ Rupes* when sheltering from the rain in the artificial ruin now known as Swift's Tower. In June, 1725, he wrote to Dr. Sheridan, ' Mr. Townshend of Cork will do you any good office on my account without any letter.'

P. 151. John Townshend, of Shepperton, gave up the seat of Dingle on receiving 'a place of profit.' A very lovely portrait of his wife, Mary Morris, is preserved at Drishane.

P. 152. Richard Townshend sat for Dingle before he became member for Cork County.

P. 193, Table II. Richard Neville, second son of Thomas Somerville and Mary Townshend of Derry, married Letitia Hungerford of the Island, and had a son, Richard Neville, who married Elizabeth Townshend Somerville, and had with other daughters Agnes, who married Rev. Horace Townshend of Kilcoe.

Table IX. The younger children of Thomas Somerville and Elizabeth Townshend of Shepperton have the following children:—
  Admiral Philip H. T. Somerville has three sons: (1) David Maitland Critchon; (2) Thomas Townshend; (3) Maitland.
  Doctor James Edward Somerville has: (1) Thomas Townsend; (2) John French; (3) Henry; (4) James Fitz-James; (5) Edward

## ADDENDA.

Richard; (6) Philip; (7) Mary Cornelia; (2) Elizabeth Townsend; (3) Ellen; (4) Grace French; (5) Ada Charlotte Augusta.

Morris Townshend Somerville has: (1) Anquitil Fitz-Townshend, married Mary Cotterell, with issue; (2) Richard Neville; (3) Philip Horatio Townshend.

P. 209. *Read* Mary or Margaret.

Table IX. Rev. Richard Jones is now Rector of Youghal.

P. 223. Miniatures of Commander Townshend and his wife are in the possession of Mrs. Edward Townshend.

P. 240. A miniature of Elizabeth Hungerford wearing a large cap and muslin handkerchief is at New Court.

Table XI. Has been drawn up with the kind help of Thomas Courteney Townshend.

Table XII. The first wife of Capt. Horace Townshend was not Jane but Elizabeth McCarthie.

Table XIII. Eliza, daughter of Dr. Edward Richard Townsend, married the Ven. Robert Wills, Archdeacon of Cloyne, and has two daughters. Horatio Hamilton Townsend of Woodside has with two sons also two daughters, Elizabeth Zena and Kathleen Mary Henrietta.

The Chetwode family is a branch of the English family Chetwode of Chetwode. John Chetwode Aikin claims the ancient title of De Wahull as representing through his mother the Chetwodes of Woodbrook, one of whom married the heiress of Baron de Wahull.

The second son of Admiral Samuel Philip Townsend is not Hugh but Ernest Neville.

## ERRATA.

P. 125, l. 18. *For* 1792 *read* 1692.
P. 128, l. 5. *For* 1637 *read* 1634.

# INDEX.

The Roman numbers refer to pedigree tables: when no surname is put the Christian name refers to a Townshend.

## A.

Agricola. *See* William R. Townsend.
Aikenhead, E., wife of General Townshend, X.
Aitkin, Chetwode, XII.
Ancram, Catherine, wife of Richard Townsend, I.
Ancram, Major, II.
Anketell, II.
Armitage, Dr., XII.
—— Francis, III.
Armstrong, Charles, 219.
—— Ellen, wife of Judge Townshend, I.
Arnop, Colonel, 97, 206.
Arundel of Trevose, 25, &c.
—— Lieut.-Col., 27.
Audley, Lord (Castlehaven), 95, 236.
Aylmer, Rose, I.
Ayscue, Sir J., 27.

## B.

Baker, Dorothea, wife of Richard B., XII.
Baldwin, Anne, wife of Ed. Mansell, XII.
—— Mercy, wife of Samuel, 235, X.
—— James, IX.
—— William, I.
Baltimore, sack of, 92.
Barclay or Berkeley, Captain, 198.
Barry, Annabella Harriet, wife of Norman Lionel, XI.
—— Catherine, wife of John of Skirtagh, 216, IX.
—— Col. Jack, 82, 197.
—— Col. James, of Lisnagar, 200, III (196).

Barry, James Redmond, 199.
—— Lady Catherine, 108, 198, 199, III (196).
—— Redmond, 216.
—— Smith, 199.
Barrymore, title, 197, 199, 218.
—— Alicia, Countess of, 197.
—— Earls of, 198, 199.
—— David, Earl of, 193.
—— Susan, Countess of, 197.
Batten, Admiral, 25.
Beamish, 104, 111, 132.
—— Amelia, V (204).
—— Frances, IV (201).
—— Rev. Adam Newman, XI.
—— Townsend, IV (201).
—— William, VIII.
Becher pedigree, 104, 132, 145, VI (205).
—— Charlotte, X. VI.
—— Elizabeth, wife of Horatio, 203, V (204), VI.
—— Elizabeth, wife of Richard of Castle Townshend, 150, and VI.
—— Helena, X. VI.
—— Henry, 213.
—— John, IX. VI.
—— John, 207.
—— Susanna, 205, 241.
—— Thomas, 96, 105, 111, 116, 121, 205.
Benduff Castle, 226.
Bennett, Col. R., 27.
Berkeley, Sir J., 4.
Bernard, A., 116, 123.
Betteridge, Lieut. F., 84.
Blake, Robert, 7, &c., 87.
Bligh, Neville, 27.
Blunt, Col., 49, 57.
Boultbee, Rev., XII.
Bourdillon, Rev., XII.

# INDEX.

Bowdler, Marg. 209, VIII.
—— Capt., 209.
Boyle, Margaret, 158.
—— Mary, 148.
Brandon, Lord, 158.
Bridges, Emma, wife of Adm. Samuel, XIII.
—— Sir W., 49, 58.
Bristol, surrender of, 1.
Brocker, Lieut.-Col., 27.
Broderick, St. John, 78.
Broghill (Orrery), 49, 69, 81, 88, 90, 105, 110, 114, 162.
Brown, Adelaide Helen, wife of Thomas Courteney, XI.
—— Geoffry, 67.
—— Major, 58.
Bryan, name of, 127, 145, 219.
Bryanite Club, 147.
Bunbury, Alice, wife of Thomas, XII.
Burgh, Hussey, 154.
—— Jane Adaliza De, wife of Henry John, 187, I.
Bush, Mary C., wife of Henry Fitzjohn, I.

## C.

Cadogan, Eliza, wife of Sam Thomas, XIII.
Cameron, Archdeacon, 193, II.
—— Judith, II.
Campbell, Jane, wife of Sam Philip, XIII.
Carew, Peter, 81, 84.
Carleton, Webber, XII.
Carr, Elizabeth, wife of Thomas, XI.
Castlehaven, Castle, 97, 124, 193, 262.
Castle Town, mansion of, 108, 123.
Ceely, Thomas, 3, 7, 17, 24, 25, 28.
Charles I., King, 1, 25, 34, 63, 77.
—— II., King, 77, 113.
Chetewood, Henrietta Maria, wife of Horatio, XIII.
Cholmondly, Capt., XII.
Chute, A. E., wife of Maurice Fitzgerald, 185, I.
Clare's Dragoons, 157.
Clarke, Louisa, wife of Horatio Uniacke, XI.
Clubmen, 18.

Coghill, Adelaide, II.
Colkitto (Sir A. Macdonald), 50, 61.
Coote, M. A. H., 266, XI.
—— Sir Charles, 77, 80 (note).
Copinger, Domenic, 133, 201, 207, 213.
—— Sir Walter, 213.
Corbett, Rev. John Reginald, XI.
Cork, surrender of, 85-88.
Corker family, 105, 265.
Corker, Catherine, wife of Horatio, 260, XII.
Cotton, Sir Stapleton, 174.
Cox, family of, 104, 116, 124.
Crawford, Annie, wife of Horace Webb, XIII.
Crighton, Mary, II.
Crispe, Lieut.-Col. 49, 57.
Crofton, Henry Morgan, X.
Cromwell, Oliver, 31, 63, 71, 94.
Cromwell's letter on Col. Townesende, 88.
—— Henry, 102.
Crosbie, Elizabeth, 158.
Cuff, Joseph, 141.
Cust, Sir Pury, 121.

## D.

Dalrymple, Ida, wife of Charles Eyre Coote, XI.
Daunt family, 132, V (204).
Daunt, George Digby, V (204).
—— Joseph, 116.
—— Mildred, wife of Richard, XIII.
—— Rev. Achilles, V (204)
—— Rev. Thomas, 150, I.
—— Thomas, V (204).
Davis, Dean, 120.
Deane, Col., 87.
—— Rt. Hon. Joseph, 158.
Delap, Mary, wife of Philip, 219, IX.
Denny, Arabella, wife of Richard Hungerford, XI.
Desmond, Earls of, 156, 157, &c.
D'Esterre, Jane, V (204).
Devereux, J. P., XI.
Digby, Jane, wife of Jonas Morris, I.
Digby, W., I.
D'Oyley, Anne, of Shottisham, 4.

# INDEX. 283

D'Oyley, Dorothy, of Wallingford, 4.
—— Dorothy, of Testerton, 128.
—— Col. Edward, 4, 72, 80, 92.
—— Major Charles, 4, 70, 75.
Doneraile, Lord, 159.
Donovan, Jeremy, 104.
Down, Survey, 97.
Downes, Bishop Dives, 198, 203.
Driscol, Colonel, 122.
Dundas, Sir David, 171.
Dunscombe, Niblett, III (196).
—— Noblett, 105.
Dyke, Elizabeth, wife of Sealy Uniacke, XI.

## E.

Eames, Captain, 78.
Egerton, Lady Alice, 97.
Essex, Earl of, 13, 17.

## F.

Fairfax, General, 20, 22, &c., 71, 79, 95.
Famine, Irish, of 1847, 224.
Fanshaw, Lady, 80, 86.
—— Sir Richard, 76.
Farmer, Major, 84.
Fealane, Major J. 58.
Fenton, Sir W., 68, 88.
—— Captain, 68.
Fiennes, 1.
Fitch, Lieut.-Col. Thomas, 27.
Fitzgerald, Elizabeth, wife of Richard, 156, 158, I.
—— Emma, wife of Dean of Tuam, XIII.
—— Knight of Kerry, &c., 156, &c.
Fitzmaurice, 157.
Fleming family, 104, 265.
—— Becher, XII.
—— Horace, XII.
—— Judith, 225, XII.
—— Lionel John, II, XII.
Fortescue, Col. Richard, 23, 27, 30, 35.
Foulke, 84, 78 (note), 104.
Frazer, Henrietta, wife of William C., XI.
Freake, Capt. John, 111.
Freeman, Jane, XII.
—— Rev. David, 152, I.

Freke, Helena, 218, IX.
French, family of, 104, 254, 266.
—— Michael, 266, XI.
—— Philip, V (204).

## G.

Gahan, Beresford, I.
Galway, Helena, 207.
Gay, Susanna, wife of Richard, 216, IX.
Gayson, Lucia, XII.
Gibson, Emily, wife of Chambré Corker, XII.
Gifford or Jefford, 80, 82, 85, 89, 104, 111, 141.
Gillett, Evelyn, I.
—— Rev. Hugh, I.
Gooking, Robert, 78 (note), 101, 111, 116.
—— Vincent, 116.
Gosse, Rev. R., X.
Granger, Lieut. Peter, 85.
Gray, Adjutant, 36, 45, 49, 57.
Gunn, Frances, 119.
—— Townsend, 119.
—— William, 117.
Gwyn, Captain, 151, 231, I.

## H.

Hamilton, Duke of, 71.
Hancock, Anne, wife of John Sealy, XI.
Harris, Lieut., XIII.
—— R., 111.
Hart, Dr. T. B., 277.
Haytubbe, Capt. R., 99.
Herbert family, 104, 132.
—— Helena, V (204).
—— Mary, wife of John Henry, I.
—— Rev. A., 151, I.
Herle, Capt. Edward, 27.
Hibbert, Laura, wife of Richard, XII.
Hill, Rev. Lion, XIII.
Homan, Anne, wife of H. O. Becher, I.
Honnor, Catherine, wife of Francis 200, IV (201).
Hopton, Sir Ralph, 20.
Horatio, name of, 127.
House or Hough, Dr. John, 148.
Hughes, George, X.

# INDEX.

Hull, R., 104, 110, 111, 117.
Hume, Harriet, wife of Richard, XIII, 268.
Humphries, Elizabeth, wife of Ed. Richard, XIII.
Hungerford, Colonel, 36.
—— Elizabeth, wife of Richard B., IX.
—— Helena, IX.
—— Thomas, II.
Hungerford of Caermore, 148.
—— —— Mary, 266.
Hungerford of the Island, 104, 145, 206.
—— —— Elizabeth, 240, XI.
—— —— Mary, 267, XII.
Hyde of Purton, 130.
—— Hildigardis, wife of Colonel Richard, 129.

## I.

Inchiquin, Lord, 5, 15, 40, 69, 84.

## J.

James II., King, 115, 118.
Jarvis of Braad, 155, 241.
Jefford, *see* Gifford.
Jennings, Col. C., 27.
—— Major T., 27.
Jennison, Miss, wife of Richard, IX.
—— Francis, 219.
Jephson, 103.
Jeune, Joseph, 27.
Jeynes, Caroline, wife of Thomas, XIII.
Johnson, 84, 87.
Jones, Bishop, 106, 132.
—— Colonel, 44.
—— Rev. Jones, X.
Joy, Amelia Dora, wife of John Hume, D.D., XIII.

## K.

Keightly, Thomas, 129.
Kenny, Sarah Anne, wife of Horatio, XII.
Killigrew, Susan, Countess of Barrimore, 197.
Kingston, Baron, 104, 131, 251, 267.

Kingston, James of Clonakilty, 130.
—— Mary, 130.
—— Samuel of Skeat, 130.
Kirby, Mary, wife of Horace, XII.
Knocknones or Knockincross, battle of, 48, &c.

## L.

Lawless, Hon. Cecil John, I.
Lifford, Lord, 266.
Limerick, W., II.
Lisle, Sir G., 71.
Loudon, Lord, 242.
Louisburg, siege of, 248.
Lucas, Sir C., 71.
Lyme Regis, 2, &c.

## M.

Mackinnon, Katherine, wife of Richard, M.D., XI.
Macknamara, 58.
Mansell, Dorothea, wife of Samuel, 230, X.
—— Maria Frances, wife of Richard, XIII.
—— Miss, XIII.
Mardyke, John Townshend of, 241.
Marston Moor, battle of, 16.
Martin, Judge, 118.
Mason, Annie Roberts, wife of William C., XI.
Massey, 35.
Maunsell, Katherine Hare, wife of R. Newman, M.D., XI.
Maurice, Prince, 1, 5, 14.
Maynard, Capt. W., 27.
McBride, Captain, 156.
McCarthie, Reagh, 106.
—— Jane, wife of Horatio, XII.
McCullagh, Maye, wife of John, XI.
Meade of Balintober, 148.
—— Archdeacon, VIII (208).
—— Helena, wife of Horatio, 260, XII.
—— Rev. John, XIII.
Mellifont, Barbara, wife of Richard, I.
—— Eliza, wife of Richard M., I.
Meares, John, X.
Meath, Earl of, his regiment, 125.

# INDEX.

Mildmay, Captain, 87.
Miller, Professor Thomas, XII.
—— John Chambré, XII.
Mills, Miss, 261.
Minchin, Catherine, wife of Philip Uniacke, XI.
—— Francis Catherine, XI.
—— Miss, wife of Richard, IV (201).
Monsereda, Prince of, 155.
Moore, Edward, 115.
—— Emanuel, 110, 111.
—— Henry, XI.
—— Mary, 240.
—— Sir Charles, 267.
—— Sir Samuel, 116.
More, William, 60.
Morgan, Edward Percival, XII.
—— Edward Strachan, XII.
—— Henrietta, wife of Sam Nugent, X.
—— Hugh Townshend, XII.
Morris of Benduff, 210, 219, 226, IX.
—— Catherine, wife of Horatio, XIII.
—— Fortunatus, 226.
—— Jonas, 227, IX.
—— Mary, wife of John, 254, I.
—— William, 227, IX.
Mundy, General Pierrepont, 187, &c., I.
Murphy, Joannah, 210, VII.
—— Thomas, 211.
Myhill, Captain, 85, 86.

## N.

Napier, Sir W., 171.
Naseby, battle of, 18.
Neville, Anne, 193, II.
Newenham, Henrietta, wife of Richard Boyle, 162, 182, I.
Newman, Adam, XIII.
—— Helena, wife of Samuel Philip, XIII.
—— Mary, wife of Richard, M.D., XI.
Newton, Judge, XII.
Nisbit, Mary, 148.

## O.

O'Brien, Catherine, 130.

O'Brien, M., 130.
O'Driscol, 111, 123.
O'Donovan, 111, 145.
O'Hea, 145, 209.
O'Neil, Owen Roe, 38, &c.
O'Regan, 132.
Ogilevie, Maude, wife of Thos. Loftus Uniacke, XI,
Oliver family, 266.
—— Eliza, wife of Chambré Corker, 263, XII.
Ormonde, Marquess of, 39, 67, 72, 77, 89.
Orpen family, 132, 213, VIII (208).
Orrery. *See* Broghill.
Ossory, Earl of, 112, 114.
Owen, Col., 104, 133, 206, 213.
Oxford, Earl of, 186.

## P.

Palmer, Eliz., wife of Philip, XIII.
Pendennis Castle, 20-29.
Peel, Sir Robert, 161, 184.
Perry, 193.
Phaire, Col., 68, 88, 100.
Piggot, Capt., 63, 78 (note).
Pine, Capt. Thomas, 6, &c., 12.
Pitt, 161.
Powell, Rev. J. P., XI.
Poole of Mayfield, XII.
—— Joanna, wife of Horace, XII.
Poyer, Col., 69.
Proctor, Rev., H. P., X.
Preston, 38, 67.
Purdon, Major, 88, 89.

## R.

Raban, Rev. R., XII.
Raglan Castle, 29.
Randolf, Capt., 49, 57.
Rathfarnham, battle of, 80.
Reddish, Elizabeth, wife of John, 217, IX.
Reeves (Ryves), Col., 86, 194.
—— family, II.
—— Somerville, 255, II.
Richards, Anne, wife of Horatio, 210, VIII (206).
Riggs, Edward, 115, 116, 193.
Rinucini, nuncio, 37, &c., 70.
Roberts, Anna Maria, wife of Ch. Uniacke, XI.

## INDEX.

Robinson family, 217.
—— Dorothea, wife of Richard, 217, IX.
—— Dorothea, wife of Ed. Mansell, X.
—— Helena, wife of Sam Philip, XIII.
—— Rev. Thomas, X.
Rollo, Colonel, 242.
Rupert, Prince, 1, 16, 82.

### S.

Salmon, Capt., 97,
Schomburg, 120.
Scravenmore, 121.
Sealy, Eleanor, wife of Richard, 254, XI.
Shannon, Lord, 153, 259.
Shipman, Sir A., 27.
Shute, Sir C., 150.
Skippon, 33, 35.
Slaughter, Col. W., 27.
Smith, Sir Percy, 82, 87.
Sneyd, H. F., X.
Somerville, Agnes, wife of Horatio, II, IX, XI.
—— Dr. J., 266, II.
—— family, 193, II.
—— Judith, 225, II.
—— Mary, wife of Jonas Morris, I, II.
—— Rev. W., 193, II.
—— Thomas, 183, 191, 193, II.
Southwell, Arthur, 176, 177.
—— Capt., 49, 57.
—— Sir Thomas, 117.
St. Aubyn, Col. John, 27.
St. Lawrence, Rev. R., 183, I.
St. Leger, Louise, X.
Stephens, Abigail, 185.
—— family, 185.
Stewart, Frances Vere, wife of Chambré Corker, XII.
Stewart, family, 132.
—— W. of Welfield, 202.
Stirling, Col., 44, 86.
Strawson, Maria, wife of Oliver, XII.
Strode, 2.
Sweet, Capt. John, 105, 209.
—— Jane, 209.
Swift, Dean, 150.
Sykes, Emmeline, II.
Symes, G., 111.

Synge family, 148.
—— Charles, 175.
—— Edward, Bishop of Cork, 106, 114, 149.
—— George, Bishop of Cloyne, 68, 116, 143, 148.
—— Mary, wife of Bryan, 143, 149.
—— Mary, wife of Richard, 150, I.

### T.

Taaf, Lord, 45, 47, 50, 67, 70.
Tanner, Margaret, VIII.
Temple, Col., 47, 49, 75.
—— Sir W.
Thomas, Catherine, wife of Sam Townshend, X.
Thomond, Earl of, 157.
Tottenham Anna Maria, wife of Charles U., XI.
Tower, Catherine, wife of John Hancock, XI.
Townshend, Viscount, 153.
—— Baron, 127.
TOWNSHEND or TOWNESEND :—
Abraham Boyle, 172, 183, I.
—— Morris, 192, I.
Ada Elizabeth, XI.
Adam Newman, XI.
Alice Gertrude (Vernon), 187, I.
—— Katherine, XI.
—— Mary (Townshend), IX, I.
—— X.
Alicia Hewitt (Morgan), XII.
—— Maud (Maunsell), XII.
—— Uniacke, XI.
Anna Jane (Croasdaile), XI.
—— Maria E., XI.
—— Maria, X.
Anne (Becher), X.
—— Johnson (Jones), X.
—— (Murphy), 211, VIII (206).
—— (Orpen), VIII (206).
—— X, I.
—— XI.
—— XII.
—— XIII.
Arthur Barry, XI.
—— Fitzhenry, I.
—— Henry, V (204).
Aubrey de Vere (Rev.), 268, XIII.
Aubrey L. Hume, XIII.
Augusta Matilda (Warren), X.
Barbara (Hungerford), 148, 241.

# INDEX.

TOWNSHEND or TOWNESEND:
Barbara (Baldwin), IX.
—— (Becher), IX.
—— Mellifont, I.
—— 217, IX.
Brian, XII.
Brook Young, 274, XIII.
Butler, 202, IV (201).
Bryan of Castle Townshend, 80, &c., 111, 114, 117, 125, 134, 143, 215.
—— 145, 147.
—— 219, IX.
—— 224, IX.

(Katherine is entered under C for convenience of reference.)
Catherine (Armitage), XII.
—— Corker, XII.
—— (Gahan), XII.
—— Granville, XIII.
—— (Gunn), 117, 133.
—— Helena 209, I.
—— Helena (Baldwin), I.
—— Mary, XI.
—— Morris, IX.
—— (Newton), XII.
—— (Wakeham), XII.
—— III (196).
—— XII.
—— 148.
—— 263, XII.
Caroline Edith (Hutt), XI.
—— (Miller), XII.
—— (Powell), XI.
Caroline, XII.
—— XIII.
Chambré Corker, XII.
—— Corker, Rev., 263, XII.
—— Walker, XIII.
Charlotte (Hughes), X.
—— Becher, X.
—— I.
—— XII.
—— XIII.
Charles Loftus Uniacke, XI.
—— Uniacke, XI.
—— William, XIII.
—— IX.
Christopher, XI.
Cicily, XII.
Constance, XI.
Cornelius, 111, 207, VIII (208).

TOWNSHEND or TOWNESEND:
Cornelius of Bridgemount, 202 VIII (208).
—— of Clogeen, VIII (208).
—— XIII.
Cuthbert, XIII.
Cyril, XII.

David, III (196).
Delia C. Grace, XI.
Digby, I.
Dora, XII.
Dorothea (Beamish), VIII (208).
—— (Busteed), IX.
—— (Copinger), 133, 213.
—— (Keiley), X.
—— Robinson, wife of Richard, 217, IX.
—— (1 Robinson, 2 Wright), X.
—— 217.
Dorothy, XI.
—— of Devonshire, 128.
—— 202, IV (201).
Dulcibella, XIII.

Edward Carr, XI.
—— H. of Whitehall, 238, X.
—— Hume, 268, 270, XIII.
—— James, IX.
—— Major, XIII.
—— Mansell, XIII.
—— of Keamore, 111, 132.
—— Professor, XIII.
—— R. N., XIII.
—— Richard, M.D., XIII.
—— Richard, M.D., 274, XIII.
—— son of Bryan, 147.
—— (Splendid Ned), 234, X.
—— Synge, 211, 268, XIII.
—— IX.
—— 93.
Edwin, 225, XIII.
Eleanor, wife of Commissioner John, 222, IX, XI.
Eleanor, XI.
Eileen Blanche, XI.
Elizabeth Anne (St. Lawrence), 183, 184, I.
—— (Cummings), XII.
—— (Dunscombe), 200, III (196).
—— (Fleming), XII.
—— (Green), IX.

## INDEX.

TOWNSHEND or TOWNESEND:
Elizabeth (Gwyn), 151, I.
—— (Harris), XI.
—— Helen Fitzgerald, XI.
—— Henrietta, I.
—— Henrietta (Somerville), I, II.
—— Hildegarde (Warren), I.
—— (Morris), IX.
—— (Smith), XIII.
—— (Stewart), 202, IV (201).
—— Trelawney, wife of Horatio, 232, X, XIII.
—— (Udaile), IX.
—— V (204).
—— wife of Edward Synge, XIII, 93, 213.
Eleonor (Moore), XI.
Ellen Beatrice, XI.
Ellinor Hilaire Fitzgerald, XI.
Emma (Wadsworth), XI.
Emily Mabel, XIII.
Ernest, XI.
Ethel Hare, XI.
Eva Mary, XI.

Florence, XI.
—— XII.
Francis, 120, 132, 134, 200, IV (201).
—— (Daunt), V (204).
—— Dorothea, wife of J. Crew Townsend, XIII.
—— Georgina (Browne), I.
—— Horatio, XIII.
—— of Clogeen, 202, IV (201).
—— son of Bryan, 148.
—— VIII (207).
Frederick Trench, General, 265, XI.

George, XI.
—— Robert, XIII.
—— XII.
Georgiana (Hill), XIII.
Gerald, XI.
Geraldine Henrietta Townshend (Mundy), 187, 189, I.
—— Mary Newman, XI.
—— XI.
Gertrude M. Fitzgerald, XI.
—— (Townshend), XI.
Gladys Mary, XI.
Godfrey T. Mason, XI.

TOWNSHEND or TOWNESEND:
Grace (Anstis), 93.
—— (Meade), VIII (208).

Harriett (Freeman), 152, I.
—— (Gahan), I.
Helen Agnes, XI.
—— Marianne Barry, XI.
—— (Meares), XI.
Helena (Becher), X.
—— (Daunt), XIII.
—— (Herbert), 152, 252, I.
—— (Holder), XI.
—— (Meade), 148.
—— (McDermot), XIII.
—— (Penrose), XIII.
—— X, XIII.
—— XII.
Henrietta, Anne Margaret (Somerville), I.
—— (Crofton), XIII.
—— (Raban), XIII.
—— XII.
—— XIII.
Henry Becher, XIII.
—— Denny, XII.
—— Fitzjohn, I.
—— John, 187, I.
—— Owen Becher, I.
—— XIII.
—— 151, 191, I.
—— 183, I.
Herbert, XII.
Herbert Eyre, XI.
Hildegardis, XI.
—— XIII.
Honora Maria (Whitla), XI.
Horace Montague Dimock, XI.
Horatio Crawford, XIII.
—— Hamilton, XIII.
—— I. Uniacke, XI.
—— of Coolmona, 148, 151, 267, XIII.
—— of Derry, 159, 258, XII.
—— S., XI.
—— Thomas, IX.
—— Uniacke, XI.
—— Webb, XIII.
—— IX.
—— XII.
—— XIII.
—— 120, 122, 132, 134, 203, V (202).
—— 210, VIII (208).

# INDEX.

TOWNSHEND or TOWNESEND:
Hugh, XIII.
James Edward, IX, X.
—— of Baltimore, 218, IX.
—— Richard, XI.
—— 217, IX.
Jane, 201.
—— (Grey), XIII.
Janet Mary (Galwey), XI.
Joanna (Poole), XII.
John C., XI.
—— Chambré, XII.
—— Colonel, 165, 180, &c., I.
—— Commander, 268 XIII.
—— Commissioner, R.N., 220, &c., IX.
—— Crew Chetwood, XIII.
—— Fitz Cornelius, 134, 209, VIII (209).
—— Fitzhenry, Judge, 151, 192, I.
—— Hancock, XI.
—— Hume, XIII.
—— of Carmullane, 217, IX.
—— of Courtmacsherry, 197, III (196).
—— of Shepperton, 151, 191, I.
—— of Skirtagh, 146, 216, &c., IX.
—— Sealy, 224, IX.
—— Sealy (Master in Chancery), 264, XI.
—— IX.
—— XIII.
—— 217, IX.
—— 225, XIII.
Jonas Morris, 192, I.
Judith, wife of Ed. Townshend, 225, IX, XIII.
Judith, IX.

Kathleen, XI.
—— Audrey, XI.
—— Francis, XI.
—— Synge, XIII.
Kingston, 120, 132.
—— VIII (260).

Laura (Bourdillon, XII.
Lilian, XIII.
Louisa Elizabeth, XI.
Lucy (Chetwood Aikin), XIII.

Mabel Louise, XI.

TOWNSHEND or TOWNESEND:
Margaret, wife of Richard, VIII (208), XI.
Maria (Somerville), II, XII.
Marianne Oliver (Townshend) XII, XIII.
Marion Francis, XI.
—— Hungerford, XIII.
—— (Sneyd), X.
Maria (Devereux), XI.
—— Eliz. Coote, XI.
Martha (Carré Williams), IX.
—— Eleonor (Corbett), XI.
—— (Gosse), XI.
—— Uniacke, XI.
—— 217, IX.
Mary Alice (Townshend), 219 IX, X.
—— Amelia, XI.
—— Baldwin, X.
—— (Boultbe), XII.
—— (Daunt), 150, I.
—— H. Maunsell, XIII.
—— (Harris), XIII.
—— (House), 148.
—— Hungerford, XIII.
—— Maunsell, XIII.
—— (Molloy), XI.
—— (Morris), IX.
—— (Robinson), IX.
—— (Somerville), 254, 262, II, XI.
—— (Tuckey) XIII.
—— Young, XIII.
Maud, XIII.
—— Alicia, XI.
Maurice E. Hume, XIII.
—— FitzGerald, 177, 184, I.
—— Fitzgerald Stephens, 187, I.
Mercy, X.
Mildred (Carleton), XIII.
—— Ethel, XI.
—— Louisa, XI.
Muriel Florence Uniacke, XI.

Nathaniel W. Oliver, XII.
Norman FitzGerald, XI.
—— Lionel, XI.
—— Singleton Barry, XI.

Patrick, III (196).
Penelope (French), 203, V (204).
Percy Dalrymple, XI.

# INDEX.

TOWNSHEND or TOWNESEND:
Philip of Derry, 146, 148, 151, &c., 239, &c., XI, XII.
—— of Fern Hill, XIII.
—— Uniacke, XI.
—— William Uniacke, XI.
—— 107, 132, 134, 137, 206, VII (207).
—— 211, VIII (208).
—— 219, IX.

Redmond, John Uniacke, XI.
—— Uniacke, XI.
Townesend, Richard, takes Bridport, 7; wounded at Lyme Regis, 13; defeats the clubmen, 20; becomes Lieut.-Col., 25; treats for the surrender of Pendennis, 27; reports the same to Col. Ceely, 28; returns to Dorset, 30; ordered to Ireland, 36; commands the 'main battle' at Knocknones, 49; routs Colkitto, 61; signs the Remonstrance, 65; treats with the Derby House Committee, 75; disowned by Inchiquin, 76; attempts to seize Youghal, 82, 84; made prisoner by Bettridge, 84; leads the revolt of the garrison of Cork, 85; brings the submission of Cork to Cromwell, 87; settles in West Carbery, 94; supplies the 'Little Charity' with horsemeat, 99; reports the plundering of the 'Patience,' 101; permitted to raise sunken guns, 102; receives a patent from Charles II, 105; elected member for Baltimore, 105; becomes heir to Mr. McCarthie Reagh, 106; receives a commission in the militia, 111; made High Sheriff, 114; chosen sovereign of Clonakilty, 116; defends Castletown, 122; his death and burial, 125; his possible origin, 127; the names of his two wives, 129, 130; list of his children, 132, 133; copy of his will, 134, 135; list of lands

TOWNSHEND or TOWNESEND:
belonging to him, 136, 137, 138; extracts from his patent for Skibbereen manor, 139, 140; copy of his deposition, 140, 141; deed signed by him, 142.
Richard Baxter, XII.
—— Boyle of Castle Townshend, 159, &c., I.
—— Boyle, Rev., 223, IX.
—— Fellow T.C.D., 218, IX.
—— FitzGerald, 163, 194, I.
—— Fitzjohn, 134, 138, 144, 198.
—— Harvey, XI.
—— Hume, XIII.
—— Hungerford, XIII.
—— Hungerford Denny, XI.
—— married at Brackinashe, 128.
—— M.D., 241, 254, XI.
—— Mellifont, 192, 200, I.
—— Newman, M.D., XI.
—— of Devonshire, 128.
—— of Ditchford, 128.
—— of Kinneagh, 93.
—— of Northampton, 125.
—— of Palace Town, 268, XIII.
—— of Schull, 216, IX.
—— of the Point, 192, I.
—— Staplyton Barry, XI.
—— 2nd of Castle Townshend, 137, 146, 147, 149, 151, 191, I.
—— 3rd of Castle Townshend (Munster Peacock), 152, &c., I.
—— VIII (208).
—— XII.
—— 202, IV (201).
Robert, Captain, 78.
—— P. Loftus, XI.
—— Sir, of Chester, 78.
—— Uniacke FitzGerald, XI.
Roger, Sir, of Raynham, 4, 79.

Samuel, General, 230, 232, X.
—— Henry, X.
—— Irwin, X.
—— Nugent, 233, 239, X.
—— Philip, Admiral, 274, XIII.
—— Philip, Colonel, 274, XI.
—— Thomas, X.
—— of Dereeney, X.

TOWNSHEND or TOWNESEND:
  Samuel, of Firmount, 267, XIII.
  —— of Garrycloyne, XIII.
  —— of Whitehall, 146, 147, 151, 215, 229, 252, X.
  —— 2nd of Whitehall, 233, 234, X.
  —— 3rd of Whitehall, X.
  —— 150, I.
  Sealy Uniacke, XI.
  Sophia Elizabeth, XI.
  Susan Constantia, XI.
  —— (Hodgson), XII.
  —— (Townshend), XII, XIII.
  Susanna (French), 254, 266, XI.

  Thomas Achilles, XIII.
  —— Commodore, 218, IX.
  —— Courteney, XI.
  —— Crofton Croker, XI.
  —— Dyke, XI.
  —— Hungerford Denny, XI.
  —— Loftus Uniacke, XI.
  —— of Braconashe, 4, 128.
  —— of Clyda, XI.
  —— of Derry, 241, 254, XI.
  —— of Innistogue, XI.
  —— of Mayo, XIII.
  —— Philip Barry, XI.
  —— Richard, I.
  —— Somerville, I.
  —— William FitzGerald, XI.

  Victoria (Chambers), I.

  Walter of Hinton, 128.
  William Chambers (Dean of Tuam), 274, XIII.
  —— of Derry, 254, 257, &c.
  —— Richard, I.
  —— Richard Newman, XI.
  —— Robinson, 272, XIII.
  —— son of Bryan, 148.
  —— son of Col. Richard, 108, 132, 134.
  —— Tower, XI.
  —— Uniacke, XI.
  —— X.
  —— XI.
  —— XII.
  Wilmot, XII.

Travers, Sir R., 58.
Tremaine, Col. Lewis, 27.
Trench, Helena, wife of Richard, XI.
—— W. Stuart, XI.
Tuckey, Major, X.

U.

Uniacke, Isabel, II.
—— Redmond, 165, XI.
Ussher, Adelaide, II.

V.

Veres, the fighting, 127.
Vernon, Hon. and Rev. Courteney, 189, I.
—— Courteney, Robert, I.
—— Sidney, C. FitzG., I.

W.

Wadsworth Ch., XI.
Wakeham, Rev. T., X.
Warden, 82, 87, 89, 105, 141.
Warren, Alicia, wife of John, 217, IX.
—— Capt. R., X.
—— Mary, Carré, wife of Ed. Henry, X.
Warwick, Earl of, 4, 11.
Water, Lieut. George, 141.
Wellington, Duke of, 171, 174, 175.
Were, Col., 6.
Westropp, Bella, wife of Henry, X.
White, Mrs., of Glengariffe, 163.
Wilkinson, Miss, 217, IX.
Williams, Carré Columbine, 217.
—— Martha, wife of John, IX.
Wolff, General, 253, 254.
Wogan, Col., 82.
Woodbiffe, Antony, 111.
Worcester, Marquess of, 170, 172.
Wrey, M., II.
Wright, W., X.

Y.

Youghal, 80, 83, 88.
Young, Jessie, wife of Edward Mansell, XIII.

# LIST OF SUBSCRIBERS.

ARMITAGE, Mrs. Breckenbrough, Emu Bay, Tasmania (2 *copies*).
ARNOLD, C. T., Stanford House, Wimbledon (2 *copies*).
BAKER, Miss, Covert Side, Hasfield, Gloucester (6 *copies*).
BARTER, Rev. W. E. B., 1 Grafton Street, Berkeley Square, W.
BEAMISH, W. H., 8 The Crescent, Queenstown, Co. Cork.
BECHER, Rev. H., The Rectory, Castle Haven, Skibbereen.
BOULTBEE, Mrs., The Vicarage, Chesham, Bucks.
CLOYNE, The Dean of, The Deanery, Cloyne, Co. Cork.
COLEMAN, James, H. M. C,. M.R.S.A., 41 Manchester Street, Southampton.
COPPINGER, W. A., The Priory, Manchester.
DUNN, T. W., Bath College, Bath.
EVANS, Richardson, Wimbledon.
FLEMING, Mrs., New Court, Skibbereen (2 *copies*).
GIBBON, Mrs., Leinster House, Wimbledon (2 *copies*).
GILLMAN, Herbert Webb, J.P., B.L., Clontiadmore, Coachford, Co. Cork.
GORT, Viscount, East Cowes Castle, Isle of Wight.'
HODGSON, Brian H., F.R.S., D.C.L., Alderley Grange, Wootton-under-Edge (2 *copies*).
HUNGERFORD, Miss, The Island, Clonakilty, Co. Cork.
KING, Gilbert, Pallastown, Kinsale, Co. Cork.
KINGTON-OLIPHANT, J. L., Gask, Auchterarder (3 *copies*).
L'ESTRANGE, Mrs., 27 Royal York Crescent, Clifton.
    „     Rev. A. G., 26 Cumberland Terrace, Regent's Park.
MARSH, Mrs. Howard, 30 Bruton Street, W.

MILLER, Professor, Göttingen, Germany.
MUNDY, Mrs. Pierrepoint, Castle Townshend, Co. Cork (25 *copies*).
PEARSON, Lady, Rozel, Wimbledon.
REEVES, Miss, Tramore, Douglas, Cork (2 *copies*).
ROSS, The Dean of, Glandore House, Leap, Co. Cork.
SHERWOOD, Rev. W. E., Magdalen College School, Oxford.
SOMERVILLE, Col., J.P., D.L., Drishane, Skibbereen, Co. Cork.
„ Aylmer, Drishane, Skibbereen, Co. Cork.
„ Lieut. Boyle T., R. N.
„ Miss Henrietta, The Clock House, Farnborough, R. S. O. (2 *copies*).
„ James, M.D., Park Cottage, Leap, Co. Cork.
„ Thomas Townshend, Christiania.
STAVELEY, Canon, The Vicarage, Killiney, Dublin.
TOWNSEND, Charles Eyre Coote, Mount Coote, Kilmallock.
„ Horatio Hamilton, Woodside, Co. Cork.
„ Rev. John Hume, D.D., St. Mark's House, Tunbridge Wells (3 *copies*).
„ Martin, Troy, New York.
„ N. L., Resident Magistrate, Armagh.
„ Richard Hungerford, M.B., 13 Westbourne Terrace, Queenstown.
„ Robert U. F., Stone View, Blarney.
„ Admiral Samuel, The Grange, Farnham, Hants. (2 *copies*).
„ Mrs. W. Uniacke, Walcot, Bray, Co. Wicklow.
TOWNSHEND, Rev. A. G., 32 Effra Road, Rathmines, Dublin.
„ Mrs. Chambré Corker (20 *copies*).
„ Chambry C., Frenchgate, Richmond (8 *copies*).
„ C. B., M.D., 456 King's Road, Chelsea.
„ Charles Loftus, 15 Molesworth St., Dublin (2 *copies*).
„ Charles Hervey, Raynham, New Haven, Connecticut (2 *copies*).
„ Charles Uniacke, 15 Molesworth Street, Dublin.
„ Professor Edward, Queen's College, Galway (3 *copies*).
„ Major Henry Fitzjohn, Seafield, Castle Townshend.

TOWNSHEND, Capt. Horace, Courtmacsherry, Co. Cork.
,, Mrs. Horatio, Kilcoe, Skibbereen.
,, Jas. Richard, 31 Walham Terrace, Blackrock, Dublin.
,, Mrs. John Hancock, Myross Wood, Leap, Co. Cork.
,, Mrs. John Sealy, 90 Lower Drumcondra Road, Dublin.
,, Miss Katharine Corker.
,, Capt. R. A., Friendly Cove House, Durrus, Bantry.
,, Mrs. Richard Newman, Innishannon, Co. Cork.
,, Samuel Nugent, St. Kames, Schull, Co. Cork.
,, Thomas Courtenay, White Hall, Fox Rock (2 *copies*).
,, W. Charles, 22 Lower Pembroke Street, Dublin.
TUAM, The Dean of, The Deanery, Tuam.